Clean Eating Cookbook for Beginners

Eat Better, Feel Better, 500 No-Fuss Clean Recipes Incl. Whole Foods, Diabetic Recipes with 21-Meal Plan to Fuel Your Life

Eric Baker

Content

Chapter 3: Vegetables 33

Chapter 4: Grain and Beans... 45

Chapter 5: Poultry 54

Chapter 6: Pork, Beef and Lamb 67

Chapter 7: Fish and Seafood 80

Chapter 8: Salads 92

Chapter 9: Soup and Stew 101

Chapter 10: Sides 114

Chapter 11: Appetizers and Snacks 126

Chapter 12: Desserts 139

Chapter 13: Drink and Smoothie.................................... 154

Chapter 14: Sauces and Dressing 164

Appendix 1: Measurement Conversion Chart 173

Appendix 2: Dirty Dozen and Clean Fifteen 174

Appendix 3: Recipes Index... 175

Introduction

Ever since we have stepped into this new era, processed and packaged food products have taken over food markets, and over-reliance on frozen and pre-made, ready-to-cook meals has increased up to many folds. Frequent intake of such products has been affecting our health, and it is found  to be one of the major causes of nutritional deficiencies, obesity and several chronic diseases. Considering all the ill effects of processed food, nutritional experts around the world have started recommending the "clean eating" diet to everyone who is seeking good health. The idea is to start consuming food in its organic and un-processed form to get maximum nutritional benefits out of it. It is not an entirely new dietary concept; rather, it came up as more of a reset program which simply reminds us to eat what is actually healthy for the body. To eat clean, you need to start looking at your food differently, restock the pantry, adopt new habits and make use of healthy, clean recipes with organic ingredients. And this cookbook, with its variety of recipes and a comprehensive guide on the principles of clean eating, can make that possible for you.

Chapter 1: Basics of Clean Eating

Although there are many different types of clean eating, generally speaking, it refers to consuming foods that are unprocessed, raw, whole or organic. This forces us to prepare our meals from scratch in an effort to make them as "clean" as possible. The primary driver for adopting a clean eating diet is the health benefits of consuming nutrient-dense, naturally grown foods that are not unduly processed. The majority of Americans consume a diet high in processed meals created from artificial ingredients, which are loaded with sodium, chemicals, fat, sugar, preservatives, food colours, and other additives that your body is ill-equipped to deal with. These extras could be harmful to your general health and well-being.

Principles of Clean Eating

Clean eating provides your body with nourishment in the form of wholesome foods. Clean meals give your body a wealth of vitamins and minerals, healthy fats, and quality proteins, all of which improve your cardiac and brain health, aid in weight loss, fortify your immune system and give you more energy. The flavor of naturally prepared foods is also greater. This approach sets out a few basic codes for eating clean, such as:

- **Pick Whole Foods**

Choosing foods that are consumed in their natural state is the fundamental principle of clean eating. So choose fresh, whole foods instead of packaged, boxed, or bagged ones. Consider fresh blueberries or a whole chicken instead of fruit-flavored gummy candies or frozen chicken meatballs. You can avoid their extra sugar, calories, salt, and saturated fat when you steer clear of highly processed foods like cookies, chips, and ready-to-eat meals.

- **Eat More Whole Grains**

Refined carbohydrates that lose nutrients during manufacture such as pasta, white bread, and rice are not good for the health. They can be replaced with brown or wild rice, whole wheat bread, and pasta. Alternately, pick a different whole grain like popcorn, bulgur, barley, or oatmeal. This change may have a major impact because studies show that eating a lot of whole grains can lower your risk of cardiac diseases, type 2 diabetes, and colon cancer.

- **Load Up on Fruits and Veggies**

Two essentials of clean eating are organic fruits and veggies. All your produce should, according to some clean eaters, be fresh. Others, however, contend that because frozen and canned foods have the same amount of nutrients, they are the next best thing. To be sure you aren't consuming additional sugar or salt, simply read the label. Go for whole fruits as opposed to juices, which have more sugar and less fibre. Try to consume five to nine servings of fruits and vegetables each day, depending on how many calories you require and how active you are.

● Beware of Added Sugar and Salt

Since salt and sugar aren't present in clean foods by nature, adding them goes against the as-natural-as-possible tenet. By avoiding processed foods, which are a major source of them, you can lower your intake. Otherwise, read food labels carefully to look for extra salt and sugar, even in seemingly healthful items like yoghurt or tomato sauce. Keep track of the amount you add to your meals and beverages. Think about flavoring instead of using herbs and spices.

● Don't Use Artificial Ingredients

Artificial sweeteners, colours, preservatives, and other artificial ingredients have no place in a clean-eating diet. To spot fake ingredients on grocery store products and avoid them, read the labels.

● Drink Lots of Water

Don't consume sugar-rich juices and soft drinks and try to prefer ow-calorie options like water and herbal tea. Water can make you feel full, and that helps you stop eating excessively, and it can also help you feel active and fight lethargy.

● Reconsider Using Alcohol and Caffeine

Some clean eaters completely avoid caffeine and alcohol and depend on consuming lots of water. Others claim that they can be consumed in moderation. Whether you're a clean eater or not, experts advise limiting your daily caffeine intake to 400 milligrams, as well as your alcohol intake to one serving for women and two for men. Likewise, avoid the added sweeteners in the drinks. Choose simple tea or coffee instead of sugary alcoholic mixers.

● Choose Whether to Go Organic

It is believed that eating organic fruit is the healthiest option since organic growers employ natural pesticides instead of synthetic ones. You get to choose how significant it is to your diet. If you want to learn what kinds of pesticides the vendors at your neighborhood farmers market use, you may also shop there. Another suggestion is to choose non-organic items with peels and skins you don't consume, such as avocados, corn, and onions, since pesticides typically get up on the exterior of fruits and vegetables.

● Know Your Meat and Dairy Sources

Meat, dairy goods, and eggs you buy at the grocery store may come from animals that were given antibiotics and growth hormones. Clean eaters avoid them and choose organic foods or locally produced meat from farmers who treat their animals humanely. At a farmer's market, you can learn more about the sources of your meat and dairy. Because it isn't usually labelled as organic, look for seafood that is low in mercury and is caught using sustainable fishing techniques.

Try to eat smaller healthy nutri-dense meals throughout the day. In between meals, eat snacks at least three times per day. You are more prone to make bad food decisions if you wait too long to eat. Keep healthy organic snacks in your bag or purse as a backup, like nuts and seeds, granola or cookies made out of whole grains and no added sugar.

Why Eat Clean?

The health benefits of eating clean food can never be over-emphasized. There are endless advantages to eating food in its authentic, organic and unprocessed form. Since I can't possibly list them all, let me tell you about the benefits that I have experienced and learned from others who have tried consuming nothing but a clean diet.

Budget-Friendly:

When you receive the nutrients you need by eating clean, authentic food, you can say goodbye to medical bills and sick days. Buying locally and in-season makes financial sense. Making a list and following it will ensure that there is no danger of overspending at the supermarket when you plan clean meals for the week. You then also set your budget, not just your waistline, and then you avoid expensive meals and unhealthy takeout orders.

Longer Lifespan:

Numerous studies have demonstrated that eating clean foods can increase your life expectancy. Eating more whole grains, especially nutrient-dense grains like teff, amaranth, millet, and sorghum, per day results in a 5 per cent decreased chance of dying from any cause. Additionally, European researchers discovered that raising your daily produce intake to more than 569 grams lowers your risk of mortality by approximately 10 per cent.

Strengthens Mind:

Eating a balanced and healthy diet high in fruits, vegetables, fish, and nuts makes our minds sharper and our memory stronger by 24%. Our brains also work better when we consume nutrients like omega-3 fatty acids, but they sputter and slow down when we consume sweets, alcohol, fast food, and unhealthy fats. A balanced diet promotes greater brain health.

Great for The Planet:

According to an often cited statistic, food in the United States travels 1,500 miles on average from the farmer to the consumer. You may lessen your carbon impact by following Clean Eating's guidelines to eat locally and seasonally. Want to have even more of an impact? Make an effort to eat vegetarian occasionally. Leaning toward a Lacto-ovo vegetarian diet which includes dairy and eggs, can help preserve the resources of the planet, even if you don't entirely give up meat, fish, and fowl.

Groups of Clean-Eating Foods

When your refrigerator, freezer, and cabinets are stocked with healthy, clean items, eating clean is much simpler. Whole foods like vegetables and fruits are obvious options while following a clean diet. A clean-eating diet can also include foods with few ingredients and minimal processing. Pick meals that contain whole grains, healthy fats, and little or no added sugar or salt. You might be wondering which items to actually eat when you're eating clean, from the fruit section to the butcher counter, from sweets to drinks. Here is some advice on how to stock your kitchen with things that make eating healthy simpler.

1. Fruits

Fruit is often a good choice. Though some people are concerned about fruit's sugar level, fruit is also a great source of fiber, vitamins, and minerals. Natural sugars are generally not a reason for concern among health professionals because it's difficult to consume too much of them while still receiving healthy nutrients. Fruits in cans and dried fruits should have labels checked for added sugars. You can count fruit juice as part of your required daily fruit intake as well; just make sure it's 100% juice. You might wish to limit your intake because even 100% fruit juices lack the healthy fibre found in whole fruits.

2. Vegetables

The foundation of your clean-eating meals should be vegetables because they are a rich source of fiber, vitamins, and minerals. Vegetables that are canned or frozen are also nutritious, but make sure to choose those without sauces and always check the label because even foods that appear to be plain may have salt added. When you don't have enough time to prepare or cook a meal, there are several easy methods to eat vegetables. In addition to frozen options, supermarkets provide a selection of pre-cut vegetables and even pre-spiralized veggie noodles. We're all for quick fixes that make it simpler to incorporate vegetables into your diet but beware of vegetarian chips and veggie spaghetti that may just contain a light dusting of actual vegetables.

3. Whole Grains

The good-for-you carbohydrates that provide fibre and nourishment are whole grains. Whole grains are largely unprocessed and include just one ingredient, including brown rice, quinoa, barley, oats, farro, or millet. They are as healthy as it gets. Other whole-grain options include whole-wheat varieties of bread, pasta, English muffins, and refrigerated pizza dough; just make sure whole-wheat flour is the first component, and there isn't sugar in the ingredient list. Even popcorn is a whole grain; purchase the kernels, pop them on the stove or in an air popper, and have a healthy snack free of the additives and fattening calories found in microwave packages.

4. Dairy

To improve your nutrition, pick plain yoghurt, either ordinary or Greek, instead of fruit- and vanilla-flavored yoghurts, which are high in added sugar. Dairy products, like cheese and milk, have two different uses; they can be consumed on their own or used as ingredients in healthier homemade versions of dishes like pizza and macaroni & cheese. Choosing non-dairy substitutes like soy, coconut, and almond milk? To eliminate extra sugar, look for kinds that are unsweetened. Additionally, ensure that reduced- and low-fat dairy products don't contain any strange substances or a ton of fillers. Dairy products made with plain, whole milk are healthy.

5. Protein

Meat provides iron, vitamin B12, and protein. Bologna, pepperoni, salami, and hot dogs should be avoided if you want to eat healthier because they are processed foods. These and other processed meat products may also contain artificial colours and preservatives and are often heavy in sodium. You can clean eat by selecting ecologically sustainable protein when it is possible. Many fish species include heart-healthy omega-3 fats, making fish and shellfish excellent sources of protein. When it's possible, pick seafood that is caught sustainably.

Eggs are a terrific option; just make sure you consume the yolk in order to get the extra protein and minerals. For plant-based proteins, consider nuts, seeds, and beans. Just remember to search out lower-sodium alternatives when you can.

6. Desserts

You decide how "clean" your diet is by restricting the added sugar, salt and preservatives. You can restrict additional sugar or completely eliminate it. When you're eating healthy, the majority of packaged conventional desserts don't meet the bill. Usually, they are produced with refined flour and a lot of extra sugar. You don't have to avoid sweets from your life, though. You can make snacks at home using fruit, whole grains, and less sugar, or you can prepare some fruit-based delights completely without any added sugar.

7. Drinks

Drinks have a high added sugar content. Avoid sodas, sweetened tea, and flavored coffee drinks. Water, seltzer, unsweetened tea, and coffee are all healthy options. Make your drink a bit more special by adding a dash of juice and serving it in a glass. If you're eating healthily, you might want to avoid alcohol, but you don't have to. You should set limits; for women, this means no more than one drink per day, and for men, no more than two. Wine and beer are allowed, but if you prefer cocktails, be cautious of sugary mixers.

Are you ready to start eating healthy? Well, this is going to be one great change to make in your lifestyle, but once you start eating clean food, you will feel more healthy and active. It is a great step to take a new start and work on your physical health. To switch to this diet, you just need the intent and will to do so. I am telling you, once you make up your mind about something, it's going to happen for you. The great thing about this clean eating approach is that it is not complicated; it allows you to eat a variety of food from different food groups with complete freedom; you just have to look for the organic, raw, and whole varieties of the products then you are good to go.

21-Day Meal Plan

Here, I create a 21-Day meal plan as an example, this will help discipline you're eating habits, and you will be able to feel more control over your dietary choices. You can create a meal plan as per your weekly requirements after this meal plan. Now, go ahead, give my clean eating, healthy recipe collection a try and let me know through your feedback which ones of them you really liked! Then share your experience with people around you.

Meal plan	Breakfast	Lunch	Dinner	Snack/Dessert
Day-1	Nutty Fruits Bowl (page 24)	Healthy Root Veggies (page 40)	Spring Shrimp Rolls (page 83)	Spicy Mixed Nuts (page 129)
Day-2	Glazed Strawberry Pop-Tarts (page 11)	Pea and Chicken Stew (page 47)	Pork Tenderloin (page 71)	Cinnamon and Apple Chips (page 135)
Day-3	Apple Oat Breakfast Bowl (page 15)	Marinara Chickpea Meatballs Sub (page 46)	Baked Acorn Squash and Arugula Salad (page 97)	Crunchy Homemade Chickpeas (page 134)
Day-4	Breakfast Almond Oats (page 17)	Sheet-Pan Chicken Fajitas (page 62)	Avocado Cucumber Feta Salad (page 99)	Maple-Yogurt Chia Pudding (page 152)
Day-5	Blueberry Pecan Cheesecake Bars (page 23)	Apple, Brie and Onion Burger (page 68)	Easy Baked Fish and Chips (page 83)	Chunky Monkey Chocolate Waffles (page 147)
Day-6	Apple-Cranberry Quinoa (page 27)	Adzuki Bean and Celery Soup (page 45)	Baked Hawaiian Pork Kebabs (page 67)	Berries Oat Crisp (page 139)
Day-7	Veggies Breakfast Bowl (page 15)	Baked Salmon and Asparagus (page 86)	Pasta Vegetables Stew (page 108)	Spinach and Banana Smoothie (page 159)
Day-8	Potato, Tomato and Egg Strata (page 28)	Classic Moroccan Beef in Lettuce Cups (page 71)	Healthy Rainbow Salad (page 94)	Fruit & Nut Chocolate Bark (page 151)
Day-9	Simple Poached Eggs (page 27)	Easy Baked Chicken (page 63)	Wild Rice and Mushroom Soup (page 102)	Raisin Rice Pudding (page 151)
Day-10	Baked Berries Oatmeal (page 26)	Homemade Crispy Baked Wings (page 56)	Parmesan Salmon with Root Vegetables (page 90)	Crispy Chili-Lime Popcorn (page 128)
Day-11	Maple-Pecan Beet and Oats (page 19)	Healthy Beef Stroganoff (page 67)	Cheesy Broccoli and Carrot Soup (page 104)	Spicy Mole Chicken Bites (page 135)
Day-12	Healthy Veggie Sandwich (page 14)	Pork Chops and Carrot (page 72)	Chicken Enchiladas (page 55)	Lemon Kale and Mango Smoothie (page 155)

Day-13	High Protein Breakfast Box (page 18)	Classic Jambalaya (page 65)	Taco Pasta (page 68)	Spinach Stuffed Mushrooms (page 126)
Day-14	Savory Spinach Oatmeal (page 28)	Roast Pork with Red Cabbage (page 76)	Hearty 7-Layer Taco Salad (page 93)	Spicy Broccoli Pizza Crust (page 133)
Day-15	Loaded Avocado Toast with Eggs (page 26)	Tuna and Carrot Salad (page 99)	Delicious Chicken Marsala (page 62)	Baked Seasoned Chickpeas (page 134)
Day-16	Apple Sausage Patties (page 27)	Mustard Beef Brisket (page 67)	Healthy Veggie Minestrone Soup (page 104)	Vanilla Almond Milk (page 156)
Day-17	Honey Granola (page 23)	Linguine with Clams (page 81)	Feta Lamb Burgers (page 72)	Tuna and Carrot Lettuce Cups (page 133)
Day-18	Blueberry Pecan Cheesecake Bars (page 23)	Thai Beef Roast and Veggies (page 70)	Garlicky Cilantro Grilled Shrimp (page 86)	Mocha Ricotta Mousse (page 147)
Day-19	High-Protein Breakfast Egg Muffins (page 20)	Breaded Chicken Tenders (page 57)	Beef and Mushroom Lo Mein (page 74)	Raspberry Cherry Dessert Bowl (page 139)
Day-20	Fried Rice Bowl (page 12)	Mushroom Shrimp Scampi (page 88)	Lemon Chicken and Zucchini Soup (page 106)	Baked Eggs with Zoodles (page 130)
Day-21	Mixed Nuts Berry Granola (page 28)	Chicken Broccoli Dijon Rice (page 61)	Pork, Sweet Potato and Corn Chowder (page 110)	Vanilla Latte (page 156)

Chapter 2: Breakfasts

Healthy PB&J Overnight Oats

Prep time: 15 minutes, Cook time: 26 minutes, Serves 4

Ingredients

Raspberry Jam:
2 cups fresh raspberries, plus more for topping
2 to 2½ tbsps. chia seeds, divided
2 to 4 tsps. pure maple syrup, divided
DIY Peanut Butter:
2 cups raw, shelled peanuts
⅛ tsp. sea salt
Oats:

1½ cups rolled oats
1½ cups unsweetened almond milk
2 tbsps. pure maple syrup
2 tbsps. chia seeds
For Serving:
Natural peanut butter (optional)
Chopped peanuts (optional)

Directions

Make the Jam:
1. In a medium saucepan over medium heat, cook the raspberries until the raspberries break down and release juices, about 5 to 10 minutes. Use the back of a spatula or a potato masher to mash the fruit, until it reaches your desired texture, lumpy or smooth.
2. Take the pan from the heat, and stir in 2 tsps. of the maple syrup. Taste the jam, and place more of the remaining 2 tsps. of maple syrup, a tsp. at a time, if needed for additional sweetness.
3. Put 2 tbsps. of the chia seeds to the jam, and stir to combine. Allow the jam to stand for about 5 to 10 minutes, or until thickened. The jam will continue to thicken, especially after it's refrigerated, but if you'd like thicker jam, toss in the remaining ½ tbsp. of chia seeds. Allow the jam to cool to room temperature, then take it to a jar with a lid or sealable container.

Make the Peanut Butter:
4. Preheat your oven to 350ºF (180ºC), and carefully line a rimmed baking sheet with parchment paper. Place the peanuts to the baking sheet, and roast for 8 to 10 minutes, until they are lightly golden and glossy with oil.
5. Take the peanuts from the oven, and take them to a food processor, along with the salt. Process the nuts for about 5 to 6 minutes, stopping to scrape down the sides and bottom of the bowl, as needed. The peanut butter is ready when it is completely smooth.

Make the Oats:
6. In a mixing bowl, combine ⅓ cup of the peanut butter, the maple syrup, and the milk. Toss in the oats and chia seeds.
7. Put about 2 tbsps. of the raspberry jam in the bottom of four 8-ounce jars with lids or sealable containers. Add one-quarter of the peanut butter–oat mixture over the raspberry jam in each jar. Cover and refrigerate overnight, or for at least 4 hours.
8. Place the raspberries and, if desired, the chopped peanuts and peanut butter on the oats. The oats can be enjoyed cold or heated in the microwave for 1 to 2 minutes.

Nutritional Info per Serving
calories: 595, fat: 38g, protein: 26g, carbs: 57g, fiber: 18g, sugar: 22g, sodium: 154mg

Chocolate Banana and Quinoa Breakfast Bowl

Prep time: 5 minutes, Cook time: 28 minutes, Serves 4

Ingredients

1 banana, sliced
1 cup quinoa, rinsed and drained
1 cup unsweetened almond milk
1 cup coconut milk
¼ cup fresh blueberries

2 tbsps. cacao powder
2 tbsps. cacao nibs
2 tbsps. organic maple syrup
1 tbsp. hemp seeds
½ tsp. pure vanilla extract
Pinch sea salt

Directions

1. In a small saucepan over medium heat, place the quinoa and toast it for about 3 minutes, stirring constantly. Pour in the unsweetened almond milk, coconut milk, and salt. Raise the heat to high and bring the liquid to a boil, stirring constantly.
2. Turn the heat to low and allow the quinoa to simmer for about 20 to 25 minutes, stirring occasionally.
3. Once the liquid is fully absorbed and the quinoa is tender, take the pan from the heat. Place the cacao powder, maple syrup, and vanilla extract. Stir to combine well.
4. Divide the quinoa evenly between 2 bowls and garnish with the banana, blueberries, cacao nibs, and hemp seeds. Enjoy!

Nutritional Info per Serving
calories: 408, fat: 18g, protein: 9g, carbs: 54g, fiber: 6g, sugar: 18g, sodium: 97mg

Glazed Strawberry Pop-Tarts

Prep time: 14 minutes, Cook time: 30 minutes, Makes 4 to 6 tarts

Ingredients
Crust:
½ cup coconut oil, frozen and chopped into small pieces
¾ cup whole-wheat pastry flour
½ cup spelt flour
1 egg, beaten
6 to 8 tbsps. ice cold water, divided
2 tsps. coconut sugar
½ tsp. sea salt
Strawberry Jam Filling:
2 to 4 tsps. raw honey or maple syrup
2 cups diced fresh strawberries
2 to 2½ tbsps. chia seeds
Glaze:
⅓ cup plain full-fat Greek yogurt
1 tbsp. pure maple syrup
¼ tsp. beet powder, for coloring (optional)
¼ tsp. vanilla extract

Directions
Make the Crust:
1. In a food processor, process the whole-wheat pastry flour, spelt flour, coconut sugar, and salt, until it's mixed well.
2. Pour in the coconut oil, and process until it is broken down into the size of peas.
3. Place the cold water, 1 tbsp. at a time, to the flour mixture, and pulse the food processor until the dough begins to come together. Shape the dough into a disc with your hands. Use plastic wrap to cover it and refrigerate it for at least 30 minutes, or until it is hard enough to hold together when it's rolled out.
4. While the dough is chilling, make the jam. In a large saucepan over medium heat, cook the strawberries for about 5 to 10 minutes, until they break down and release juices.
5. Use the back of a spatula or a potato masher to mash the fruit, leaving the texture of the jam lumpy or mashing it until smooth, as you prefer.
6. Take the pan from the heat, and stir in 2 tsps. of the honey. Taste, and place the remaining 2 tsps. of honey if it's needed for sweetness.
7. Put 2 tbsps. of the chia seeds to the pan, and stir them in. Allow the jam to stand for 5 to 10 minutes, or until thickened. The jam will continue to thicken after it's refrigerated, but if you want a thicker consistency, stir in the remaining ½ tbsp. of chia seeds. When the jam has cooled to room temperature, take it to a jar with a lid or sealable container.
Make the Tarts:
8. Take the dough from the fridge for about 10 minutes before you want to use it, so it softens just slightly.
9. On a lightly floured surface, roll the dough into a rectangle ⅛ inch thick with a rolling pin. Cut smaller rectangles to the size you want. Reroll the scraps and cut more rectangles.
10. With a pastry brush, brush the egg lightly over the pieces of dough. Place about 2 tbsps. of the strawberry jam filling on half of the rectangles, leaving a ½-inch border. Top each jam-covered rectangle with a second piece. Use the tines of a fork to press the sides of each tart together, then poke some holes on the top to let air escape while baking.
11. Arrange the tarts on a baking sheet, and refrigerate them for at least 30 minutes or up to 2 hours.
12. Preheat the oven to 350ºF (180ºC). Bake the tarts for about 20 minutes, until they are golden brown.
13. Make the glaze when the tarts are cooling from the oven. Whisk together the yogurt, vanilla, maple syrup, and beet powder, if desired. Coat the glaze evenly over the tarts. Enjoy!

Nutritional Info per Serving
calories: 311, fat: 20g, protein: 6g, carbs: 30g, fiber: 4g, sugar: 9g, sodium: 213mg

Breakfast Pistachio Muesli and Pear Bowl

Prep time: 5 minutes, Cook time: 20 minutes, Serves 2

Ingredients
2 cups gluten-free rolled oats
1 cup unsweetened almond milk
1 Anjou pear, sliced
½ cup shelled pistachios
2 tbsps. organic maple syrup
2 tbsps. sesame seeds
2 tbsps. poppy seeds
1 tsp. pure vanilla extract
¼ tsp. ground ginger
¼ tsp. sea salt

Directions
1. Preheat the oven to 375ºF (190ºC).
2. Combine the oats, pistachios, maple syrup, poppy seeds, sesame seeds, vanilla, ginger, and salt in a medium bowl.
3. Place the mixture onto a rimmed baking sheet and bake for about 10 minutes. Stir the muesli, rotate the pan, and bake for another 10 minutes or until golden brown.
4. Take the muesli from the oven and scoop into 2 bowls. Garnish with the unsweetened almond milk and the sliced Anjou pear. Serve immediately.

Nutritional Info per Serving
calories: 475, fat: 23g, protein: 23g, carbs: 80g, fiber: 21g, sugar: 32g, sodium: 432mg

Maple-Glazed Baked Vanilla Donuts

Prep time: 10 minutes, Cook time: 34 minutes, Makes 6 donuts

Ingredients
Baked Donuts:
3 tbsps. cooled, melted coconut oil, plus more for greasing the pan
3 eggs
1 cup almond flour
⅓ cup pure maple syrup
¼ cup coconut flour
¼ cup unsweetened almond milk
1 tbsp. arrowroot starch
1 tsp. vanilla extract
½ tsp. baking soda

¼ tsp. ground cinnamon
¼ tsp. sea salt
Maple Glaze:
1 tbsp. cooled, melted coconut oil
½ cup raw pistachios, crushed
2 tbsps. coconut butter
2 tbsps. pure maple syrup
½ tsp. vanilla extract
¼ tsp. ground cinnamon

Directions
1. Grease a donut pan lightly with coconut oil, and preheat the oven to 350ºF (180ºC). Prepare a cooling rack and place in a rimmed baking sheet.
2. Whisk together the almond flour, coconut flour, arrowroot starch, baking soda, salt, and cinnamon in a large mixing bowl.
3. In another mixing bowl, whisk together the eggs, coconut oil, almond milk, maple syrup, and vanilla.
4. Add the milk mixture into the flour mixture, and stir until entirely incorporated, taking care not to overmix.
5. Use a piping bag, ziplock bag with a corner cut off, or a spoon to pour the mixture into the donut-pan cavities until they're about three-quarters full.
6. Lightly tap the pan to release any air bubbles and smooth out the dough. Bake the donuts for about 20 to 24 minutes, or until they're golden and a toothpick inserted into the center comes out clean.
7. Allow the donuts to sit in the pan for 5 minutes, then take them to the prepared cooling rack.
8. Make the glaze while the donuts are cooled. In a heat-safe bowl, mix the coconut butter, coconut oil, maple syrup, and vanilla and microwave in 20-second increments until it's smooth. You can also heat the glaze in a double boiler.
9. One at a time, dip each donut into the glaze by a twisting motion, and then take the donut back to the rack, glazed side up. Scatter the glaze with the pistachios and cinnamon, and allow the donuts to stand until the glaze is hard, about 5 minutes. Enjoy!

Nutritional Info per Serving
calories: 395, fat: 30g, protein: 9g, carbs: 26g, fiber: 4g,
sugar: 18g, sodium: 254mg

Fried Rice Bowl

Prep time: 18 minutes, Cook time: 15 minutes, Serves 4

Ingredients
2 cups cooked brown rice, cooled
¼ cup vegetable broth
¼ cup coconut aminos
1 tsp. garlic, minced
1 tsp. lime juice, freshly squeezed
1 tbsp. grated peeled fresh ginger, divided
½ tsp. honey
2 tbsps. sesame oil,

divided
4 large eggs, beaten
½ cup chopped scallions, white and green parts separated
2 cups green cabbage, shredded
1 cup red cabbage, shredded
2 cups carrots, shredded

Directions
1. Whisk the vegetable broth, coconut aminos, garlic, lime juice, 1 tsp. of ginger, and honey in a large bowl.
2. Heat a large skillet or wok over medium-high heat. Add 1 tbsp. of oil and the eggs. Stir immediately to prevent the oil from burning. Scramble the eggs for about 1 minute into small pieces until cooked. Remove the eggs from the pan.
3. Adjust the heat to high. Place the scallion whites in the center of the skillet and cook until softened, for 1 minute, stirring constantly. Push the scallions to the outer edges of the skillet.
4. Place the cabbage in the center of pan. Cook for 1 minute, until slightly tender, stirring constantly. Push the cabbage with the scallions.
5. Repeat the process used in steps 4 and 5 for the remaining vegetables. Work in the following order: red cabbage, carrots, and, finally, the remaining 2 tsps. of ginger.
6. Once the ginger is fragrant, add the remaining oil and the cooked rice. Cook, stirring constantly, for 1 minute until the fried rice starts to smell toasted.
7. Still in all the vegetables from the edges of the skillet. Mix well to incorporate.
8. Pour in the sauce from step 2 and stir. Cook for about 2 minutes until reduced by roughly half. Remove the pan from the heat. Stir in the scrambled eggs and scallion greens.
9. Evenly portion the fried rice into 4 single-compartment glass meal-prep containers Cover the lids and refrigerate.

Nutritional Info per Serving
calories: 315, fat: 12g, protein: 9g, carbs: 35g, fiber: 6g,
sugar: 8g, sodium: 172mg

Homemade Cinnamon Rolls

Prep time: 16 minutes, Cook time: 25 minutes, Makes 10 rolls

Ingredients

Dough:
3 tbsps. coconut oil, plus more for greasing the pan
2½ to 3 cups whole-wheat pastry flour, divided
1 cup unsweetened almond milk
1 packet instant yeast or rapid-rise yeast
1 tbsp. coconut sugar
¼ tsp. sea salt
Filling:

3 tbsps. melted coconut oil
⅓ cup coconut sugar
2 tbsps. pure maple syrup
1½ tbsps. ground cinnamon
Frosting:
2½ tbsps. pure maple syrup
1½ cups plain full-fat Greek yogurt
1 tsp. vanilla extract
½ tsp. maple extract

Directions

Make the Dough:

1. In a large saucepan, heat the almond milk, coconut sugar, and coconut oil until warm and melted, but not boiling. Take the mixture from the heat, and allow it to cool for 5 minutes. Transfer the milk mixture to a large mixing bowl, and scatter the yeast across the surface. Let it sit for about 10 minutes to allow the yeast to activate.

2. Add the salt and ½ cup flour to the bowl, and stir it in. Continue to add the remaining flour, ½ cup at a time, stirring as you go. The dough will be sticky. Once the dough is too thick to stir, take it to a lightly floured surface, and knead it for a minute or so, until it forms a loose ball (be careful not to overmix). Continue to add flour a little at a time, as needed, until the dough no longer sticks to your hands. You may not need all the flour. Knead the dough for about 5 minutes, or until all the flour is entirely incorporated and the dough is smooth and springy.

3. Take the dough back to the bowl, cover it with plastic wrap or a clean dish towel, and place it in a warm place to rise for 1 hour, or until it is doubled in size.

Make the Filling:

4. In a small bowl, combine the coconut sugar and cinnamon. Combine the coconut oil and the maple syrup in a separate small bowl. Keep the bowls aside.

5. Grease an 8-inch square pan lightly with coconut oil.

6. On a lightly floured surface, gently roll out the dough into a thin, even ¼-inch rectangle. Brush with the coconut oil and maple syrup mixture. Then, generously scatter with the coconut sugar and cinnamon mixture.

7. Starting at one end, tightly roll up the dough and situate it seam side down. Cut the dough into ten 1- to 1½-inch sections with a serrated knife. Layer the rolls in the prepared pan.

8. Allow the rolls to rise while you preheat the oven to 350ºF (180ºC).

9. Once the oven is hot, bake the rolls until very slightly golden brown, for about 18 to 20 minutes. Pay close attention so they do not overcook and get too dry. Let the rolls cool in the pan for 10 minutes. While the rolls are cooling, prepare the frosting. Stir together the yogurt, vanilla, maple syrup, and maple extract. Spread the frosting on top of the rolls. Enjoy!

Nutritional Info per Serving
calories: 255, fat: 10g, protein: 7g, carbs: 37g, fiber: 4g, sugar: 14g, sodium: 96mg

Cinnamon Toast Crunch Waffles

Prep time: 7 minutes, Cook time: 15 minutes, Serves 4

Ingredients

Cooking oil spray
1 cup milk
3 large eggs
¼ cup coconut oil, melted
¼ cup coconut sugar, plus 2 tbsps. for topping (optional)

1 tsp. pure vanilla extract
2 cups flour
2 tsps. baking powder
1 tsp. cinnamon, plus 1 tsp., for topping (optional)
A pinch of salt

Directions

1. Coat a waffle iron with cooking oil spray. Preheat for 3 to 5 minutes.

2. In a large bowl, stir together the milk, eggs, coconut oil, ¼ cup sugar, and vanilla until frothy.

3. In a medium bowl, combine the flour, baking powder, 1 tsp. of cinnamon, and salt.

4. Pour the flour mixture into the milk mixture and whisk into a smooth batter.

5. Pour ¼ cup of batter evenly into the waffle iron.

6. If using, combine the remaining 1 tsp. of cinnamon and 2 tbsps. of sugar in a small bowl and mix thoroughly. Close the waffle iron briefly, about 1 second, then reopen and sprinkle the waffles with a small amount of the cinnamon and sugar mixture.

7. Close the waffle iron and cook the waffles until cooked through, or as per manufacturer instructions.

8. Top with fresh berries, yogurt, or maple syrup. Sprinkle with the cinnamon or sugar, if using.

Nutritional Info per Serving (2 waffles)
calories: 460, fat: 20g, protein: 14g, carbs: 60g, fiber: 1.8g, sugar: 10.4g, sodium: 122mg

Cinnamon Apple French Toast Bake

Prep time: 14 minutes, Cook time: 5 hours, Serves 8

Ingredients
8 eggs
10 slices whole-wheat bread, cubed
2 Granny Smith apples, peeled and diced
1 cup granola
1 cup canned coconut milk
1 cup unsweetened apple juice
¼ cup coconut sugar
2 tsps. vanilla extract
1 tsp. ground cinnamon
¼ tsp. ground cardamom

Directions
1. Grease a 6-quart slow cooker lightly with plain vegetable oil.
2. Mix the coconut sugar, cinnamon, and cardamom in a small bowl.
3. Layer the bread, apples, and coconut sugar mixture in the slow cooker.
4. Mix the eggs, coconut milk, apple juice, and vanilla in a large bowl, and mix well. Add this mixture slowly over the food in the slow cooker. Scatter the granola on top.
5. Cover the slow cooker and cook on low for 4 to 5 hours, or until a food thermometer registers 165ºF (74ºC).
6. Ladle the mixture from the slow cooker to serve.

Nutritional Info per Serving
calories: 317, fat: 9g, protein: 12g, carbs: 49g, fiber: 6g, sugar: 18g, sodium: 326mg

Warm Green and Quinoa Breakfast Bowl

Prep time: 3 minutes, Cook time: 23 minutes, Serves 2

Ingredients
2 tbsps. coconut oil, divided
1 cup quinoa, rinsed and drained
1 cup kale, chopped
1 cup baby spinach
2 eggs
1 avocado, sliced
2 cups water
2 garlic cloves, minced
2 tbsps. chopped almonds

Directions
1. In a large pot, bring the quinoa and water to a boil over high heat, stirring constantly. Turn the heat to low and allow the quinoa to simmer until al dente, for about 10 to 15 minutes, stirring occasionally. Drain well and keep aside.
2. In a cast-iron pan, heat 1 tbsp. coconut oil over medium heat. Place the garlic and almonds and cook for about 3 to 5 minutes, until the almonds become golden brown.
3. Put the cooked quinoa, kale, and spinach to the pan and cook for 3 to 5 minutes, until the leaves start to wilt. Divide the mixture evenly between 2 bowls.
4. Heat the remaining 1 tbsp. of coconut oil in the same pan. Gently crack the eggs into the pan and fry them until the whites are cooked through. Put a fried egg and half of the avocado on top of each bowl. Serve immediately.

Nutritional Info per Serving
calories: 415, fat: 29g, protein: 13g, carbs: 29g, fiber: 9g, sugar: 2g, sodium: 95mg

Healthy Veggie Sandwich

Prep time: 6 minutes, Cook time: 0 minutes, Serves 1

Ingredients
2 slices whole-grain bread
4 leaves butter lettuce
1 medium tomato, sliced
1 small carrot, julienned
½ small avocado
⅛ head red cabbage, thinly sliced
½ small cucumber, thinly sliced
¼ small red onion, thinly sliced
1½ tsps. raw sunflower seeds
⅛ tsp. black sesame seeds
⅛ tsp. sea salt
⅛ tsp. ground black pepper

Directions
1. Toast the bread until crisp, so it does not get soggy. Keep it aside.
2. Mash the avocado until it is mostly smooth in a small bowl. Combine the salt, pepper, and sesame seeds.
3. Place half of the mashed avocado over one side of each slice of toast. Scatter one slice with the sunflower seeds.
4. Layer half the lettuce over the sunflower seeds, so it evenly fits the size of bread, then place the cucumber, carrot, tomato, cabbage, and onion. Then put the remaining lettuce, and place the other slice of toast on top.
5. Tightly wrap the sandwich in parchment paper to help hold it together. Slice the sandwich in half and serve right away.

Nutritional Info per Serving
calories: 426, fat: 20g, protein: 15g, carbs: 54g, fiber: 19g, sugar: 17g, sodium: 589mg

Apple Oat Breakfast Bowl

Prep time: 4 minutes, Cook time: 15 minutes, Serves 2

Ingredients

Bowl:
1 cup gluten-free rolled oats
2 cups water
¼ tsp. ground cinnamon
¼ tsp. ground cardamom
¼ tsp. ground nutmeg
Pinch sea salt

Topping:
1 apple, sliced
¼ cup dried cranberries
¼ cup toasted pumpkin seeds
2 tbsps. chia seeds
1 tbsp. raw honey
1 tbsp. chopped crystallized ginger

Directions

1. Bring the oats, water, cardamom, cinnamon, nutmeg, and salt to a boil in a large pot over medium heat. Turn the heat to low and allow the oats to simmer for about 5 to 7 minutes, stirring occasionally, until the liquid is entirely absorbed.
2. Divide the oats evenly between 2 bowls.
3. Place the apple slices, pumpkin seeds, cranberries, chia seeds, and crystallized ginger on the oatmeal. Drizzle with the honey. Enjoy!

Nutritional Info per Serving
calories: 296, fat: 11g, protein: 13g, carbs: 58g, fiber: 12g, sugar: 20g, sodium: 89mg

Veggies Breakfast Bowl

Prep time: 5 minutes, Cook time: 9 minutes, Serves 2

Ingredients

1 tbsp. extra-virgin olive oil
2 carrots, peeled and sliced
1 beet, peeled
8 Brussels sprouts, sliced
4 kale leaves, stemmed and chopped
½ cup canned chickpeas, drained
½ avocado, sliced
2 tbsps. pomegranate seeds
1 tbsp. water
1½ tsps. miso paste

Directions

1. Whisk together the miso paste and water in a small bowl and keep aside.
2. In a cast-iron pan, heat the olive oil over medium heat. Place the beet, carrots, Brussels sprouts, kale, and chickpeas. Cook for about 5 to 7 minutes, until the kale starts to wilt.
3. Stir in the miso mixture and sauté for an additional 2 minutes. Take the pan from the stove.
4. Divide the vegetables equally between 2 bowls and

garnish with pomegranate seeds and avocado slices. Enjoy!

Nutritional Info per Serving
calories: 400, fat: 18g, protein: 15g, carbs: 50g, fiber: 14g, sugar: 12g, sodium: 230mg

Healthy Blueberry Chia Jam and Oatmeal Breakfast Bowl

Prep time: 8 minutes, Cook time: 15 minutes, Serves 2

Ingredients

Blueberry Chia Jam:
2 cups frozen blueberries
1 tbsp. chia seeds
1 tbsp. organic maple syrup
1 tsp. freshly squeezed lemon juice
1 tsp. pure vanilla extract
Pinch sea salt
Oatmeal:
1 tbsp. coconut oil
2 cups gluten-free rolled oats

1½ cups plus 2 tbsps. water
½ cup unsweetened almond milk
¼ tsp. ground cinnamon
Pinch sea salt
Topping:
2 tbsps. unsweetened coconut flakes
2 tbsps. chopped toasted almonds
1 tbsp. flaxseed
1 tbsp. chia seeds

Directions

Make the Blueberry Chia Jam:
1. Add the blueberries, maple syrup, vanilla, lemon juice, and salt in a food processor, and combine until smooth. With the food processor running, gently add the chia seeds and process until completely incorporated, 5 to 10 seconds.
2. Scrape the jam into a glass jar, and put it in the refrigerator until gelled, about 15 to 20 minutes.

Make the Oatmeal:
3. In a large skillet, heat the coconut oil over medium heat. Place the oats and toast for about 6 to 8 minutes, stirring occasionally.
4. In a large pot, bring the unsweetened almond milk, water, salt, and cinnamon to a boil over medium heat.
5. Toss the oats into the liquid. Cover the pot, turn off the heat and allow the oats to sit for about 7 minutes.
6. Take the oats from the stove, stir them, and evenly divide between 2 bowls. Swirl in the blueberry chia jam and garnish with the coconut, almonds, chia seeds, and flaxseed. Enjoy!

Nutritional Info per Serving
calories: 444, fat: 22g, protein: 20g, carbs: 80g, fiber: 22g, sugar: 28g, sodium: 225mg

Green and Banana Blueberry Yogurt Bowl

Prep time: 12 minutes, Cook time: 0 minutes, Serves 2

Ingredients
Bowls:
2 cup baby spinach
1 cup plain full-fat Greek yogurt
1 ripe banana
Small handful of kale, stems removed
½ avocado
2 tbsps. almond butter

1 tsp. matcha powder
For Serving:
1 cup fresh blueberries
Unsweetened shredded coconut (optional)
Sliced kiwi (optional)
Raw pepitas (optional)
Hemp seed hearts (optional)

Directions
1. In a food processor or high-speed blender, combine the spinach, yogurt, kale, banana, avocado, almond butter, and matcha powder. Blend until smooth and creamy, then evenly divide between two bowls.
2. For serving, place the blueberries, pepitas, coconut, kiwi, and hemp seed hearts (if desired) on the yogurt mixture.

Nutritional Info per Serving
calories: 313, fat: 21g, protein: 9g, carbs: 26g, fiber: 6g, sugar: 17g, sodium: 116mg

Savory Mushroom and Oat Breakfast Bowl

Prep time: 3 minutes, Cook time: 12 minutes, Serves 2

Ingredients
2 eggs
1 tsp. coconut oil, divided
1 cup gluten-free rolled oats
¼ cup mushrooms
1 red bell pepper, cored and diced

½ onion, chopped
2 cups water
2 tbsps. chopped scallions
¼ tsp. sea salt
¼ tsp. freshly ground black pepper

Directions
1. In a large pot, bring the oats, water, salt, and pepper to a boil over medium heat. Turn the heat to low and allow the oats to simmer for about 5 to 7 minutes, stirring occasionally, until the liquid is absorbed.
2. In a cast-iron pan, heat ½ tsp. coconut oil over medium-high heat. Place the pepper, onion, and mushrooms to the pan and cook for about 3 to 5 minutes, until tender. Scoop the pepper and onion over the cooked oats.
3. In the same pan over medium heat, heat the remaining ½ tsp. coconut oil. Gently crack the eggs into the pan and fry them until the whites are cooked through.
4. Divide the oats and vegetables evenly between 2 bowls and place a fried egg and the scallions on top. Enjoy!

Nutritional Info per Serving
calories: 223, fat: 10g, protein: 15g, carbs: 37g, fiber: 8g, sugar: 4g, sodium: 365mg

Blackberry Cobbler Granola with Greek Yogurt Bowl

Prep time: 16 minutes, Cook time: 30 minutes, Serves 4

Ingredients
Blackberry Cobbler Granola:
2 tbsps. melted coconut oil
2 cups rolled oats
1½ cups fresh blackberries, plus more for topping
½ cup raw pepitas
½ cup sliced raw

almonds
3 tbsps. raw honey
½ tsp. vanilla extract
½ tsp. ground cinnamon
Bowls:
2 tbsps. raw honey, plus more for topping
2 cups plain full-fat Greek yogurt
½ tsp. vanilla extract

Directions
1. Preheat the oven to 350ºF (180ºC), and carefully line a rimmed baking sheet with parchment paper.
Make the Granola:
2. Combine the oats, almonds, pepitas, honey, coconut oil, vanilla, and cinnamon in a large mixing bowl, and toss to coat well. Gently stir in the blackberries. Take the granola to the baking sheet and spread it out evenly.
3. Bake for about 25 to 30 minutes, stirring one or two times. The granola is done when the oats smell toasted and are golden brown. Let the granola cool completely—it will harden as it cools.
Make the Bowls:
4. In a large mixing bowl, mix the yogurt, honey, and vanilla, until it is combined well.
5. For serving, evenly divide the flavored yogurt mixture between two bowls, and then place the blackberry cobbler granola, fresh blackberries, and honey on top, if desired.

Nutritional Info per Serving
calories: 507, fat: 27g, protein: 20g, carbs: 69g, fiber: 13g, sugar: 31g, sodium: 63mg

Strawberry Shortcake Overnight Oats

Prep time: 5 minutes, Cook time: 0 minutes, Serves 2

Ingredients
1 cup rolled oats
1 cup strawberries, diced, plus more for serving
1 cup unsweetened almond milk
¼ cup plain full-fat Greek yogurt, plus more for serving
2 tsps. raw honey
½ tsp. vanilla extract
½ tsp. almond extract

Directions
1. Mix the oats, milk, strawberries, yogurt, honey, almond extract, and vanilla until well combined in a small bowl. Divide the mixture evenly between two 8-ounce jars with lids or sealable containers. Refrigerate overnight, or for at least 4 hours.
2. When ready to serve, place additional strawberries and yogurt on the oats. The oats can be enjoyed cold or heated in the microwave for 1 to 2 minutes.

Nutritional Info per Serving
calories: 259, fat: 8g, protein: 14g, carbs: 51g, fiber: 9g, sugar: 18g, sodium: 77mg

Breakfast Almond Oats

Prep time: 10 minutes, Cook time: 0 minutes, Serves 2

Ingredients
Oats:
½ cup unsweetened coconut milk
½ cup rolled oats
1 tbsp. cooled, melted coconut butter
1 tbsp. pure maple syrup
1 tbsp. chia seeds
1 tbsp. dark cocoa powder
¼ tsp. almond extract
For Serving:
1 tbsp. almond butter
1 tsp. unsweetened shredded coconut
1 tsp. raw sliced almonds
1 tsp. dark chocolate chips

Directions
1. In a mixing bowl, add the oats, coconut milk, chia seeds, coconut butter, dark cocoa powder, maple syrup, and almond extract. Stir well to combine. Evenly divide the oats into two 8-ounce jars with lids or sealable containers.
2. Refrigerate the oats overnight, or for at least 4 hours. The oats can be served straight from the refrigerator or can be heated in the microwave for about 30 to 60 seconds.
3. For serving, place the almond butter, chocolate chips, almonds, and coconut on the oats.

Nutritional Info per Serving
calories: 407, fat: 32g, protein: 10g, carbs: 33g, fiber: 8g, sugar: 10g, sodium: 17mg

Freezer V-Egg-ie Burritos

Prep time: 7 minutes, Cook time: 18 minutes, Serves 4

Ingredients
Vegetables:
1 tbsp. olive oil
4 garlic cloves, minced
1 yellow onion, chopped
1 bell pepper, chopped
1 medium sweet potato, diced
½ tsp. paprika
½ tsp. garlic powder
Salt
Pepper

Eggs:
8 eggs
Pinch paprika
Salt
Pepper
1 tbsp. water
1 cup Cheddar cheese, shredded
Burritos:
4 large burrito wraps

Directions
Make the Vegetables:
1. Heat the oil over medium heat in a large skillet. Add the garlic, onion, bell pepper, and sweet potato and stir together.
2. Cover and cook for 10 minutes, or until the potato is fork-tender. Add the paprika, garlic powder, salt, and pepper and stir to ensure all vegetables are evenly seasoned. Transfer the vegetables to a large bowl.

Make the Eggs:
3. Whisk together the eggs, spices, and water in a large bowl until frothy.
4. Return the skillet to heat (add an extra tsp. of oil if dry). Add the ready eggs to the skillet. Stir constantly until just cooked. Stir in the cheese until the cheese is melted.

Make the Burritos:
5. Spread ¼ of the vegetables and ¼ of the eggs on each wrap. Start with end closest to you and fold the left and right sides of the wrap toward the middle, then roll the burrito up tightly.
6. Cool the burritos to room temperature. Wrap each burrito tightly with parchment paper and then wrap again with aluminum foil. Place in the freezer. Before serving, remove both wraps and microwave for 60 seconds or until warm. Alternatively, warm the burrito in the oven or a toaster oven. Garnish with avocado and hot sauce.

Nutritional Info per Serving
calories: 557, fat: 28g, protein: 25g, carbs: 48g, fiber: 3.2g, sugar: 7.8g, sodium: 624mg

High Protein Breakfast Box

Prep time: 7 minutes, Cook time: 0 minutes, Serves 4

Ingredients
2 cups full-fat plain Greek yogurt
1 cup blueberries, fresh
1 cup fresh strawberries, sliced
1 cup granola
8 large hard-boiled eggs, peeled
½ cup almonds, divided

Directions
1. Portion ½ cup of yogurt into the largest compartment of 4 large three-compartment glass meal-prep containers. Top the yogurt with ¼ cup of blueberries, ¼ cup of strawberries, and ¼ cup of granola.
2. Place 2 hard-boiled eggs in one of the small compartments of each container.
3. Portion 2 tbsps. of almonds into the other small compartment. Cover and refrigerate.

Nutritional Info per Serving
calories: 486, fat: 24g, protein: 26g, carbs: 41g, fiber: 8g, sugar: 13g, sodium: 227mg

Autumn Harvest Bowl

Prep time: 14 minutes, Cook time: 35 minutes, Serves 4

Ingredients
2 cups cooked quinoa
2 small delicata squash, halved, seeded, and cut into ½-inch-thick half-moons
1 (15½-ounce / 439-g) can chickpeas, drained and rinsed
2 tsps. extra-virgin olive oil
½ tsp. salt
½ tsp. black pepper, freshly ground
¼ tsp. cinnamon, ground
⅛ tsp. paprika
4 thyme sprigs
¼ cup cranberries, dried
¼ cup pumpkin seeds
1 (8-ounce / 227-g) package chopped kale
¼ cup maple syrup

Directions
1. Preheat the oven to 350ºF (180ºC). Line a large baking sheet with foil.
2. In a large bowl, combine well the squash, chickpeas, oil, salt, pepper, cinnamon, paprika, and thyme sprigs. Evenly spread the mixture into a single layer on the baking sheet.
3. Roast for 30 minutes. Remove from the oven and sprinkle with the cranberries and pumpkin seeds. Bake for 5 minutes more.
4. Meanwhile, evenly portion the kale into 4 large single-compartment glass meal-prep containers with lids.
5. Evenly divide the cooked quinoa, the warm ingredients, and the maple syrup, on top of the kale. Cover and refrigerate.

Nutritional Info per Serving
calories: 448, fat: 10g, protein: 13g, carbs: 82g, fiber: 16g, sugar: 23g, sodium: 447mg

Vegetable Ratatouille Bake

Prep time: 16 minutes, Cook time: 1 hour, Serves 8

Ingredients
1 tsp. extra-virgin olive oil plus 1 tbsp.
1 (12-ounce / 340-g) eggplant cut into ¼-inch rounds
2 tsps. salt, divided
1 (28-ounce / 794-g) can diced tomatoes and juices
2 tbsps. balsamic vinegar
2 tbsps. garlic, minced
½ cup thinly sliced scallions, white and green parts
¼ cup loosely packed fresh basil, chopped
½ tsp. herbes de Provence
¼ tsp. black pepper, freshly ground
⅛ tsp. red pepper flakes (optional)
1 or 2 zucchinis, cut into ¼-inch rounds
1 or 2 yellow squash, cut into ¼-inch rounds

Directions
1. Preheat the oven to 375ºF (190ºC). Brush a 9-by-13-inch glass baking dish with 1 tsp. of oil.
2. Lay out the eggplant slices. Sprinkle with 1 tsp. of salt and let sit.
3. In a large bowl, stir together the tomatoes and their juices, vinegar, garlic, scallions, basil, remaining 1 tsp. of salt, herbes de Provence, black pepper, and red pepper flakes, if using. Transfer half the mixture to the baking dish, evenly spreading it in a layer.
4. Blot the salted eggplant with a clean towel to remove excess moisture. Stack the eggplant, zucchini, and yellow squash in 3 or 4 rows, alternating in a pattern to fill the baking dish.
5. Cover the vegetables with the remaining tomato mixture. Drizzle with the remaining 1 tbsp. of oil.
6. Cover with foil and bake for 40 minutes. Remove the foil and bake for 20 minutes.
7. Portion half the ratatouille into 4 single-compartment glass meal-prep containers. Cover and refrigerate. Portion the remaining half into 4 airtight freezer-safe containers. Cover and freeze.

Nutritional Info per Serving
calories: 81, fat: 2.6g, protein: 1.9g, carbs: 12g, fiber: 5g, sugar: 5g, sodium: 497mg

Maple French Toast Overnight Oats

Prep time: 3 minutes, Cook time: 0 minutes, Serves 2

Ingredients

1⅓ cups almond milk, unsweetened
1 cup rolled oats
2 tbsps. flax meal
2 tbsps. maple syrup

2 tsps. chia seeds
1½ tsps. cinnamon
Fresh berries, maple syrup, or walnuts, for topping (optional)

Directions

1. In a medium bowl, combine almond milk, oats, flax meal, maple syrup, chia seeds and cinnamon and mix well.
2. Divide the oatmeal mixture evenly into two 2-cup containers with lids, for storage.
3. Cover and keep for 8 hours or overnight in fridge.
4. Remove the overnight oats from the refrigerator, add the toppings you prefer, and enjoy.

Nutritional Info per Serving
calories: 273, fat: 8.1g, protein: 8g, carbs: 46g, fiber: 7.8g, sugar: 19g, sodium: 110mg

Easy Green Shakshuka

Prep time: 8 minutes, Cook time: 16 minutes, Serves 6

Ingredients

1 tbsp. extra-virgin olive oil
1 yellow onion, chopped
1 green bell pepper, chopped
3 garlic cloves, minced
4 cups kale, chopped
¼ cup fresh parsley, chopped

1 (7-ounce / 198-g) can mild green chiles
6 large eggs
6 ounces (170 g) feta, crumbled
1 avocado, sliced for topping
1 jalapeño, seeded and sliced in rings for topping

Directions

1. Preheat the oven to 375ºF (190ºC).
2. Heat the oil over medium heat in a large oven-safe skillet. Add the onion and sauté until the onion starts to become translucent, for 3 minutes.
3. Add the green pepper and garlic. Sauté for another 2 to 3 minutes.
4. Add the kale, parsley, and green chiles, stirring until the kale is wilted.
5. Make 6 wells in the pepper-and-onion mixture with a spatula.
6. Crack 1 egg into each well.
7. Place the skillet in the oven and bake for 10 minutes, or until the whites of the eggs are set.
8. Top with the crumbled feta, sliced avocado, and jalapeño rings and serve.

Nutritional Info per Serving
calories: 262, fat: 17g, protein: 12g, carbs: 13g, fiber: 5.3g, sugar: 3.1g, sodium: 502mg

Maple-Pecan Beet and Oats

Prep time: 7 minutes, Cook time: 10 minutes, Serves 2

Ingredients

Oats:
2 medium raw beets, peeled and diced
1 cup rolled oats
1 cup unsweetened almond milk
2 tbsps. pure maple syrup
1 tbsp. chia seeds
1 tsp. vanilla extract

Maple-Pecan Topping:
1 tbsp. pure maple syrup
¼ cup pecans, plus more for topping
½ tsp. ground cinnamon
Greek Yogurt Topping:
1 tbsp. pure maple syrup
⅓ cup plain full-fat Greek yogurt
¼ tsp. vanilla extract

Directions

1. In a food processor or blender, process the beets, milk, maple syrup, and vanilla until smooth.
2. Combine the oats and chia seeds in a large mixing bowl, and stir to mix well. Place the beet mixture, and stir to combine well. Divide the mixture evenly between two 8-ounce jars with lids or sealable containers. Refrigerate overnight, or for at least 4 hours.

Make the Maple-Pecan Topping:
3. Toast the pecans. Heat a skillet over medium heat, then place the pecans. Cook, tossing constantly, until the pecans turn darker brown and turn aromatic, about 4 to 6 minutes. Then pour in the maple syrup and cinnamon, and stir frequently for about 3 to 4 minutes, or until the syrup crystallizes and turns into a powder.
4. Take the pan from the heat immediately, and let the nuts cool. Store the topping in an airtight container if you make it ahead.

Make the Yogurt Topping:
5. In a small bowl, stir together the yogurt, maple syrup, and vanilla. Refrigerate, covered, if you make it ahead.
6. Place the yogurt mixture, maple pecans, and raw pecans on the refrigerated oats. Enjoy!

Nutritional Info per Serving
calories: 426, fat: 18g, protein: 18g, carbs: 66g, fiber: 13g, sugar: 28g, sodium: 153mg

High-Protein Breakfast Egg Muffins

Prep time: 6 minutes, Cook time: 20 minutes, Serves 6

Ingredients
Cooking oil spray
8 large eggs
½ cup plain unsweetened Greek yogurt
½ tsp. salt
¼ tsp. black pepper
½ cup Cheddar cheese, shredded
2 cups raw vegetables, chopped

Directions
1. Preheat the oven to 350ºF (180ºC). Coat the muffin cups of a 12-cup muffin tin with cooking oil spray.
2. In a large bowl, whisk the eggs, Greek yogurt, salt, and pepper until the eggs are frothy and no large clumps are visible.
3. Fold the cheese into the egg mixture. Set aside.
4. Evenly distribute the vegetables among the muffin cups.
5. Pour about ¼ cup of the egg over the vegetables in each muffin cup.
6. Bake until cooked through, for 20 minutes.

Nutritional Info per Serving (2 muffins)
calories: 160, fat: 12g, protein: 11g, carbs: 2.8g, fiber: 1.1g, sugar: 0.4g, sodium: 374mg

Blueberry Oatmeal Pancakes

Prep time: 10 minutes, Cook time: 10 minutes, Serves 4

Ingredients
2 eggs
1 cup plain unsweetened Greek yogurt
¼ cup maple syrup
½ cup milk of choice
1 tsp. pure vanilla extract
1½ cups rolled oats
2 tbsps. flax meal
1 tsp. baking powder
½ tsp. cinnamon
A pinch of salt
1 cup blueberries
Cooking oil spray

Directions
1. In a large bowl, combine the eggs, yogurt, maple syrup, milk, and vanilla and whisk until frothy.
2. In a medium bowl, stir the oats, flax meal, baking powder, cinnamon, and salt and until well blended.
3. Add the oat mixture into the wet ingredients and whisk until well combined.
4. Fold the blueberries into the batter.
5. Heat a skillet or griddle over medium heat. Coat the surface with cooking oil spray.
6. Pour ¼ cup of the batter onto a hot skillet. Cook for 2 to 3 minutes or until bubbles form on the surface and begin to pop. Flip and cook for another 60 to 90 seconds.
7. Remove from the heat and set aside. Repeat with the remaining batter.

Nutritional Info per Serving (2 to 3 pancakes)
calories: 315, fat: 12g, protein: 10g, carbs: 45g, fiber: 5.2g, sugar: 19g, sodium: 132mg

Sweet Potato Crust Quiche

Prep time: 12 minutes, Cook time: 1 hour 5 minutes, Serves 6

Ingredients
Crust:
Cooking oil spray
1 large (16- to 20-ounce / 454- to 567-g) sweet potato, sliced into ⅛-inch slices
Salt
Pepper
Filling:
1 tbsp. olive oil
1 small onion, chopped
2 garlic cloves, minced
1 bell pepper, chopped
6 large eggs
½ cup milk
2 tsps. dried basil
Salt
Pepper
Red pepper flakes (optional)
½ cup Mozzarella cheese, shredded
1 cup kale, chopped

Directions
Make the Crust:
1. Preheat the oven to 350ºF (180ºC).
2. Spray the inside of a 9-inch round pan or pie dish with cooking oil spray. Place the sweet potatoes round on the bottom and sides of pan, overlapping heavily. Sprinkle with salt and pepper. Lightly spray cooking oil on the top of sweet potatoes.
3. Bake for 30 minutes. Note that the sweet potato will shrink somewhat.
Make the Filling:
4. While the crust is cooking, heat the olive oil in a medium saucepan. Add the onion and garlic. Cook for 1 minute, or until translucent. Add the bell pepper and cook for 3 to 4 minutes more, or until the bell pepper is tender.
5. In medium bowl, whisk together the eggs, milk, basil, salt, pepper. Stir in red pepper flakes, if desired. Combine the egg mixture with the ready peppers and onions. Add the cheese and kale and stir.
6. Pour the egg mixture on top of the crust. Bake for 30 minutes or until eggs are set. Slice into 6 pieces.

Nutritional Info per Serving
calories: 215, fat: 9g, protein: 10g, carbs: 20g, fiber: 2.7g, sugar: 3.2g, sodium: 188mg

Banana and Pecan Breakfast Bowl, page 24

Breakfast Almond Oats, page 17

Apple Sausage Patties, page 27

Loaded Avocado Toast with Eggs, page 26

Blueberry Porridge Breakfast Bowl

Prep time: 8 minutes, Cook time: 10 minutes, Serves 2

Ingredients

Porridge:
1 cup fresh blueberries, plus more for topping
1 cup rolled oats
1 cup whole milk
1 cup water
2 tbsps. chia seeds
2 tbsps. pure maple syrup, plus more for topping

2 tsps. vanilla extract
¼ tsp. ground cinnamon, plus more for topping
⅛ tsp. sea salt
For Serving:
Milk (optional)
Chopped almonds (optional)
Plain full-fat Greek yogurt (optional)

Directions

1. In a medium saucepan, place the oats, water, milk, blueberries, chia seeds, maple syrup, cinnamon, and salt. Stir to combine well.
2. Cook over medium heat, stirring occasionally, until the mixture comes to a boil, about 5 minutes. Reduce the heat, and simmer for about 5 more minutes, until the oats have thickened and most of the berries have popped, turning the porridge purple. Transfer the porridge from the heat, and stir in the vanilla.
3. For serving, take the porridge into two bowls, and place blueberries, syrup, and cinnamon on top. Serve with the chopped almonds, a little milk, and a dollop of yogurt for additional texture, if desired.

Nutritional Info per Serving

calories: 346, fat: 11g, protein: 14g, carbs: 66g, fiber: 13g, sugar: 27g, sodium: 217mg

Baked Pumpkin Spice Oatmeal Bars

Prep time: 10 minutes, Cook time: 45 minutes, Serves 6

Ingredients

Cooking oil spray
2 cups rolled oats
1 tsp. baking powder
1 tsp. cinnamon
A pinch of salt
1 cup puréed pumpkin

¾ cup milk of choice
¼ cup maple syrup
1 large egg
1 tsp. pure vanilla extract
½ cup walnuts (optional)

Directions

1. Preheat the oven to 350ºF (180ºC). Coat the inside of an 8-by-8-inch baking dish with cooking oil spray.
2. Mix together the oats, baking powder, cinnamon, and salt in a large bowl.
3. In a medium bowl, combine the pumpkin, milk, maple syrup, egg, and vanilla. Stir until well blended and smooth.
4. Add the pumpkin mixture to the dry ingredients and stir until well combined.
5. Carefully fold in the walnuts, if using.
6. Pour the batter into the prepared baking dish. Bake for 45 minutes or until a toothpick inserted in the center comes out clean. Cut into 12 squares. Refrigerate in a sealed, airtight container and serve or keep for up to 5 days.

Nutritional Info per Serving (2 bars)

calories: 185, fat: 3.5g, protein: 6g, carbs: 31g, fiber: 4g, sugar: 10.2g, sodium: 57mg

Apple Cinnamon Oatmeal Cake

Prep time: 15 minutes, Cook time: 45 minutes, Serves 4

Ingredients

Nonstick cooking spray
2 ripe bananas
2 large eggs
1¼ cups milk
1 tbsp. honey
1 tbsp. chia seeds
1 tbsp. cinnamon, ground
1 tsp. baking powder

½ tsp. salt
½ tsp. nutmeg, ground
2 cups old-fashioned rolled oats
½ cup walnuts, crushed
1 red apple, thinly sliced
2 cups fresh strawberries, sliced

Directions

1. Preheat the oven to 400ºF (205ºC). Coat a 9-by-9-inch glass baking dish with cooking spray.
2. In a high-speed blender, combine the bananas, eggs, milk, honey, chia seeds, cinnamon, baking powder, salt, and nutmeg. Blend on high in 30-second intervals until smooth, scraping down the sides if needed.
3. Put the oats in a large bowl. Pour the blender mixture over the oats and stir until fully incorporated. Pour the batter to the prepared baking dish and top with the walnuts and apple slices.
4. Bake until golden brown, for 45 minutes. Insert a toothpick into the center coming out clean. Set aside to cool and then cut into 8 slices.
5. Portion 2 slices of cake into the bigger side of 4 large two-compartment glass meal-prep containers with lids. Place the strawberries in the adjacent compartment. Cover and refrigerate.

Nutritional Info per Serving

calories: 453, fat: 13g, protein: 12g, carbs: 72g, fiber: 16g, sugar: 27g, sodium: 357mg

Blueberry Pecan Cheesecake Bars

Prep time: 8 minutes, Cook time: 0 minutes, Makes 10 (2-inch) square bars

Ingredients

Cheesecake Filling:
1½ cups raw cashews
1 cup fresh blueberries
⅔ cup full-fat coconut milk, refrigerated
⅓ cup melted coconut oil
⅓ cup pure maple syrup
2 cups water, boiled

Freshly squeezed juice of 2 medium lemons
Crust:
1 cup raw pecans
12 pitted dried dates
2 tbsps. rolled oats, plus more for topping
⅛ tsp. sea salt

Directions

1. For the filling, cover the cashews with the water and allow them to soak for at least 1 hour, or up to overnight. It's necessary to soak them to soften them.
2. Make the crust when the cashews soak. Process the pecans, dates, oats, and salt in a food processor or high-speed blender. The mixture will first be a consistency of cornmeal. Continue to process it until a small ball forms, and then until the mixture resembles a loose dough.
3. Line a 9 × 5-inch loaf pan or an 8-inch square pan with parchment paper. A pan with shallow sides will make the crust easier to press, but it is not required. Carefully use your fingers to pack down the date-pecan mixture evenly.
4. To continue with the filling, drain the soaked cashews, and put them in a blender. Spoon the hardened coconut milk from the top of the can, leaving the clear liquid underneath (you can reserve the water for another use, if desired). Pour the solid coconut milk, lemon juice, coconut oil, and maple syrup into the blender. Blend the mixture together until very smooth; the smoother this mixture is, the creamier your cheesecake will be. Carefully fold in the blueberries, and place the mixture on top of the prepared crust.
5. Freeze the mixture in the pan for about 1 to 2 hours to let it set. When it's solid, take the bars from the freezer, and slice them into 2-inch squares.
6. Store the bars in an airtight container in the freezer and use parchment paper to separate the bars so they don't stick to each other. To serve, thaw the bars for about 5 minutes at room temperature, so they soften slightly.

Nutritional Info per Serving (1 bar)
calories: 336, fat: 26g, protein: 5g, carbs: 24g, fiber: 3g, sugar: 14g, sodium: 38mg

Homemade Strawberry Shortcake Overnight Oats

Prep time: 4 minutes, Cook time: 0 minutes, Serves 2

Ingredients
1 cup milk
1 cup rolled oats
½ cup small-curd cottage cheese
2 tbsps. honey

1 tbsp. chia seeds
2 tsps. strawberry jam or jelly (optional)
1 tsp. pure vanilla extract
1 cup strawberries, sliced

Directions
1. In a medium bowl, combine all ingredients except for strawberries. Mix well.
2. Divide the oatmeal mixture evenly into two 2-cup containers with lids, for storage.
3. Cover and keep for 8 hours or overnight in fridge.
4. Remove the overnight oats from the refrigerator the next morning. Top each serving with ½ cup of freshly sliced strawberries.

Nutritional Info per Serving
calories: 406, fat: 10g, protein: 16g, carbs: 60g, fiber: 7.8g, sugar: 29g, sodium: 291mg

Honey Granola

Prep time: 6 minutes, Cook time: 45 minutes, Makes 3 cups

Ingredients
2 tbsps. coconut oil
2 cups gluten-free rolled oats
½ cup almonds, sliced
½ cup raw honey

¼ cup cashews, chopped
1 tbsp. pure vanilla extract
1 tbsp. ground cinnamon

Directions
1. Preheat the oven to 300ºF (150ºC).
2. Combine the oats, almonds, cashews, and cinnamon in a large bowl.
3. Combine the honey, coconut oil, and vanilla in a small bowl. Add this over the oat mixture and toss until well coated.
4. Cover a large baking sheet with parchment paper. Spread the oat mixture evenly on the baking sheet.
5. Bake the granola for about 45 minutes, stirring it every 15 minutes. Let it cool completely before serving.

Nutritional Info per Serving (½ cup)
calories: 444, fat: 17g, protein: 12g, carbs: 64g, fiber: 7g, sugar: 24g, sodium: 4mg

Nutty Fruits Bowl

Prep time: 6 minutes, Cook time: 0 minutes, Serves 1

Ingredients
½ cup Greek yogurt
½ cup papaya
½ cup sliced honeydew melon
¼ cup fresh blueberries
¼ cup fresh raspberries
½ tbsp. unsweetened shredded coconut
½ tbsp. sliced almonds
½ tbsp. pumpkin seeds

Directions
1. Scoop the Greek yogurt into a bowl of your choice.
2. Spread the raspberries, blueberries, papaya, and melon on top of the yogurt.
3. Place the pumpkin seeds, almonds, and coconut on the top. Serve immediately.

Nutritional Info per Serving
calories: 243, fat: 6g, protein: 11g, carbs: 41g, fiber: 7g, sugar: 30g, sodium: 138mg

Baked Eggs and Ramps Breakfast Bowl

Prep time: 5 minutes, Cook time: 35 minutes, Serves 2

Ingredients
1 tbsp. extra-virgin olive oil
½ white onion, diced
1 garlic clove, minced
½ cup ramps, rinsed
1 (15-ounce / 425-g) can
crushed tomatoes
½ tsp. paprika
¼ tsp. red pepper flakes
¼ tsp. sea salt
2 eggs

Directions
1. Preheat the oven to 400ºF (205ºC).
2. In a large saucepan, heat the olive oil over medium-low heat. Place the onion and cook it for about 7 to 8 minutes, until translucent and tender. Put the garlic and cook for an additional 2 to 3 minutes.
3. Put the ramps to the pan and sauté for about 3 to 5 minutes, until they begin to wilt. Stir in the tomatoes, red pepper flakes, paprika, and salt. Turn the heat to low and allow to simmer for about 10 to 12 minutes.
4. Divide the sauce evenly between 2 oven-safe bowls. Gently crack an egg over the top of each bowl.
5. Put the bowls in the oven and bake for about 8 to 10 minutes, or until the egg whites are cooked through but the yolks are still soft. Serve hot.

Nutritional Info per Serving
calories: 226, fat: 12g, protein: 10g, carbs: 23g, fiber: 6g, sugar: 8g, sodium: 384mg

Banana and Pecan Breakfast Bowl

Prep time: 3 minutes, Cook time: 2 minutes, Serves 1

Ingredients
2 bananas, sliced
¼ cup chopped pecans
½ cup coconut milk
2 tbsps. unsweetened shredded coconut
1 tsp. ground cinnamon

Directions
1. Combine all the ingredients in a microwave-safe bowl. Mix well.
2. Heat on high for about 2 minutes or until the mixture is entirely warmed. Stir and serve.

Nutritional Info per Serving
calories: 465, fat: 24g, protein: 6g, carbs: 65g, fiber: 13g, sugar: 29g, sodium: 131mg

French Asparagus and Zucchini Omelet

Prep time: 16 minutes, Cook time: 4 hours, Serves 6

Ingredients
12 eggs, beaten
1 cup chopped fresh asparagus
1 small zucchini, peeled and diced
1 yellow bell pepper, stemmed, seeded, and chopped
½ cup grated Parmesan
cheese
⅓ cup 2% milk
2 shallots, peeled and minced
½ tsp. dried tarragon leaves
½ tsp. dried thyme leaves
¼ tsp. salt

Directions
1. Grease the inside of a 6-quart slow cooker lightly with plain vegetable oil.
2. Mix the eggs, milk, thyme, tarragon, and salt in a large bowl, and mix well with an eggbeater or wire whisk until well combined.
3. Place the asparagus, zucchini, bell pepper, and shallots. Put into the slow cooker.
4. Cover the slow cooker and cook on low for 3 to 4 hours, or until the eggs are set.
5. Scatter with the Parmesan cheese, cover and cook for another 5 to 10 minutes or until the cheese starts to melt. Enjoy!

Nutritional Info per Serving
calories: 205, fat: 12g, protein: 17g, carbs: 7g, fiber: 1g, sugar: 3g, sodium: 471mg

Banana Bread Oatmeal with Pecan

Prep time: 13 minutes, Cook time: 8 hours, Serves 6

Ingredients

4 cups coconut milk
3 ripe bananas, peeled and mashed
2 cups steel cut oats
1 cup chopped pecans
4 cups water
⅓ cup coconut sugar
2 tsps. ground cinnamon
2 tsps. vanilla extract
½ tsp. ground nutmeg

Directions

1. In a 6-quart slow cooker, combine the coconut milk and water. Place the steel cut oats, bananas, coconut sugar, cinnamon, vanilla, nutmeg, and pecans.
2. Cover the slow cooker and cook on low for 7 to 8 hours or until the oats are very soft. Stir well before eating.

Nutritional Info per Serving

calories: 545, fat: 35g, protein: 9g, carbs: 50g, fiber: 7g, sugar: 17g, sodium: 21mg

Spicy Eggs in Purgatory

Prep time: 14 minutes, Cook time: 8 hours, Serves 10

Ingredients

2½ pounds (1.1 kg) Roma tomatoes, chopped
8 large eggs
1 cup vegetable broth
2 onions, chopped
2 red chili peppers, minced
2 garlic cloves, chopped
½ cup chopped flat-leaf parsley
1 tsp. paprika
½ tsp. ground cumin
½ tsp. dried marjoram leaves

Directions

1. Mix the tomatoes, onions, garlic, paprika, cumin, marjoram, and vegetable broth in a 6-quart slow cooker, and stir to mix well. Cover the slow cooker and cook on low for 7 to 8 hours, or until a sauce has formed.
2. One at a time, gently break the eggs into the sauce; do not stir.
3. Cover and cook on high until the egg whites are fully set and the yolk is thickened, for about 20 minutes. Scatter the eggs with the minced red chili peppers.
4. Garnish with the parsley and serve warm.

Nutritional Info per Serving

calories: 116, fat: 5g, protein: 8g, carbs: 10g, fiber: 2g, sugar: 5g, sodium: 112mg

Garlic Root Vegetable Hash

Prep time: 18 minutes, Cook time: 8 hours, Serves 8

Ingredients

2 tbsps. olive oil
4 Yukon Gold potatoes, chopped
3 large carrots, peeled and chopped
2 russet potatoes, chopped
1 large parsnip, peeled and chopped
2 onions, chopped
2 garlic cloves, minced
¼ cup vegetable broth
1 tsp. dried thyme leaves
½ tsp. salt

Directions

1. Mix all the ingredients in a 6-quart slow cooker. Cover the slow cooker and cook on low for 7 to 8 hours.
2. Stir the hash well and serve warm.

Nutritional Info per Serving

calories: 150, fat: 4g, protein: 3g, carbs: 28g, fiber: 4g, sugar: 4g, sodium: 176mg

Tropical Fruits Overnight Oats

Prep time: 4 minutes, Cook time: 0 minutes, Serves 2

Ingredients
Oats:
1 ripe banana
1 cup rolled oats
1 cup unsweetened coconut milk
½ cup diced fresh mango, plus more for topping
¼ cup diced fresh
pineapple, plus more for topping
2 tsps. chia seeds
1 tsp. vanilla extract
For Serving:
2 tbsps. unsweetened shredded coconut
1 tbsp. raw sliced almonds

Directions

1. In a blender, place the coconut milk, banana, and vanilla and blend until smooth.
2. Mix well the oats and chia seeds in a mixing bowl. Add the banana mixture into the bowl, and stir to combine well. Put the mango and pineapple, and fold in until evenly mixed.
3. Divide the oat mixture evenly between two 8-ounce jars with lids or sealable containers. Refrigerate overnight, or for at least 4 hours.
4. Place the mango, pineapple, coconut, and almonds on the oats. Enjoy the oats cold, or heat them in the microwave for 1 to 2 minutes.

Nutritional Info per Serving

calories: 298, fat: 8g, protein: 13g, carbs: 62g, fiber: 10g, sugar: 25g, sodium: 72mg

Loaded Avocado Toast with Eggs

Prep time: 4 minutes, Cook time: 7 minutes, Serves 2

Ingredients
2 slices bread
½ avocado, smashed
1 tbsp. hemp or flax seed
2 slices tomato
2 poached eggs
Salt
Pepper
Hot sauce (optional)

Directions
1. Toast the bread until ready.
2. Spread the smashed avocado evenly on the toast. Sprinkle the seeds over the avocado and press them into the avocado with the back of a fork.
3. Top each toast with a slice tomato and a poached egg.
4. Sprinkle salt and pepper and drizzle on hot sauce as needed.

Nutritional Info per Serving
calories: 291, fat: 14g, protein: 14g, carbs: 26g, fiber: 8.7g, sugar: 2.7g, sodium: 324mg

Mediterranean Spinach Strata

Prep time: 16 minutes, Cook time: 7 hours, Serves 10 to 12

Ingredients
2 tbsps. olive oil
8 cups whole-wheat bread, cut into cubes
2 cups chopped baby spinach leaves
4 eggs
2 egg whites
1½ cups 2% milk
1 cup shredded Asiago cheese
2 red bell peppers, stemmed, seeded, and chopped
1 onion, finely chopped
3 garlic cloves, minced

Directions
1. Mix the bread cubes, onion, garlic, bell peppers, and spinach in a 6-quart slow cooker.
2. Mix the eggs, egg whites, olive oil, and milk in a medium bowl, and beat well. Add this mixture into the slow cooker. Sprinkle with the cheese.
3. Cover the slow cooker and cook on low for 5 to 7 hours, or until a food thermometer registers 165ºF (74ºC) and the strata is set and puffed.
4. Ladle the strata out of the slow cooker to serve.

Nutritional Info per Serving
calories: 385, fat: 11g, protein: 16g, carbs: 55g, fiber: 8g, sugar: 11g, sodium: 572mg

Cookie Dough Overnight Oats

Prep time: 6 minutes, Cook time: 0 minutes, Serves 2

Ingredients
1 cup rolled oats
¾ cup milk
½ cup plain unsweetened Greek yogurt
2 tbsps. almond butter
2 tbsps. coconut sugar
2 tbsps. dark chocolate
chips
1 tsp. pure vanilla extract
A pinch of salt
Coconut flakes, sliced almonds, or walnuts, for topping (optional)

Directions
1. In a medium bowl, combine all of the ingredients except for the optional toppings and mix well.
2. Evenly divide the oatmeal mixture into two 2-cup containers with lids.
3. Cover and store in fridge for 8 hours or overnight.
4. Remove the overnight oats from the refrigerator the next morning. Add the toppings if desired, and enjoy.

Nutritional Info per Serving
calories: 398, fat: 22g, protein: 13g, carbs: 59g, fiber: 7.1g, sugar: 21g, sodium: 165mg

Baked Berries Oatmeal

Prep time: 10 minutes, Cook time: 6 hours, Serves 14

Ingredients
2 tbsps. melted coconut oil
7 cups rolled oats
1½ cups dried blueberries
1 cup dried cherries
4 eggs
1½ cups almond milk
⅓ cup honey
1 tsp. ground cinnamon
¼ tsp. ground ginger
¼ tsp. salt

Directions
1. Grease a 6-quart slow cooker lightly with plain vegetable oil.
2. Add the rolled oats in a large bowl.
3. Mix the eggs, almond milk, coconut oil, honey, salt, cinnamon, and ginger in a medium bowl. Mix until combined well. Add this mixture over the oats.
4. Slowly stir in the dried blueberries and dried cherries. Pour into the prepared slow cooker.
5. Cover the slow cooker and cook on low for 4 to 6 hours, or until the oatmeal mixture is set and the edges start to brown. Enjoy!

Nutritional Info per Serving
calories: 368, fat: 7g, protein: 9g, carbs: 68g, fiber: 6g, sugar: 33g, sodium: 97mg

Simple Poached Eggs

Prep time: 2 minutes, Cook time: 5 minutes, Serves 1

Ingredients

6 cups water
A pinch of salt
1 tsp. vinegar
2 large eggs

Directions

1. Add the salt and the vinegar to a medium saucepan with water and bring it to a boil over high heat.
2. Crack each egg in its own small bowl.
3. When reaching a boil, turn down the heat until it comes to a slow and steady simmer.
4. Swirl the water in a circle with a spoon to create a vortex and slide the egg(s) into water.
5. Cook for 4 minutes and then remove the eggs with a slotted spoon.
6. If you prefer your yolks on the runnier side, cook for 3 minutes. If you prefer them hard, cook longer, for 5 to 6 minutes.

Nutritional Info per Serving

calories: 152, fat: 9g, protein: 12g, carbs: 0.8g, fiber: 0g, sugar: 0.2g, sodium: 298mg

Kale and Quinoa Egg Casserole

Prep time: 13 minutes, Cook time: 8 hours, Serves 6 to 8

Ingredients

11 eggs
3 cups chopped kale
3 cups 2% milk
1½ cups quinoa, rinsed and drained
1½ cups shredded Havarti cheese
1½ cups vegetable broth
1 leek, chopped
1 red bell pepper, stemmed, seeded, and chopped
3 garlic cloves, minced

Directions

1. Grease a 6-quart slow cooker lightly with vegetable oil and keep aside.
2. Mix the milk, vegetable broth, and eggs in a large bowl, and beat well with a wire whisk.
3. Stir in the kale, quinoa, leek, bell pepper, garlic, and cheese. Add this mixture into the prepared slow cooker.
4. Cover the slow cooker and cook on low for 6 to 8 hours, or until a food thermometer registers 165ºF (74ºC) and the mixture is set. Serve warm.

Nutritional Info per Serving

calories: 483, fat: 27g, protein: 25g, carbs: 32g, fiber: 3g, sugar: 8g, sodium: 462mg

Apple-Cranberry Quinoa

Prep time: 12 minutes, Cook time: 8 hours, Serves 12

Ingredients

3 cups quinoa, rinsed and drained
4 cups canned coconut milk
2 cups unsweetened apple juice
1½ cups dried
cranberries
2 cups water
¼ cup honey
1 tsp. ground cinnamon
1 tsp. vanilla extract
½ tsp. salt

Directions

1. Mix all the ingredients in a 6-quart slow cooker. Cover the slow cooker and cook on low for 6 to 8 hours or until the quinoa is creamy. Serve warm.

Nutritional Info per Serving

calories: 284, fat: 4g, protein: 6g, carbs: 55g, fiber: 4g, sugar: 25g, sodium: 104mg

Apple Sausage Patties

Prep time: 8 minutes, Cook time: 20 minutes, Serves 4

Ingredients

2 to 3 tbsps. coconut oil, divided
½ cup apple, minced
½ cup yellow onion, minced
1 pound (454 g) pork,
ground
1 tsp. cinnamon, ground
½ tsp. garlic powder
½ tsp. salt
¼ tsp. black pepper, ground

Directions

1. In a large skillet, heat 1 tbsp. of the oil over medium heat. Add the apple and the onion. Sauté until soft, 3 to 5 minutes.
2. Meanwhile, mix ground pork with the cinnamon, garlic powder, salt, and black pepper in a medium bowl. Set aside.
3. Remove the apples and onions from the heat. Cool for 5 minutes.
4. When cool, stir the apples and onions into pork mixture. Form 12 even-size patties.
5. Heat 1 tbsp. of oil in the skillet over medium heat and add the patties in batches. Cook 4 to 5 minutes per side or until internal temperature reaches 160ºF (71ºC) and the centers are no longer pink.

Nutritional Info per Serving (3 sausages)

calories: 375, fat: 30g, protein: 18g, carbs: 5.1g, fiber: 0.8g, sugar: 2.2g, sodium: 356mg

Savory Spinach Oatmeal

Prep time: 12 minutes, Cook time: 8 hours, Serves 6 to 8

Ingredients
3 cups steel-cut oatmeal
2 cups chopped baby spinach leaves
½ cup grated Parmesan cheese
5 cups vegetable broth
1 cup water
2 shallots, peeled and minced
2 tbsps. chopped fresh basil
1 tsp. dried basil leaves
½ tsp. dried thyme leaves
¼ tsp. salt
¼ tsp. freshly ground black pepper

Directions
1. Mix the oatmeal, shallots, vegetable broth, water, basil, thyme, salt, and pepper in a 6-quart slow cooker. Cover the slow cooker and cook on low for 7 to 8 hours, or until the oatmeal is soft.
2. Stir in the spinach, Parmesan cheese, and basil, and allow to stand, covered, for another 5 minutes. Stir and serve warm.

Nutritional Info per Serving
calories: 262, fat: 5g, protein: 8g, carbs: 43g, fiber: 6g, sugar: 2g, sodium: 172mg

Mixed Nuts Berry Granola

Prep time: 11 minutes, Cook time: 5 hours, Makes 20 cups

Ingredients
10 cups rolled oats
2 cups whole walnuts
2 cups whole almonds
2 cups macadamia nuts
2 cups dried blueberries
2 cups dried cherries
½ cup honey
1 tbsp. vanilla extract
2 tsps. ground cinnamon
¼ tsp. ground cardamom

Directions
1. Mix the oatmeal, almonds, walnuts, and macadamia nuts in a 6-quart slow cooker.
2. Mix the honey, cinnamon, cardamom, and vanilla in a small bowl. Pour this mixture over the oatmeal mixture in the slow cooker and stir with a spatula to coat well.
3. Partially cover the slow cooker. Cook on low for 3½ to 5 hours, stirring twice during the cooking time, until the oatmeal and nuts are completely toasted.
4. Transfer the granola from the slow cooker and lay on two large baking sheets. Place the dried blueberries and cherries to the granola and stir carefully.
5. Allow the granola to cool, then store in an airtight container at room temperature up to one week.

Nutritional Info per Serving (½ cup)
calories: 255, fat: 12g, protein: 6g, carbs: 33g, fiber: 4g, sugar: 16g, sodium: 14mg

Potato, Tomato and Egg Strata

Prep time: 18 minutes, Cook time: 8 hours, Serves 10 to 12

Ingredients
8 eggs
8 Yukon Gold potatoes, peeled and diced
3 Roma tomatoes, seeded and chopped
1½ cups shredded Swiss cheese
2 red bell peppers, stemmed, seeded, and minced
1 cup 2% milk
2 egg whites
1 onion, minced
3 garlic cloves, minced
1 tsp. dried marjoram leaves

Directions
1. Lay the diced potatoes, onion, bell peppers, tomatoes, garlic, and cheese in a 6-quart slow cooker.
2. Mix the eggs, egg whites, marjoram, and milk well with a wire whisk in a medium bowl. Add this mixture into the slow cooker.
3. Cover the slow cooker and cook on low for 6 to 8 hours, or until a food thermometer registers 165ºF (74ºC) and the potatoes are soft.
4. Scoop the strata out of the slow cooker to serve.

Nutritional Info per Serving
calories: 305, fat: 12g, protein: 17g, carbs: 33g, fiber: 3g, sugar: 5g, sodium: 136mg

Egg and Mushroom Wild Rice Casserole

Prep time: 15 minutes, Cook time: 7 hours, Serves 6 to 8

Ingredients
11 eggs
3 cups plain cooked wild rice
2 cups sliced mushrooms
1½ cups shredded Swiss cheese
1 red bell pepper, stemmed, seeded, and chopped
1 onion, minced
2 garlic cloves, minced
1 tsp. dried thyme leaves
¼ tsp. salt

Directions
1. Layer the wild rice, mushrooms, bell pepper, onion, and garlic in a 6-quart slow cooker.
2. Beat the eggs with the thyme and salt in a large bowl. Pour into the slow cooker. Place the cheese on top.

3. Cover the slow cooker and cook on low for 5 to 7 hours, or until a food thermometer registers 165ºF (74ºC) and the casserole is set. Serve warm.

Nutritional Info per Serving
calories: 360, fat: 17g, protein: 24g, carbs: 25g, fiber: 3g, sugar: 3g, sodium: 490mg

Bean and Rice Burrito with Pico de Gallo

Prep time: 17 minutes, Cook time: 55 minutes, Serves 4

Ingredients
Pico de Gallo Salsa:
2 large tomatoes, diced
1 jalapeño pepper, seeded and finely chopped
½ small red onion, diced
⅓ cup roughly chopped fresh cilantro
1 clove garlic, minced
1 tbsp. freshly squeezed lime juice
⅛ tsp. ground cumin
⅛ tsp. sea salt
⅛ tsp. ground black pepper
Cilantro-Lime Rice:
1 cup brown rice
2 cups low-sodium vegetable broth
Juice of 1 lime
2 tbsps. chopped fresh cilantro
⅛ tsp. sea salt
Spicy Black Beans:

1 tbsp. olive oil
1 (15-ounce / 425-g) can black beans with no salt added, drained and rinsed
1 jalapeño pepper, seeded and minced
½ small red onion, finely diced
2 cloves garlic, minced
1 tsp. chili powder
½ tsp. ground cumin
½ tsp. sea salt
Burritos:
4 large cassava flour tortillas or whole-grain wraps
Avocado slices (optional)
Shredded cheese (optional)
Plain full-fat Greek yogurt (optional)
Salsa (optional)

Directions
1. To make the pico de gallo, combine the tomatoes, onion, cilantro, jalapeño, garlic, lime juice, salt, pepper, and cumin in a large mixing bowl. Refrigerate for 30 minutes to allow the flavors to meld.
2. For the rice, in a medium saucepan with a tight-fitting lid, bring the rice and vegetable broth to a boil over high heat. Lower the heat to a simmer, and simmer the rice for about 30 to 40 minutes, or until it's tender. Allow the rice to stand for 10 minutes, covered, then fluff it with a fork. Take 2 cups of the rice from the pan, and put it in a large mixing bowl. Place the cilantro, lime juice, and salt to the bowl, and toss to combine well.
3. For the beans, in a large skillet over medium-high

heat, heat the olive oil. Put the onion, garlic, and jalapeño, and cook, stirring occasionally, for about 6 to 8 minutes, or until the onion is soft.
4. Place the beans, chili powder, cumin, and salt to the skillet, and stir to combine well. Cook about 4 to 6 minutes, until heated through.
5. For the burritos, warm the tortillas by using a paper towel to wrap them and microwaving them for about 10 to 20 seconds, until they are pliable. You can also briefly heat them in an ungreased skillet over high heat. Place one-quarter of the beans and rice onto each tortilla. Put the cheese, avocado, salsa, and yogurt, if desired. Fold up opposite sides of the tortilla, and then the bottom, and gently roll up to enclose the filling. Wrap the burritos in parchment paper or aluminum foil to keep them from opening. Enjoy!

Nutritional Info per Serving
calories: 502, fat: 10g, protein: 15g, carbs: 88g, fiber: 6g, sugar: 5g, sodium: 835mg

Vanilla Pumpkin Pie Baked Oatmeal

Prep time: 14 minutes, Cook time: 8 hours, Serves 10

Ingredients
3 cups steel-cut oats
1 (16-ounce / 454-g) can solid pack pumpkin
2 cups canned coconut milk
1 cup granola
4 cups water
¼ cup honey
2 tsps. vanilla extract
1 tsp. ground cinnamon
½ tsp. ground ginger
¼ tsp. salt

Directions
1. Grease a 6-quart slow cooker lightly with plain vegetable oil.
2. Add the oats into the slow cooker.
3. In a medium bowl, mix the coconut milk and canned pumpkin with a wire whisk until blended. Then stir in the honey, water, vanilla, salt, cinnamon, and ginger. Mix until combined well. Pour this mixture into the slow cooker over the oats and stir well. Place the granola on top.
4. Cover the slow cooker and cook on low for 6 to 8 hours, or until the oatmeal is tender and the edges start to brown. Enjoy!

Nutritional Info per Serving
calories: 278, fat: 5g, protein: 7g, carbs: 51g, fiber: 7g, sugar: 13g, sodium: 77mg

Honey Carrot Cake Oatmeal

Prep time: 12 minutes, Cook time: 8 hours, Serves 6

Ingredients
2 tbsps. melted coconut oil
3 cups steel-cut oats
1 (8-ounce / 227-g) BPA-free can unsweetened crushed pineapple in juice, undrained
2 cups finely grated carrot
2 cups almond milk

4 cups water
¼ cup honey
2 tsps. vanilla extract
1 tsp. ground cinnamon
¼ tsp. salt

Directions
1. Grease a 6-quart slow cooker lightly with plain vegetable oil.
2. Mix the steel-cut oats, carrot, and pineapple in the slow cooker.
3. Mix the almond milk, water, coconut oil, honey, vanilla, salt, and cinnamon in a medium bowl. Mix until combined well. Add this mixture into the slow cooker.
4. Cover the slow cooker and cook on low for 6 to 8 hours, or until the oatmeal is tender and the edges start to brown. Enjoy!

Nutritional Info per Serving
calories: 132, fat: 8g, protein: 8g, carbs: 58g, fiber: 7g, sugar: 17g, sodium: 133mg

Grain Granola with Dry Cherries

Prep time: 12 minutes, Cook time: 5 hours, Serves 40

Ingredients
5 cups regular oatmeal
4 cups barley flakes
3 cups buckwheat flakes
2 cups whole walnuts
2 cups whole almonds

2 cups golden raisins
2 cups dried cherries
½ cup honey
2 tsps. ground cinnamon
1 tbsp. vanilla extract

Directions
1. Mix the oatmeal, barley flakes, buckwheat flakes, almonds, and walnuts in a 6-quart slow cooker.
2. Mix the honey, cinnamon, and vanilla in a small bowl, and combine well. Pour this mixture over the food in the slow cooker and stir with a spatula to coat well.
3. Partially cover the slow cooker. Cook on low for 3½ to 5 hours, stirring twice during the cooking time, until the oatmeal, barley and buckwheat flakes, and nuts are completely toasted.
4. Remove the granola from the slow cooker and lay on two large baking sheets. Place the raisins and cherries to the granola and stir slowly.
5. Allow the granola to cool, then store in an airtight container at room temperature.

Nutritional Info per Serving
calories: 214, fat: 8g, protein: 6g, carbs: 33g, fiber: 4g, sugar: 13g, sodium: 17mg

Green Tea & Ginger Overnight Oats

Prep time: 9 minutes, Cook time: 0 minutes, Serves 5

Ingredients

2½ cups quick-cooking oats
5 tsps. chia seeds
5 tsps. honey

1¼ tsps. fresh ginger, peeled and minced
5 green tea bags
5 cups boiling water

Directions

1. In each of 5 pint-size drinking jars with lids, place ½ cup of oats, 1 tsp. of chia seeds, 1 tsp. of honey, ¼ tsp. of ginger, and 1 green tea bag.
2. Pour 1 cup of boiling water in each jar and secure the lids. Shake well to combine.
3. Refrigerate for at least 4 hours or overnight, before serving.

Nutritional Info per Serving

calories: 202, fat: 3.7g, protein: 5g, carbs: 34g, fiber: 7g, sugar: 5.8g, sodium: 13mg

Peanut Butter Chocolate Chip Chickpea Cookie Dough

Prep time: 7 minutes, Cook time: 0 minutes, Makes 3 cups

Ingredients

1 (15-ounce / 425-g) can no-salt-added chickpeas, drained, rinsed, and patted dry
½ cup natural peanut butter
⅓ cup dark chocolate chips
2½ tbsps. pure maple syrup

2 tbsps. rolled oats
1 to 2 tbsps. unsweetened almond milk, divided
2 tsps. vanilla extract
½ tsp. ground cinnamon
⅛ tsp. sea salt

Directions

1. In a food processor, place the chickpeas, peanut butter, vanilla, maple syrup, oats, cinnamon, salt, and 1 tbsp. of the milk.
2. Blend the mixture until it is smooth and creamy. If it is too thick, pour in some or all of the remaining tbsp. of milk to achieve cookie-dough texture.
3. Take the cookie dough to a mixing bowl, and gently fold in the chocolate chips. Refrigerate the cookie dough in an airtight container for up to 5 days.

Nutritional Info per Serving

calories: 558, fat: 28g, protein: 21g, carbs: 61g, fiber: 14g, sugar: 24g, sodium: 202mg

Chapter 3: Vegetables

Spicy Eggplant Gyro with Tzatziki Sauce

Prep time: 12 minutes, Cook time: 10 minutes, Serves 4

Ingredients
Tzatziki Sauce:
½ large cucumber, diced
½ cup raw cashews
1 clove garlic
2 to 3 tbsps. unsweetened almond milk, divided
2 tbsps. freshly squeezed lemon juice
2 tsps. chopped fresh dill
1 tbsp. tahini
1 tbsp. hemp seeds
2 tsps. chopped fresh Italian parsley
½ tsp. sea salt
¼ tsp. ground black pepper
Eggplant:

1 tbsp. olive oil
2 medium eggplants, cut into ½-inch slices
1½ tsps. dried oregano
½ tsp. sea salt
½ tsp. ground black pepper
Gyros:
4 warmed whole-wheat pitas or Naan bread
1 large tomato, sliced
½ large cucumber, thinly sliced
½ medium red onion, thinly sliced
2 tbsps. chopped fresh Italian parsley, plus more for garnish (optional)

Directions
Make the Tzatziki Sauce:
1. In a medium bowl, cover the cashews with boiling water, and allow to stand for 1 hour, or up to overnight, to soften them.

Make the Eggplant:
2. Combine the salt, pepper, and oregano in a small mixing bowl. Scatter this seasoning mixture on all sides of the eggplant to coat it evenly.
3. In a skillet over medium-high heat, heat the olive oil. Place the eggplant slices, in batches so as not to crowd them, and cook for about 8 to 10 minutes, or until the eggplant is mostly soft. Keep the eggplant aside.
4. To finish the tzatziki sauce, combine the drained soaked cashews, tahini, garlic, cucumber, hemp seeds, 2 tbsps. of the almond milk, dill, lemon juice, parsley, salt, and pepper in a food processor, and process until smooth. The mixture should be thick, but pourable. If you desire a thinner consistency, add more of the remaining 1 tbsp. of milk, as needed.

Make the Gyros:
5. Divide the eggplant evenly among the pita breads and top it with the tomato, cucumber, onion, and parsley. Spread the tzatziki sauce over the gyro.
6. Tightly Wrap the gyros in foil to help them hold together, and serve right away. Garnish with parsley, if desired.

Nutritional Info per Serving
calories: 427, fat: 24g, protein: 13g, carbs: 48g, fiber: 13g, sugar: 13g, sodium: 597mg

Roasted Hummus Panini for Veggie

Prep time: 6 minutes, Cook time: 15 minutes, Makes 4 sandwiches

Ingredients
1 eggplant, sliced lengthwise (ends removed)
1 yellow squash, sliced lengthwise (ends removed)
1 red bell pepper, sliced
2 tbsps. olive oil, divided
½ tsp. salt, divided

½ tsp. pepper, divided
5 garlic cloves, minced
¼ cup hummus
2 ounces (57 g) goat cheese
8 slices bread, toasted (unless using panini press)

Directions
1. Preheat the oven to 450ºF (235ºC). Line a baking sheet with aluminum foil.
2. Put the eggplant, squash, and bell pepper on the baking sheet in a single layer. Spray or brush oil over the vegetables with about 1 tbsp. oil. Sprinkle half of the salt, pepper and garlic on the surface the vegetables. Roast for 10 minutes.
3. Remove the vegetables from the oven and flip over. Brush or spray the flipped surface with the remaining oil and season with the other half of salt and pepper. Return to the oven and cook for 5 minutes.
4. Remove from the oven and cool for 5 minutes.
5. Spread 1 tbsp. of hummus on each slice of bread. Assemble each sandwich with a quarter of the vegetables and ½ ounce (14 g) of goat cheese.
6. If you have a panini press, press the sandwich; otherwise, eat as is.

Nutritional Info per Serving
calories: 415, fat: 15g, protein: 18g, carbs: 61g, fiber: 14g, sugar: 8g, sodium: 672mg

Cheese Stuffed Tomatoes

Prep time: 13 minutes, Cook time: 7 hours, Serves 6

Ingredients

6 large tomatoes
1½ cups shredded Colby cheese
1 yellow bell pepper, stemmed, seeded, and chopped
¾ cup low-sodium whole-wheat bread crumbs
1 red onion, finely chopped
½ cup vegetable broth
¼ cup finely chopped flat-leaf parsley
3 garlic cloves, minced
1 tsp. dried thyme leaves

Directions

1. Cut the tops off the tomatoes. Use a serrated spoon to core the tomatoes, reserving the pulp. Keep the tomatoes aside.
2. Mix the onion, bell pepper, garlic, bread crumbs, cheese, parsley, thyme, and reserved tomato pulp in a medium bowl.
3. Stuff this mixture into the tomatoes, and put the tomatoes in a 6-quart slow cooker. Add the vegetable broth into the bottom of the slow cooker.
4. Cover the slow cooker and cook on low for 6 to 7 hours, or until the tomatoes are tender. Serve warm.

Nutritional Info per Serving
calories: 187, fat: 7g, protein: 9g, carbs: 22g, fiber: 4g, sugar: 6g, sodium: 143mg

Delicious Chickpea Tofu Marsala

Prep time: 11 minutes, Cook time: 18 minutes, Serves 4

Ingredients

¼ cup cornstarch, for dredging, plus 1 tbsp.
16 ounces (454 g) extra-firm tofu, cut into 8 slices and pressed
1 tbsp. olive oil
2 cups mushrooms, sliced
1 yellow onion, sliced
1 tsp. thyme
1 tsp. oregano
3 garlic cloves, minced
¼ cup Marsala wine
2 cups vegetable broth
1 (15½-ounce / 439-g) can chickpeas, drained and rinsed
2 tbsps. butter or ghee
Salt
Pepper

Directions

1. Place ¼ cup of cornstarch in a shallow bowl. Dredge the tofu in the cornstarch, shaking any excess back into the bowl.
2. Heat the oil over medium heat in a large skillet until sizzling. Sauté the tofu until it is brown on both sides,

2 to 3 minutes per side. Remove from the skillet.
3. Add the mushrooms, onion, thyme, and oregano, and sauté for 2 to 3 minutes. Add the garlic and sauté for 1 minute.
4. Pour in the Marsala and simmer for 3 minutes.
5. Add the remaining 1 tbsp. of cornstarch and mix well. Stir in the broth and the chickpeas.
6. Whisk in the butter and simmer for 3 to 5 minutes, or until sauce thickens. Add the tofu to the sauce, gently pressing down so it becomes completely immersed.
7. Remove from the heat and serve over rice or pasta.

Nutritional Info per Serving
calories: 418, fat: 16g, protein: 18g, carbs: 41g, fiber: 7g, sugar: 5g, sodium: 552mg

Fresh Vegetable Risotto

Prep time: 7 minutes, Cook time: 22 minutes, Serves 6

Ingredients

2 tbsps. olive oil, divided
½ red onion, diced
3 garlic cloves
1 bunch asparagus, ends trimmed and chopped into thirds
1 red bell pepper, thinly sliced
1 cup Arborio rice
4 cups vegetable broth
⅓ cup Parmesan cheese
Salt
Pepper
4 cups chopped kale
Lemon juice

Directions

1. Heat 1 tbsp. of oil over medium heat in a large saucepan. Add the onion and garlic and sauté for 3 minutes. Then, add the asparagus and bell pepper and stir. Cook for 3 to 5 minutes. Transfer the vegetables to a large bowl.
2. Return the pan to the heat, add the remaining tbsp. of oil and toast the rice, stirring continuously, for 1 minute.
3. Pour ½ cup of broth over the rice and stir frequently. When the liquid is mostly absorbed, add another ½ cup of broth and stir until most of the broth is absorbed. Repeat until all of broth is absorbed and the rice is creamy and tender.
4. Stir in the Parmesan cheese and season with salt and pepper.
5. Add the kale until wilt. Turn off the heat and continue stirring.
6. Stir in the vegetables and a squeeze of fresh lemon juice.

Nutritional Info per Serving
calories: 235, fat: 6g, protein: 9g, carbs: 36g, fiber: 3.8g, sugar: 3.1g, sodium: 758mg

Beet Veggie Burger

Prep time: 7 minutes, Cook time: 55 minutes, Serves 8

Ingredients

2 to 3 medium beets, peeled and grated
1 cup rolled oats
¼ cup flax meal
1 large egg
1 (14-ounce / 397-g) can black beans, drained and rinsed
½ cup yellow onion, roughly chopped
2 garlic cloves, peeled and smashed
½ tsp. salt
¼ tsp. black pepper
8 hamburger buns
Avocado, lettuce, pickled onion, and tomato, for topping (optional)

Directions

1. Preheat the oven to 350ºF (180ºC). Line baking sheet with parchment paper.
2. Shred the beets.
3. Add the oats, flax meal, egg, black beans, onion, garlic, salt, and pepper to the beets in the bowl of the food processor. Process for 30 seconds, then scrape down the sides of the bowl. Continue to pulse until well combined.
4. Form the patty mixture into 8 patties and place them on the baking sheet. Bake for 25 minutes. Remove from the oven, flip each patty over, then return the baking sheet to the oven and cook for 25 to 30 minutes, or until the outside is slightly golden brown.
5. Serve on a bun with toppings you desire.

Nutritional Info per Serving

calories: 302, fat: 3.6g, protein: 12g, carbs: 53g, fiber: 5g, sugar: 4g, sodium: 465mg

Homemade Spaghetti Squash

Prep time: 12 minutes, Cook time: 7 hours, Serves 12

Ingredients

2 tbsps. butter or coconut oil
1 (4- to 5-pound / 1.8- to 2.3-kg) whole spaghetti squash, washed and dried
¼ cup water
½ tsp. salt
⅛ tsp. freshly ground black pepper

Directions

1. Use a sharp knife to poke the spaghetti squash for about 10 to 12 times so it doesn't explode in the slow cooker.
2. Tear off two 20-inch strips of foil. Gently fold each strip in half lengthwise, then in half again. In a 6-quart slow cooker, arrange the strips in an "X," leaving the ends draped over the outside of the appliance.
3. Put the squash onto the foil X in the slow cooker and add the water. Cover the slow cooker and cook on low for 5 to 7 hours, or until the squash is soft.
4. Carefully, lift the squash out of the slow cooker by using the strips and put it on the counter to cool for 20 minutes.
5. Slice the squash in half crosswise. Remove the seeds with a spoon, and separate the strands with a fork. Use a large spoon to scoop the strands out of the squash.
6. Toss in the butter, salt and pepper, and serve warm.

Nutritional Info per Serving

calories: 110, fat: 4g, protein: 2g, carbs: 18g, fiber: 4g, sugar: 7g, sodium: 214mg

Squash Butternut Mac and Cheese

Prep time: 11 minutes, Cook time: 37 minutes, Serves 4

Ingredients

1 small butternut squash, peeled, seeded, diced (about 2 cups)
½ tsp. cinnamon
8 ounces (227 g) uncooked pasta (a small size like shells or elbows)
1 cup milk
2 tbsps. unsalted butter
4 ounces (113 g) goat cheese, crumbled
1 tsp. garlic powder
½ tsp. salt
¼ tsp. pepper

Directions

1. Preheat the oven to 425ºF (220ºC). Line a baking sheet with parchment paper.
2. Place the butternut squash on the baking sheet. Sprinkle with the cinnamon. Roast in the oven for 20 to 25 minutes, or until tender.
3. Meanwhile, boil 2 quarts of water over medium-high heat in a large stockpot. Once the water boils, cook the pasta for 8 to 12 minutes, or according to package directions, until tender. Drain the pasta.
4. Return the stockpot to the stove. Heat the milk and butter over low heat until the butter has melted.
5. Add the butternut squash to the milk and butter. Blend until smooth with an immersion blender. Alternatively, use a blender to blend—in batches, if necessary—then return to the pot.
6. Add the goat cheese and stir until melted.
7. Fold in the pasta and add the garlic powder, salt, and pepper.

Nutritional Info per Serving

calories: 452, fat: 18g, protein: 17g, carbs: 58g, fiber: 5.2g, sugar: 4g, sodium: 475mg

Delicious Cauliflower Curry

Prep time: 6 minutes, Cook time: 17 minutes, Serves 4

Ingredients

1 tbsp. olive oil
1 yellow onion, chopped
3 garlic cloves, minced
1 jalapeño, seeded and diced
1 large head cauliflower, cut into florets
1 (13½-ounce / 383-g) can full-fat coconut milk
1 (28-ounce / 794-g) can tomatoes, diced
1 tbsp. curry powder
1 tsp. cumin
½ tsp. cinnamon
½ tsp. turmeric
¼ cup fresh parsley, chopped (optional)

Directions

1. Heat the oil over medium heat in a large stockpot. When the oil is shimmering, add the onion and cook for 2 minutes. Add the garlic and jalapeño and cook for 2 to 3 minutes.
2. Stir in the cauliflower and sauté for an additional 2 minutes.
3. Add the coconut milk, the diced tomatoes, curry powder, cumin, cinnamon, and turmeric and stir.
4. Simmer the curry for 10 minutes, or until the cauliflower becomes soft. Garnish with the parsley, if desired.

Nutritional Info per Serving
calories: 318, fat: 22g, protein: 9g, carbs: 27g, fiber: 12g, sugar: 10g, sodium: 412mg

Italian Eggplant Parmesan

Prep time: 14 minutes, Cook time: 9 hours, Serves 8 to 10

Ingredients

2 tbsps. olive oil
5 large eggplants, peeled and sliced ½-inch thick
2 (8-ounce / 227-g) BPA-free cans low-sodium tomato sauce
½ cup grated Parmesan cheese
½ cup chopped toasted almonds
2 onions, chopped
6 garlic cloves, minced
1 tsp. dried Italian seasoning

Directions

1. Layer the eggplant slices with the onions and garlic in a 6-quart slow cooker.
2. Mix the tomato sauce, olive oil, and Italian seasoning in a medium bowl. Add the tomato sauce mixture into the slow cooker.
3. Cover the slow cooker and cook on low for 8 to 9 hours, or until the eggplant is soft.
4. Mix the Parmesan cheese and almonds in a small bowl. Scatter over the eggplant mixture and serve warm.

Nutritional Info per Serving
calories: 206, fat: 8g, protein: 10g, carbs: 28g, fiber: 11g, sugar: 14g, sodium: 283mg

Tex-Mex Burger

Prep time: 7 minutes, Cook time: 48 minutes, Serves 8

Ingredients

1 tbsp. olive oil
1 small red onion, chopped
1 carrot, chopped
1 celery stalk, chopped
2 garlic cloves
1 (15-ounce / 425-g) can black beans, drained and rinsed
8 ounces (227 g) mushrooms, roughly chopped
½ cup walnuts
1 tbsp. flax meal
1 large egg
1 tbsp. soy sauce
1 tsp. chili powder
1 tsp. cumin
Salt
Pepper
Cooking oil spray
8 hamburger buns (optional)
Lettuce, salsa, sliced avocado, sliced cheese, or tomatoes, for topping (optional)

Directions

1. Preheat the oven to 400ºF (205ºC). Line a baking sheet with parchment paper.
2. Heat the oil over medium heat in a large skillet. Add the onion, carrot, celery, and garlic. Sauté for 10 minutes to soften.
3. Transfer the sautéed vegetables to a food processor fit with regular blade. Add the black beans, mushrooms, walnuts, flax meal, egg, soy sauce, chili powder, cumin, salt, and pepper to the food processor or blender. Pulse for 30 seconds until smooth, about 30 seconds more.
4. Spray the parchment paper-lined baking sheet with cooking oil spray. Scoop the black bean patty mixture onto the parchment paper, forming 8 patties.
5. Spray the top of each patty lightly with cooking oil spray.
6. Bake for 20 minutes. Gently flip the patties and cook for another 15 minutes. Then turn the oven to broil and broil on high for 2 to 3 minutes, or until the outside is crispy.
7. Serve with or without a bun. Garnish with the toppings if desired.

Nutritional Info per Serving
calories: 136, fat: 6g, protein: 6g, carbs: 12g, fiber: 3.9g, sugar: 2.3g, sodium: 142mg

Roasted Colorful Bell Peppers

Prep time: 7 minutes, Cook time: 6 hours, Serves 8 to 10

Ingredients

1 tbsp. olive oil
8 to 10 bell peppers of different colors, stemmed, seeded, and
halved
1 red onion, chopped
1 tsp. dried thyme leaves

Directions

1. In a 6-quart slow cooker, put the bell pepper. Do not overfill your slow cooker. Pour in the olive oil, and top with the thyme and red onion. Cover the slow cooker and cook on low for 5 to 6 hours, stirring once if you are home, until the peppers are soft and slightly browned on the edges.
2. Remove the bell pepper skins if you'd like when they are done; and they will come off very easily. Enjoy!

Nutritional Info per Serving

calories: 59, fat: 2g, protein: 2g, carbs: 9g, fiber: 3g, sugar: 5g, sodium: 6mg

Quick Quinoa Tabbouleh

Prep time: 9 minutes, Cook time: 0 minutes, Serves 4 to 6

Ingredients

¼ cup extra-virgin olive oil
2 cups cooked quinoa
3 Persian cucumbers, cut into small cubes
1¼ cups fresh parsley, chopped
1 large red onion, chopped
Juice of ½ large lemon
½ tsp. Himalayan salt
Spice it up:
1 tbsp. dried mint flakes

Directions

1. Combine the quinoa, parsley, dried mint (if using), onion, and cucumbers in a large bowl.
2. Whisk together oil, lemon juice, and salt in a small bowl, and place it to the large bowl. Toss until everything is well coated. Enjoy!

Nutritional Info per Serving

calories: 276, fat: 16g, protein: 6g, carbs: 30g, fiber: 5g, sugar: 5g, sodium: 167mg

Kale and White Bean Soup with Tofu

Prep time: 7 minutes, Cook time: 23 minutes, Serves 4

Ingredients

3 tbsps. extra-virgin olive oil
1 (14-ounce / 397-g) package extra-firm tofu, drained and cubed
4 cups kale, coarsely chopped
1 (13-ounce / 369-g) can cannellini beans, rinsed and drained
1 large yellow onion, thinly sliced
4 cups vegetable stock
4 cups water
1 tsp. Himalayan salt
Spice it up:
½ tsp. crushed red pepper flakes
½ tsp. garlic powder

Directions

1. In a medium saucepan, heat the olive oil over medium heat. Place the onion and cook until translucent.
2. Place the stock, kale, beans, and water, and bring it to a boil. Put the tofu, salt, and garlic powder (if using). Sauté for 20 minutes, partly covered.
3. Sprinkle with some red pepper flakes before serving (if using).

Nutritional Info per Serving

calories: 302, fat: 17g, protein: 18g, carbs: 25g, fiber: 7g, sugar: 5g, sodium: 433mg

Spinach and Mashed Sweet Potatoes

Prep time: 4 minutes, Cook time: 19 minutes, Serves 2

Ingredients

2 tbsps. extra-virgin olive oil
2 medium sweet potatoes, cubed
3 cups baby spinach
4 tbsps. unsweetened,
plant-based milk, such as almond milk
½ tsp. Himalayan salt
Spice it up:
½ tsp. garlic powder

Directions

1. In a medium saucepan, add the sweet potatoes and just enough water to cover the potatoes. Bring to a boil and cook for about 15 minutes, until sweet potatoes are fork-tender.
2. Drain the potatoes and use a fork to mash. Keep aside.
3. Meanwhile, heat the oil and add the spinach in a small nonstick pan. Cook for just 1 minute, then put the mashed potatoes, milk, salt, and garlic powder (if using).
4. Sauté for 3 minutes to combine the flavors.
5. Turn off the heat and serve warm.

Nutritional Info per Serving

calories: 255, fat: 14g, protein: 4g, carbs: 29g, fiber: 5g, sugar: 7g, sodium: 440mg

Cheese Stuffed Tomatoes, page 34

Simple Curried Squash, page 40

Italian Eggplant Parmesan, page 36

Roasted Colorful Bell Peppers, page 37

Maple Braised Carrot Purée

Prep time: 9 minutes, Cook time: 8 hours, Serves 8

Ingredients
8 large carrots, peeled and sliced
¼ cup maple syrup
¼ cup canned coconut milk
1 red onion, chopped
2 tbsps. grated fresh ginger root
½ tsp. salt

Directions
1. Mix all of the ingredients in a 6-quart slow cooker. Cover the slow cooker and cook on low for 6 to 8 hours, or until the carrots are very soft.
2. Puree the mixture to the desired consistency with a potato masher or immersion blender.

Nutritional Info per Serving
calories: 80, fat: 2g, protein: 1g, carbs: 16g, fiber: 2g, sugar: 11g, sodium: 203mg

Healthy Portobello Tacos

Prep time: 6 minutes, Cook time: 20 minutes, Serves 4

Ingredients
1 tbsp. olive oil
1 tbsp. taco seasoning
2 portobello mushroom caps, sliced
2 bell peppers, sliced
1 small red onion, sliced
¼ cup Cotija cheese, crumbled
Juice of 1 lime
8 corn tortillas
2 cups shredded iceberg or romaine lettuce
1 avocado, sliced

Directions
1. Preheat the oven to 400ºF (205ºC). Line a baking sheet with parchment paper.
2. In a large bowl, place the oil and taco seasoning, mushrooms, peppers, and onion. Combine and toss until the vegetables are thoroughly coated with the oil and seasoning.
3. Spread the vegetables on baking sheet in a single layer. Bake for 20 minutes, or until the vegetables are soft.
4. Remove from the oven and sprinkle with the cheese and lime juice.
5. Stuff the 8 tortillas with the vegetable filling and top with the lettuce and avocado.

Nutritional Info per Serving (2 corn tortillas with filling)
calories: 287, fat: 15g, protein: 7g, carbs: 36g, fiber: 8g, sugar: 4g, sodium: 146mg

Italian Beets and Tomato

Prep time: 17 minutes, Cook time: 7 hours, Serves 10

Ingredients
2 tbsps. olive oil
10 medium beets, peeled and sliced
4 large tomatoes, seeded and chopped
2 onions, chopped
4 garlic cloves, minced
1 tsp. dried oregano leaves
1 tsp. dried basil leaves
½ tsp. salt

Directions
1. Mix the beets, tomatoes, onions, and garlic in a 6-quart slow cooker. Add the olive oil and sprinkle with the dried herbs and salt. Toss to mix well.
2. Cover the slow cooker and cook on low for 5 to 7 hours, or until the beets are soft.

Nutritional Info per Serving
calories: 100, fat: 4g, protein: 3g, carbs: 16g, fiber: 4g, sugar: 10g, sodium: 215mg

Pressure Cooker High Protein Mac and Cheese

Prep time: 6 minutes, Cook time: 12 minutes, Serves 4

Ingredients
1 tbsp. olive oil
1 small yellow onion, minced
3 garlic cloves, minced
1 bell pepper, chopped
8 ounces (227 g) uncooked gluten-free pasta shells
2 cups vegetable broth
¼ tsp. dry mustard
¼ tsp. salt
¼ tsp. pepper
¾ cup Cheddar cheese
¾ cup cottage cheese
Salt
Pepper

Directions
1. Use the sauté function of a pressure cooker, and heat the oil in the pot along with the onion and sauté until it becomes translucent, about 3 to 4 minutes.
2. Add the garlic and bell pepper and sauté for 2 to 3 minutes more.
3. Turn off the sauté function. Add the pasta, broth, and spices.
4. Set the pressure cooker on high. Cook for 5 minutes.
5. Quick release the vent, open the top and drain any excess liquid. Mix in the cheese and cottage cheese. Season with salt and pepper to taste.

Nutritional Info per Serving
calories: 382, fat: 12g, protein: 16g, carbs: 49g, fiber: 4g, sugar: 3.2g, sodium: 687mg

Tex-Mex Tomatoes and Corn

Prep time: 20 minutes, Cook time: 6 hours, Serves 10 to 12

Ingredients
4 large tomatoes, seeded and chopped
5 cups frozen corn
2 jalapeño peppers, minced
2 onions, chopped
4 garlic cloves, minced
1 tbsp. chili powder
½ tsp. salt
⅛ tsp. cayenne pepper

Directions
1. Mix all the ingredients in a 6-quart slow cooker. Cover the slow cooker and cook on low for 5 to 6 hours, or until the onions are soft. Serve warm.

Nutritional Info per Serving
calories: 124, fat: 1g, protein: 4g, carbs: 29g, fiber: 5g, sugar: 14g, sodium: 167mg

Honey Roasted Carrots and Parsnips

Prep time: 11 minutes, Cook time: 7 hours, Serves 10

Ingredients
2 tbsps. olive oil
6 large carrots, peeled and cut into 2-inch pieces
5 large parsnips, peeled and cut into 2-inch pieces
2 red onions, chopped
4 garlic cloves, minced
1 tbsp. honey
½ tsp. salt

Directions
1. Mix all of the ingredients in a 6-quart slow cooker and stir gently. Cover the slow cooker and cook on low for 5 to 7 hours, or until the vegetables are soft. Enjoy!

Nutritional Info per Serving
calories: 138, fat: 4g, protein: 2g, carbs: 26g, fiber: 6g, sugar: 10g, sodium: 199mg

Classic Spaghetti Squash

Prep time: 2 minutes, Cook time: 45 minutes, Makes 1 spaghetti squash

Ingredients
1 (2- to 3-pound / 907 g- to 1.4-kg) spaghetti squash

Directions
1. Preheat the oven to 400ºF (205ºC). Line a baking sheet with foil.
2. Cut the spaghetti squash in half lengthwise and scoop the seeds out.
3. Place the spaghetti squash cut-sides down. Bake for 45 minutes or until the skin is easy to push in and the inserted strands of a fork pull out easily.

Nutritional Info per Serving
calories: 107, fat: 1.1g, protein: 4g, carbs: 24g, fiber: 5.2g, sugar: 0.4g, sodium: 68mg

Healthy Root Veggies

Prep time: 21 minutes, Cook time: 8 hours, Serves 11

Ingredients
6 large carrots, cut into chunks
3 sweet potatoes, peeled and cut into chunks
2 medium rutabagas, peeled and cut into
chunks
2 onions, chopped
3 tbsps. honey
½ tsp. salt
⅛ tsp. freshly ground black pepper

Directions
1. Mix all the ingredients in a 6-quart slow cooker and gently stir. Cover the slow cooker and cook on low for 6 to 8 hours, or until the vegetables are soft. Enjoy!

Nutritional Info per Serving
calories: 102, fat: 0g, protein: 2g, carbs: 25g, fiber: 4g, sugar: 14g, sodium: 177mg

Simple Curried Squash

Prep time: 17 minutes, Cook time: 7 hours, Serves 6 to 8

Ingredients
3 acorn squashes, peeled, seeded, and cut into 1-inch pieces
1 large butternut squash, peeled, seeded, and cut into 1-inch pieces
⅓ cup freshly squeezed orange juice
2 onions, finely chopped
5 garlic cloves, minced
1 tbsp. curry powder
½ tsp. salt

Directions
1. Mix all of the ingredients in a 6-quart slow cooker. Cover the slow cooker and cook on low for 6 to 7 hours, or until the squash is tender when pierced with a fork. Serve warm.

Nutritional Info per Serving
calories: 88, fat: 0g, protein: 2g, carbs: 24g, fiber: 3g, sugar: 4g, sodium: 169mg

Tex-Mex Sweet Potatoes and Peppers

Prep time: 18 minutes, Cook time: 8 hours, Serves 8 to 10

Ingredients

2 tbsps. olive oil
5 large sweet potatoes, peeled and chopped
2 jalapeño peppers, minced
3 onions, chopped
5 garlic cloves, minced
⅓ cup vegetable broth
1 tbsp. chili powder
1 tsp. ground cumin
½ tsp. salt

Directions

1. Mix all of the ingredients in a 6-quart slow cooker. Cover the slow cooker and cook on low for 7 to 8 hours.
2. Stir in the mixture gently but thoroughly and serve warm.

Nutritional Info per Serving

calories: 172, fat: 5g, protein: 3g, carbs: 30g, fiber: 5g, sugar: 8g, sodium: 275mg

Tandoori Zucchini Cauliflower Curry

Prep time: 6 minutes, Cook time: 25 minutes, Serves 2

Ingredients

1 tbsp. extra-virgin olive oil
½ head cauliflower, broken into small florets
1 zucchini, cubed
1 yellow onion, sliced
2 garlic cloves, minced
2 to 3 tbsps. tandoori curry paste
¼ tsp. Himalayan salt
Spice it up:
¼ cup fresh coriander

Directions

1. In a pot of water, cook the cauliflower florets for about 5 minutes, until tender. Reserve about 2 cups of the cooking liquid.
2. In a large saucepan, heat the olive oil over medium heat. Place the onion and garlic. Cook for 2 minutes.
3. Add the zucchini and cook for an additional 3 minutes.
4. Place the cauliflower, reserved liquid, curry paste, and salt. Stir, cover, and cook for 15 minutes more.
5. Garnish with fresh coriander, if desired. Serve hot.

Nutritional Info per Serving

calories: 66, fat: 4g, protein: 2g, carbs: 7g, fiber: 3g, sugar: 1g, sodium: 94mg

Sweet and Sour Red Cabbage and Apple

Prep time: 15 minutes, Cook time: 7 hours, Serves 6 to 8

Ingredients

1 medium head red cabbage, cored and chopped (about 8 cups)
1 Granny Smith apple, peeled and chopped
1 red onion, chopped
¼ cup apple cider
vinegar
3 tbsps. honey
Pinch ground cloves
½ tsp. salt
⅛ tsp. freshly ground black pepper

Directions

1. Mix all the ingredients in a 6-quart slow cooker. Cover the slow cooker and cook on low for 5 to 7 hours, or until the cabbage is soft. Serve warm.

Nutritional Info per Serving

calories: 60, fat: 0g, protein: 1g, carbs: 15g, fiber: 3g, sugar: 11g, sodium: 161mg

Turmeric Cauliflower and Chickpea Stew

Prep time: 5 minutes, Cook time: 45 minutes, Serves 4

Ingredients

½ head cauliflower, cut into small florets
1 (13-ounce / 369-g) can chickpeas, rinsed and drained
1 medium leek, thinly sliced
1 yellow onion, thinly
sliced
6 cups water
½ tsp. turmeric
1 tsp. Himalayan salt
¼ tsp. freshly ground black pepper
Spice it up:
½ tsp. garlic powder

Directions

1. Combine the cauliflower, chickpeas, onion, leek, salt, turmeric, pepper, garlic powder (if using), and water in a medium stockpot.
2. Bring to a boil, cover, and sauté for about 30 minutes. Uncover and cook for an additional 15 minutes.
3. Serve right away, as is, or over some cooked brown rice.

Nutritional Info per Serving

calories: 138, fat: 2g, protein: 7g, carbs: 25g, fiber: 6g, sugar: 5g, sodium: 471mg

Easy Homemade Falafel

Prep time: 5 minutes, Cook time: 10 to 12 minutes, Serves 8

Ingredients
¼ cup rolled oats
1 (15-ounce / 425-g) can chickpeas, drained, rinsed, and patted dry
¼ cup fresh parsley
4 garlic cloves, minced
½ cup minced red onion
1 tbsp. sesame seeds

1 tsp. cumin
½ tsp. cayenne
½ tsp. salt
½ tsp. baking powder
1 large egg
1 tbsp. cornstarch (or more as needed for thickening)
¼ cup avocado oil for frying

Directions
1. To make oat flour, add rolled oats to blender. Pulse until oats form a flour.
2. Add the chickpeas, parsley, garlic, onion, sesame seeds, cumin, cayenne, salt, baking powder, egg, and cornstarch to blender and process until well-combined, about 30 seconds.
3. Form into 16 small patties. If the dough is sticky, chill for about 10 minutes, or until you can more easily form it into balls.
4. Heat the avocado oil over medium heat in a large skillet.
5. Working in batches, fry the falafel in batches for 2 to 3 minutes per side, as needed.

Nutritional Info per Serving (2 falafels)
calories: 163, fat: 8g, protein: 6g, carbs: 15g, fiber: 3.4g, sugar: 0.8g, sodium: 164mg

Five-Ingredient Lasagna

Prep time: 12 minutes, Cook time: 50 minutes, Serves 8

Ingredients
3 zucchinis, sliced in ½-inch rounds
½ tsp. salt, plus more for salting zucchini
Cooking oil spray
15 ounces (425 g) fresh ricotta cheese

1 large egg
¼ tsp. pepper
2 cups pasta sauce
1½ cups Mozzarella cheese, shredded

Directions
1. Place zucchinis on plate and lightly salt so that water can be drawn out for 10 minutes. Then pat with a kitchen towel to soak up any excessive moisture.
2. Preheat the oven to 375ºF (190ºC). Spray the inside of an 8-by-8-inch baking dish with cooking oil spray.
3. Whisk together the ricotta cheese, egg, salt, and pepper in a small bowl.
4. Put a ½ cup of pasta sauce in the bottom of the greased baking dish. Evenly spread it on the bottom of the dish in an layer. Top with ⅓ of the zucchinis, then another ½ cup sauce. Then add ½ of the ricotta mixture, ½ cup Mozzarella cheese, ⅓ of the zucchinis, ½ cup sauce, the remaining ricotta, and ½ cup Mozzarella cheese. Finish the lasagna with the remaining zucchinis, ½ cup sauce, and the remaining Mozzarella.
5. Cover with foil and cook for 30 minutes, remove cover, and cook for an additional 20 minutes or until the zucchini is fork-tender.

Nutritional Info per Serving
calories: 202, fat: 10g, protein: 13g, carbs: 11g, fiber: 1.7g, sugar: 3.5g, sodium: 651mg

Honey-Glazed Turnips and Fennel

Prep time: 10 minutes, Cook time: 8 hours, Serves 8 to 10

Ingredients
4 pounds (1.8 kg) turnips, peeled and sliced
4 cups chopped turnip greens
1 bulk fennel, cored and chopped
¼ cup honey

¼ cup vegetable broth
2 garlic cloves, minced
½ tsp. salt

Directions
1. Mix all of the ingredients in a 6-quart slow cooker. Cover the slow cooker and cook on low for 6 to 8 hours, or until the turnips are tender when pierced with a fork and the greens are tender too. Serve warm.

Nutritional Info per Serving
calories: 86, fat: 0g, protein: 3g, carbs: 20g, fiber: 5g, sugar: 13g, sodium: 232mg

Braised Green Cabbage and Onion

Prep time: 6 minutes, Cook time: 7 hours, Serves 8

Ingredients
1 tbsps. olive oil
1 large head green cabbage, cored and chopped
½ cup vegetable broth
3 onions, chopped

6 garlic cloves, minced
2 tbsps. apple cider vinegar
2 tbsps. honey
½ tsp. salt

Directions
1. Mix all of the ingredients in a 6-quart slow cooker. Cover the slow cooker and cook on low for 6 to 7 hours, or until the cabbage and onions are soft. Serve warm.

Nutritional Info per Serving
calories: 75, fat: 2g, protein: 2g, carbs: 14g, fiber: 3g, sugar: 10g, sodium: 171mg

Chapter 4: Grain and Beans

Barley Risotto with Mushroom

Prep time: 12 minutes, Cook time: 8 hours, Serves 6 to 8

Ingredients

1 (8-ounce / 227-g) package button mushrooms, chopped
2¼ cups hulled barley, rinsed
6 cups low-sodium vegetable broth
⅔ cup grated Parmesan
cheese
1 onion, finely chopped
4 garlic cloves, minced
½ tsp. dried marjoram leaves
⅛ tsp. freshly ground black pepper

Directions

1. Mix the barley, onion, garlic, mushrooms, broth, marjoram, and pepper in a 6-quart slow cooker. Cover with lid and cook on low for 7 to 8 hours, or until the barley has absorbed most of the liquid and is soft, and the vegetables are tender.
2. Toss in the Parmesan cheese and serve warm.

Nutritional Info per Serving

calories: 288, fat: 6g, protein: 13g, carbs: 45g, fiber: 9g, sugar: 6g, sodium: 495mg

Adzuki Bean and Celery Soup

Prep time: 6 minutes, Cook time: 35 minutes, Serves 4 to 6

Ingredients

⅛ cup extra-virgin olive oil
2 (13-ounce / 369-g) cans adzuki beans, drained and rinsed
1 large carrot, finely diced
1 long celery stalk, finely
diced
1 leek, chopped
1 small yellow onion, finely chopped
6 cups water
1½ tsps. Himalayan salt
Spice it up:
2 bay leaves

Directions

1. In a medium saucepan, heat the olive oil over medium heat. Place the leeks, onions, carrots, and celery. Cook for 5 minutes.
2. Put the salt and bay leaves (if using), then pour in the beans and water.
3. Cover and cook over medium-low heat for 30 minutes, until some of the water evaporates and the

vegetables are cooked through. If you like thinner stew, shorten the cook time a little.
4. Remove and discard the bay leaves. Serve immediately.

Nutritional Info per Serving

calories: 301, fat: 7g, protein: 13g, carbs: 47g, fiber: 13g, sugar: 3g, sodium: 640mg

Roasted Beet, Kale and Quinoa

Prep time: 4 minutes, Cook time: 55 minutes, Serves 2

Ingredients

1 tbsp. coconut oil
2 tbsps. extra-virgin olive oil
4 baby beets, scrubbed, peeled, and halved
2 cups kale, chopped
½ cup red quinoa, rinsed and drained
2 garlic cloves, minced
1 cup water
2 tbsps. freshly squeezed orange juice
1½ tsps. raw honey
1 tsp. tamari
½ tsp. balsamic vinegar
Sea salt
Freshly ground black pepper

Directions

1. Preheat the oven to 350ºF (180ºC).
2. On a baking sheet, arrange the halved beets and drizzle the coconut oil over the top. Sprinkle with salt and pepper. Roast the beets for about 30 to 35 minutes, or until they are fork-tender. Let them cool for at least 5 minutes.
3. When the beets are roasting, bring the quinoa and water to a boil over high heat in a large pot, stirring constantly. Turn the heat to low and simmer for about 15 to 20 minutes, stirring occasionally. Once the liquid is absorbed and the quinoa is tender, take the pot from the heat.
4. Combine the beets, quinoa, and the kale in a large mixing bowl, and mix well. Divide this equally between 2 serving bowls.
5. Whisk together the olive oil, orange juice, garlic, honey, tamari, and balsamic vinegar in a small bowl. Drizzle the dressing over the quinoa, beet, and kale mixture, and serve immediately.

Nutritional Info per Serving

calories: 447, fat: 23g, protein: 11g, carbs: 52g, fiber: 9g, sugar: 17g, sodium: 385mg

Marinara Chickpea Meatballs Sub

Prep time: 20 minutes, Cook time: 24 minutes, Serves 4

Ingredients

Chickpea Meatballs:
1 (15-ounce / 425-g) can no-salt-added chickpeas, drained and rinsed
½ to ¾ cup water, divided
½ to ⅔ cup almond flour, divided
1½ tbsps. ground flaxseed
1 tbsp. chopped fresh Italian parsley
2 tsps. garlic powder
2 tsps. onion powder
1 tsp. dried basil
½ tsp. sea salt
¼ tsp. ground black pepper

Marinara Sauce:
½ cup tomato paste
½ cup vegetable broth
1 tsp. pure maple syrup
1 tsp. dried basil
1 tsp. dried thyme
1 tsp. dried oregano
¼ tsp. garlic powder
½ tsp. sea salt

Subs:
4 whole-grain sub rolls, sliced in half
6 leaves fresh basil, thinly sliced

Directions

Make the Chickpea Meatballs:

1. Preheat the oven to 400ºF (205ºC), and carefully line a rimmed baking sheet with Parchment Paper.
2. In a small bowl, mix the ground flaxseed with ½ cup of the water, then keep it aside for about 5 minutes to make flax egg.
3. Add the flaxseed mixture, chickpeas, ½ cup of the almond flour, garlic powder, onion powder, parsley, salt, basil, and pepper in a food processor.
4. Process until the mixture is smooth and is the consistency that is easy to roll without sticking to your hands or cracking. If the mixture is too sticky, place more of the remaining 2 tbsps. of almond flour a little at a time. Pour in more of the remaining ¼ cup of water, a little at a time, if the mixture is too dry.
5. Form the mixture into 2-inch balls with your hands, and then arrange the balls on the prepared baking sheet. Bake for about 16 to 18 minutes, or until the meatballs begin to brown.

Make the Marinara:

6. Make the marinara when the meatballs are baking. Add the tomato paste, vegetable broth, thyme, basil, oregano, garlic powder, salt, and maple syrup in a medium saucepan. Cook for about 4 to 6 minutes over medium-high heat, until the sauce is heated through.

Make the Subs:

7. Pour the marinara sauce over the bottom of each bun. Place 3 to 4 of the meatballs, depending on the size of your roll, then top the meatballs with more marinara sauce and the basil. Serve immediately.

Nutritional Info per Serving
calories: 143, fat: 3g, protein: 7g, carbs: 24g, fiber: 5g, sugar: 8g, sodium: 596mg

Roasted Eggplant and White Bean

Prep time: 6 minutes, Cook time: 1 hour 10 minutes, Serves 2

Ingredients

1 (16-ounce / 454-g) can cannellini beans, drained and rinsed
2 small eggplants, cut into ¼-inch slices
1 cup hulled barley
1 cup arugula
3 cups water
Juice of 1½ lemons
2 garlic cloves, minced
3 tbsps. tahini, divided
2 tbsps. plus 2 tsps. extra-virgin olive oil, divided
3 tsps. tamari, divided
Sea salt
Freshly ground black pepper

Directions

1. Preheat the oven to 425ºF (220ºC).
2. In a large pot, bring the hulled barley, water, and 2 tsps. tamari to a boil over high heat. Once the barley just starts to boil, turn the heat to low and cover the pot.
3. Cook the barley for about 40 minutes without removing the lid. Take the pot from the heat when most of the water has been absorbed and the barley is tender and chewy. Drain well.
4. Pour the remaining tsp. of tamari, 1 tbsp. of tahini, and the lemon juice to the barley. Fluff with a fork, mixing all ingredients, and keep aside.
5. When the barley is cooking, arrange the eggplant slices in a single layer on a parchment paper–lined baking sheet and drizzle with 2 tbsps. olive oil. Season with the salt and pepper before putting into the oven. Bake the slices for about 20 minutes.
6. Add the arugula, the remaining 2 tsps. olive oil, garlic, and remaining 2 tbsps. Tahini in a medium skillet over medium heat. Cook for about 5 minutes.
7. Place the cannellini beans to the arugula mixture, and cook for about 5 minutes, until the beans are warm.
8. Put the rice, eggplant, and the arugula-bean mixture into three sections of each bowl, or mix all three components of this bowl together. Enjoy!

Nutritional Info per Serving
calories: 523, fat: 28g, protein: 14g, carbs: 65g, fiber: 22g, sugar: 18g, sodium: 572mg

Pea and Chicken Stew

Prep time: 8 minutes, Cook time: 47 minutes, Serves 6

Ingredients

2 tbsps. extra-virgin olive oil
1 pound (454 g) boneless, skinless chicken breast
1 pound (454 g) frozen peas
1 medium carrot, finely chopped
1 small potato, peeled and finely chopped
1 yellow onion, chopped
5 cups water
1¼ tsps. Himalayan salt
Spice it up:
½ to 1 tsp. dill

Directions

1. In a medium stockpot over medium heat, heat the olive oil. Place the onions and carrots. Cook until the onion is translucent.
2. Chop the chicken into small, bite-size cubes and place them to the pot. Cook for 5 minutes, until all sides are white and the chicken releases some water.
3. Add the peas, potatoes, salt, water, and dill (if using) to the stockpot. Stir to combine well, cover, and cook on low for about 25 to 30 minutes.
4. Uncover, and cook for 10 minutes uncovered. Most of the water will evaporate. Place the chicken to the stew, stir, and heat for about 2 minutes.
5. Sprinkle with freshly ground black pepper, if desired. Serve warm.

Nutritional Info per Serving
calories: 338, fat: 10g, protein: 33g, carbs: 28g, fiber: 8g, sugar: 6g, sodium: 362mg

Colorful Pepper Medley with Brown Rice

Prep time: 7 minutes, Cook time: 30 minutes, Serves 3

Ingredients

2 tbsps. extra-virgin olive oil
1 (13-ounce / 369-g) can whole peeled tomatoes, in liquid, chopped
1 large egg, beaten
1 cup brown rice
5 bell peppers (green, yellow, red), sliced
1 yellow onion, chopped
3 cups water, divided
1 tsp. Himalayan salt
Spice it up:
½ tsp. basil
¼ tsp. cumin
Freshly ground black pepper

Directions

1. Bring 2¼ cups of water to a boil, then place the cumin (if using), and the rice. Cover, reduce the heat to a simmer, and cook for 25 minutes.

2. Meanwhile, heat the olive oil in a sauté pan or skillet over medium heat. Put the onions and cook for bout 1 minute. Place the peppers, salt, and basil (if using), then stir, cover, and allow it to simmer for another 2 minutes.
3. Pour in the tomatoes and the remaining ¾ cup of water, then cover and simmer for 20 minutes.
4. Uncover, stir in the beaten egg, cover, and remove from the heat. Let it rest for 2 minutes.
5. Top the rice with the pepper medley. Sprinkle with black pepper if desired.

Nutritional Info per Serving
calories: 407, fat: 13g, protein: 10g, carbs: 65g, fiber: 9g, sugar: 9g, sodium: 575mg

Vegetables and Grains

Prep time: 6 minutes, Cook time: 20 minutes, Serves 2

Ingredients

1½ tbsps. extra-virgin olive oil
1 cup kale, chopped
1 cup broccoli florets
1 cup chopped Brussels sprouts
½ cup roughly chopped carrots
½ cup red quinoa, rinsed and drained
¼ cup almonds
¼ cup chopped fresh parsley
1 cup water
Juice of 1 lemon
1 tbsp. sunflower seeds
½ tbsp. Dijon mustard
1 tsp. organic maple syrup
Sea salt
Freshly ground black pepper

Directions

1. In a large pot, bring the quinoa and water to a boil over high heat, stirring constantly. Turn the heat to low and simmer for about 15 to 20 minutes, stirring occasionally. Once the liquid is absorbed and the quinoa is soft, take the pot from the heat.
2. When the quinoa is cooking, combine the broccoli florets, Brussels sprouts, kale, carrots, parsley, almonds, and sunflower seeds in a food processor. Pulse until the veggies are roughly chopped.
3. Whisk together the olive oil, mustard, maple syrup, lemon juice, salt, and pepper until well combined in a small bowl.
4. Fluff the quinoa with a fork and evenly divide it between 2 bowls. Top the quinoa with the salad mixture and pour the dressing over the top. Stir to mix or leave separated. Enjoy!

Nutritional Info per Serving
calories: 281, fat: 10g, protein: 10g, carbs: 41g, fiber: 7g, sugar: 5g, sodium: 260mg

Thai Green Bean and Soybean

Prep time: 16 minutes, Cook time: 3½ hours, Serves 8 to 10

Ingredients
1½ pounds (680 g) green beans
3 cups fresh soybeans
3 bulbs fennel, cored and chopped
1 jalapeño pepper, minced
½ cup canned coconut milk
⅓ cup chopped fresh cilantro
1 lemongrass stalk
2 tbsps. lime juice
½ tsp. salt

Directions
1. Mix the green beans, soybeans, fennel, jalapeño pepper, lemongrass, coconut milk, lime juice, and salt in a 6-quart slow cooker. Cover the slow cooker and cook on low for 3 to 3½ hours, or until the vegetables are soft.
2. Remove the lemongrass and discard. Scatter the vegetables with the cilantro and serve warm.

Nutritional Info per Serving
calories: 115, fat: 5g, protein: 6g, carbs: 11g, fiber: 6g, sugar: 4g, sodium: 154mg

Green Lentil and Carrot Stew

Prep time: 5 minutes, Cook time: 30 minutes, Serves 4

Ingredients
2 tbsps. extra-virgin olive oil
2 cups green lentils, rinsed
1 carrot, chopped
2 celery stalks, chopped
1 yellow onion, chopped
6 cups water
1 tsp. Himalayan salt
Spice it up:
1 tbsp. cumin
Freshly ground black pepper

Directions
1. In a sauté pan or skillet, heat the oil over medium heat. Place the carrots, celery, and onion. Cook until the onion is translucent.
2. Place the lentils, salt, cumin (if using), and water. Stir, cover, reduce the heat to low, and sauté for about 25 to 30 minutes.
3. Season with more salt and black pepper, if desired. Serve right away.

Nutritional Info per Serving
calories: 418, fat: 8g, protein: 24g, carbs: 65g, fiber: 12g, sugar: 4g, sodium: 324mg

Balsamic-Glazed Vegetables and Couscous

Prep time: 15 minutes, Cook time: 9 hours, Serves 10

Ingredients
5 cups cooked whole-wheat couscous
4 large carrots, peeled and cut into chunks
2 zucchinis, cut into chunks
2 sweet potatoes, peeled and cubed
2 (10-ounce / 283-g)
BPA-free cans no-salt-added artichoke hearts in water, drained
10 garlic cloves, peeled and sliced
¼ cup balsamic vinegar
2 tbsps. honey
1 tsp. dried marjoram leaves

Directions
1. Mix the sweet potatoes, garlic, carrots, zucchinis, artichoke hearts, vinegar, honey, and marjoram leaves in a 6-quart slow cooker. Cover the slow cooker and cook on low for 7 to 9 hours, or until the vegetables are soft.
2. Top over the hot cooked couscous and serve.

Nutritional Info per Serving
calories: 173, fat: 1g, protein: 5g, carbs: 36g, fiber: 5g, sugar: 9g, sodium: 53mg

Rosemary White Beans with Onion

Prep time: 8 minutes, Cook time: 8 hours, Serves 16

Ingredients
1 pound (454 g) great northern beans
2 cups low sodium vegetable broth
4 cups water
1 onion, finely chopped
3 cloves garlic, minced
1 large sprig fresh rosemary
½ tsp. salt
⅛ tsp. white pepper

Directions
1. Sort over the beans, remove and discard any extraneous material. Rinse the beans well over cold water and drain.
2. In a 6-quart slow cooker, combine the beans, onion, garlic, rosemary, salt, water, and vegetable broth.
3. Cover the slow cooker and cook on low for 6 to 8 hours or until the beans are soft.
4. Remove and discard the rosemary stem. Stir in the mixture gently and serve warm.

Nutritional Info per Serving
calories: 88, fat: 0g, protein: 5g, carbs: 17g, fiber: 5g, sugar: 0g, sodium: 362mg

Rosemary White Beans with Onion, page 48

Simple Vegetable Fried Rice, page 50

Barley Risotto with Mushroom, page 45

Herbed Black Beans, page 50

Quick Lentil Bisque

Prep time: 2 minutes, Cook time: 20 minutes, Serves 2 to 4

Ingredients

1 cup red lentils, washed and drained
1 yellow onion, chopped
2 garlic cloves, minced
4 cups water
¾ tsp. Himalayan salt
¼ tsp. freshly ground black pepper
Spice it up:
1½ tsps. cumin

Directions

1. Combine the lentils, onion, garlic, salt, cumin (if using), and water in a medium stockpot.
2. Bring to a boil, cover, reduce the heat to low and simmer for 20 minutes.
3. Serve right away with freshly ground black pepper, or blend it for a smoother texture.

Nutritional Info per Serving

calories: 370, fat: 2g, protein: 24g, carbs: 67g, fiber: 11g, sugar: 2g, sodium: 358mg

Simple Vegetable Fried Rice

Prep time: 3 minutes, Cook time: 23 minutes, Serves 4

Ingredients

3 tbsps. extra-virgin olive oil
2 cups mixed frozen vegetables
1½ cups sushi rice
1 yellow onion, chopped
2 cups water
1¼ tsps. Himalayan salt
Spice it up:
1 tsp. garlic powder

Directions

1. Add the water into a medium stockpot and bring it to a boil. Place the rice, cover, and cook for 20 minutes. Most of the liquid will evaporate.
2. Meanwhile, cook or steam the frozen vegetables. Drain well and keep aside.
3. Heat the oil and onion in a large, non-metal or cast-iron pan over medium heat. After 1 minute, put the rice. Stir well to incorporate with the onion and make sure it doesn't stick to the pan.
4. Place the vegetables, garlic powder (if using), and salt. Stir and cook for an additional 2 minutes. The rice will start to brown on the bottom—that is okay. Scrape up the browned parts from the bottom and turn off the heat. Serve warm.

Nutritional Info per Serving

calories: 428, fat: 11g, protein: 8g, carbs: 74g, fiber: 7g, sugar: 4g, sodium: 539mg

Herbed Black Beans

Prep time: 11 minutes, Cook time: 9 hours, Serves 8

Ingredients

3 cups dried black beans, rinsed and drained
6 cups low-sodium vegetable broth
2 onions, chopped
8 garlic cloves, minced
1 tsp. dried basil leaves
½ tsp. dried thyme leaves
½ tsp. dried oregano leaves
½ tsp. salt

Directions

1. Mix all the ingredients in a 6-quart slow cooker. Cover the slow cooker and cook on low for 7 to 9 hours, or until the beans have absorbed the liquid and are tender.
2. Remove the bay leaf and discard.

Nutritional Info per Serving

calories: 250, fat: 0g, protein: 15g, carbs: 47g, fiber: 17g, sugar: 3g, sodium: 253mg

Cheesy Risotto with Green Beans, Sweet Potatoes and Peas

Prep time: 10 minutes, Cook time: 5 hours, Serves 8 to 10

Ingredients

3 tbsps. unsalted butter
2 cups short-grain brown rice
1 large sweet potato, peeled and chopped
2 cups green beans, cut in half crosswise
2 cups frozen baby peas
7 cups low-sodium vegetable broth
½ cup grated Parmesan cheese
1 onion, chopped
5 garlic cloves, minced
1 tsp. dried thyme leaves

Directions

1. Mix the sweet potato, onion, garlic, rice, thyme, and broth in a 6-quart slow cooker. Cover the slow cooker and cook on low for 3 to 4 hours, or until the rice is tender.
2. Toss in the green beans and frozen peas. Cover and cook on low for about 30 to 40 minutes or until the vegetables are soft.
3. Stir in the cheese and butter. Cover and cook on low for 20 minutes, then toss and serve warm.

Nutritional Info per Serving

calories: 385, fat: 10g, protein: 10g, carbs: 52g, fiber: 6g, sugar: 10g, sodium: 426mg

Quinoa with Mushroom and Carrot

Prep time: 8 minutes, Cook time: 6 hours, Serves 8 to 10

Ingredients

2 cups quinoa, rinsed and drained
4 cups low-sodium vegetable broth
1 cup sliced cremini mushrooms
2 carrots, peeled and sliced
2 onions, chopped
3 garlic cloves, minced
1 tsp. dried marjoram leaves
½ tsp. salt
⅛ tsp. freshly ground black pepper

Directions

1. Mix all of the ingredients in a 6-quart slow cooker. Cover the slow cooker and cook on low for 5 to 6 hours, or until the quinoa and vegetables are soft.
2. Stir in the mixture and serve warm.

Nutritional Info per Serving

calories: 204, fat: 3g, protein: 7g, carbs: 35g, fiber: 4g, sugar: 4g, sodium: 229mg

Greek Cherry Tomato Quinoa Salad

Prep time: 5 minutes, Cook time: 25 minutes, Serves 4 to 6

Ingredients

Dressing:
¼ cup extra-virgin olive oil
Juice of ½ large lemon
½ tsp. Himalayan salt
Quinoa:
2 cups quinoa
1¼ cups cherry tomatoes, quartered
½ English cucumber, cubed
½ cup Kalamata olives, chopped
4 cups water

Directions

1. For the dressing: Whisk together the oil, lemon juice, and salt in a bowl, and keep aside.
2. For the quinoa: Rinse the quinoa under cold water until the water runs clear.
3. Bring 4 cups of water to a boil in a medium saucepan.
4. Place the quinoa, cover, and simmer on low for 20 minutes.
5. Open the pot, fluff the quinoa with a fork, cover, and allow it to rest for 5 minutes.
6. Take the quinoa to a large wooden or glass salad bowl and let it cool.
7. Once the quinoa cools to room temperature, put the tomatoes, cucumbers, and olives. Stir to combine well.
8. Add the dressing and toss well. Enjoy!

Nutritional Info per Serving

calories: 311, fat: 14g, protein: 9g, carbs: 39g, fiber: 5g, sugar: 1g, sodium: 184mg

Herbed Succotash with Tomato

Prep time: 14 minutes, Cook time: 9 hours, Serves 10

Ingredients

4 cups frozen corn
2 cups dry lima beans, rinsed and drained
4 large tomatoes, seeded and chopped
5 cups vegetable broth
1 red onion, minced
1 bay leaf
1 tsp. dried thyme leaves
1 tsp. dried basil leaves

Directions

1. Mix all the ingredients in a 6-quart slow cooker. Cover the slow cooker and cook on low for 8 to 9 hours, or until the lima beans are soft. Remove the bay leaf and discard. Serve warm.

Nutritional Info per Serving

calories: 128, fat: 1g, protein: 6g, carbs: 27g, fiber: 6g, sugar: 10g, sodium: 73mg

Wild Rice with Parsley

Prep time: 5 minutes, Cook time: 6 hours, Serves 8

Ingredients

3 cups wild rice, rinsed and drained
6 cups vegetable broth
1 onion, chopped
⅓ cup chopped fresh flat-
leaf parsley
1 bay leaf
½ tsp. dried thyme leaves
½ tsp. dried basil leaves
½ tsp. salt

Directions

1. Mix the wild rice, vegetable broth, onion, salt, thyme, basil, and bay leaf in a 6-quart slow cooker. Cover the slow cooker and cook on low for 4 to 6 hours, or until the wild rice is tender but still firm. You can cook this longer until the wild rice pops that will take about 7 to 8 hours.
2. Remove the bay leaf and discard.
3. Toss in the parsley and serve warm.

Nutritional Info per Serving

calories: 258, fat: 2g, protein: 6g, carbs: 54g, fiber: 5g, sugar: 3g, sodium: 257mg

Easy Three-Bean Medley

Prep time: 16 minutes, Cook time: 8 hours, Serves 10

Ingredients
1¼ cups dried black beans, rinsed and drained
1¼ cups dried kidney beans, rinsed and drained
1¼ cups dried black-eyed peas, rinsed and drained
2 carrots, peeled and chopped
6 cups low-sodium vegetable broth
1½ cups water
1 onion, chopped
1 leek, chopped
2 garlic cloves, minced
½ tsp. dried thyme leaves

Directions
1. Mix all of the ingredients in a 6-quart slow cooker. Cover with lid and cook on low for 6 to 8 hours, or until the beans are soft and the liquid is absorbed. Serve warm.

Nutritional Info per Serving
calories: 284, fat: 0g, protein: 19g, carbs: 56g, fiber: 19g, sugar: 6g, sodium: 131mg

Black Bean Wild Rice Chili

Prep time: 19 minutes, Cook time: 7 hours, Serves 10 to 12

Ingredients
2 (15-ounce / 425-g) BPA-free cans no-salt-added black beans, drained and rinsed
1½ cups wild rice, rinsed and drained
2 cups sliced cremini mushrooms
2 red bell peppers,
stemmed, seeded, and chopped
5 cups vegetable broth
3 cups low-sodium tomato juice
2 onions, chopped
3 garlic cloves, minced
1 tbsp. chili powder
½ tsp. ground cumin

Directions
1. Mix all of the ingredients in a 6-quart slow cooker. Cover the slow cooker and cook on low for 6 to 7 hours, or until the wild rice is tender. Enjoy!

Nutritional Info per Serving
calories: 288, fat: 5g, protein: 13g, carbs: 58g, fiber: 10g, sugar: 9g, sodium: 564mg

Garlic Barley and Black Beans

Prep time: 7 minutes, Cook time: 8 hours, Serves 10

Ingredients
1½ cups hulled barley
2 cups dried black beans, rinsed and drained
8 cups vegetable broth
1 onion, chopped
3 garlic cloves, minced
1 bay leaf
½ tsp. dried thyme leaves

Directions
1. Mix all the ingredients in a 6-quart slow cooker. Cover and cook on low for 7 to 8 hours, or until the barley and black beans are soft.
2. Remove the bay leaf and discard. Serve warm.

Nutritional Info per Serving
calories: 240, fat: 1g, protein: 12g, carbs: 46g, fiber: 14g, sugar: 2g, sodium: 115mg

Tomato and Beans with Baby Spinach

Prep time: 5 minutes, Cook time: 15 minutes, Serves 2

Ingredients
1 tbsp. extra-virgin olive oil
1 (13-ounce / 369-g) can white cannellini beans
2 cups baby spinach
¾ cup crushed tomatoes
½ cup chicken stock
1 large garlic clove, minced
½ tsp. dried basil
½ tsp. Himalayan salt
Freshly ground black pepper (optional)

Directions
1. In a small saucepan, heat the olive oil over medium heat.
2. Add the garlic, tomatoes, basil, and salt, and sauté for 3 minutes.
3. Place the beans, stock, and spinach.
4. Cook for 10 minutes more. The liquid will reduce by half.
5. Season with some freshly ground black pepper, if desired. Serve warm.

Nutritional Info per Serving
calories: 300, fat: 8g, protein: 17g, carbs: 44g, fiber: 12g, sugar: 8g, sodium: 333mg

Chapter 5: Poultry

Oven Chicken Thighs with Paprika

Prep time: 7 minutes, Cook time: 45 minutes, Serves 6

Ingredients
Cooking oil spray
2 pounds (907 g) boneless, skinless chicken thighs
¼ cup ghee or butter
5 to 6 garlic cloves, minced

2 tbsps. paprika
1 tbsp. oregano
½ tsp. red pepper flakes
½ tsp. dried parsley
¼ tsp. salt
¼ tsp. pepper

Directions
1. Preheat the oven to 425ºF (220ºC). Coat the inside of a 9-by-13-inch baking dish with spray.
2. Pat the chicken thighs dry and place them in the baking dish.
3. In a small saucepan, heat the ghee and whisk in the garlic, paprika, oregano, red pepper flakes, parsley, salt, and pepper. Brush the sauce over the chicken thighs.
4. Bake for 40 to 45 minutes to internal temperature of 165ºF (74ºC).

Nutritional Info per Serving
calories: 274, fat: 18g, protein: 21g, carbs: 4g, fiber: 0.7g, sugar: 0.2g, sodium: 334mg

Chicken with Squash and Mushroom

Prep time: 18 minutes, Cook time: 8 hours, Serves 10

Ingredients
1 (3-pound / 1.4-kg) butternut squash, peeled, seeded, and cut into 1-inch pieces
2 (1-pound / 454-g) acorn squash, peeled, seeded, and cut into 1-inch pieces
8 (6-ounce / 170-g) bone-in, skinless chicken breasts
1 (8-ounce / 227-

g) package cremini mushrooms, sliced
2 fennel bulbs, cored and sliced
1 cup chicken stock
½ cup canned coconut milk
3 sprigs fresh thyme
1 bay leaf
2 tbsps. lemon juice

Directions
1. Mix the butternut squash, acorn squash, fennel, mushrooms, chicken, thyme, bay leaf, chicken stock, and coconut milk in a 6-quart slow cooker. Cover the slow cooker and cook on low for 6 to 8 hours, or until the chicken registers 165ºF (74ºC) on a food thermometer.
2. Remove the thyme sprigs and bay leaf and discard. Stir in the lemon juice and serve warm.

Nutritional Info per Serving
calories: 330, fat: 8g, protein: 43g, carbs: 21g, fiber: 4g, sugar: 3g, sodium: 67mg

Better Pressure Cooker Butter Chicken

Prep time: 6 minutes, Cook time: 30 minutes, Serves 8

Ingredients
1 tbsp. butter
3 garlic cloves, minced
1 yellow onion, diced
1 tbsp. grated ginger
6 ounces (170 g) tomato paste
1 tbsp. garam masala
1 tsp. paprika
½ tsp. turmeric
½ tsp. salt

¼ tsp. pepper
¼ cup parsley, fresh
1 (13½-ounce / 383-g) can full-fat coconut milk
½ cup full-fat plain unsweetened Greek yogurt
2 pounds (907 g) chicken breast, chopped
1 tbsp. cornstarch

Directions
1. Place and whisk the butter, garlic, onion, ginger, tomato paste, garam masala, paprika, turmeric, salt, pepper, parsley, coconut milk, and yogurt into the pressure cooker.
2. Add the chicken and seal. Set pressure to high and cook for 15 minutes.
3. Allow the pressure to naturally release for 10 minutes, then quick release until you are able to open.
4. Turn on the sauté function, whisk in the cornstarch, and cook for 3 to 5 minutes, or until the sauce thickens.

Nutritional Info per Serving
calories: 351, fat: 17g, protein: 33g, carbs: 10g, fiber: 1.9g, sugar: 6g, sodium: 691mg

BBQ Pulled Chicken and Carrot Bowl

Prep time: 15 minutes, Cook time: 46 minutes, Serves 4

Ingredients

Roasted Carrots:
1 tbsp. olive oil
10 large carrots, peeled and sliced diagonally into bite-size pieces
¼ tsp. sea salt
¼ tsp. ground black pepper
BBQ Pulled Chicken:
½ tbsp. olive oil
½ pound (227 g) boneless, skinless chicken thighs
½ pound (227 g) boneless, skinless chicken breasts
½ cup no-salt tomato sauce
1 tbsp. raw honey
1 tbsp. tomato paste
1 tbsp. molasses
½ tbsp. apple cider vinegar
½ tsp. garlic powder

¼ tsp. granulated onion
⅛ tsp. sea salt
⅛ tsp. ground black pepper
Cabbage Slaw:
1 tbsp. extra virgin olive oil
½ small head green cabbage, shredded
⅓ small head red cabbage, shredded
¼ small red onion, sliced thinly
2 tbsps. plain full-fat Greek yogurt
2 tbsps. apple cider vinegar
¼ tsp. sea salt
¼ tsp. ground black pepper, to taste
For Serving:
2 green onions, sliced
Black sesame seeds

Directions

Make the Carrots:
1. Preheat the oven to 400ºF (205ºC), and carefully line a large rimmed baking sheet with parchment paper.
2. Arrange the carrots on the baking sheet, then drizzle with the olive oil, salt, and pepper. Toss until the carrots are coated, and then place them in a single layer. Roast the carrots for about 20 to 30 minutes, until they have caramelized on the edges and are easily pierced through with a fork. Toss the carrots halfway through the cooking, so they can cook evenly. Set the carrots aside.

Make the BBQ Pulled Chicken:
3. In a large skillet, heat the olive oil over medium-high heat. Place the chicken breasts and thighs, tomato sauce, granulated onion, tomato paste, garlic powder, molasses, honey, vinegar, salt, and pepper. Toss to coat the chicken evenly. Cover and cook for 12 to 16 minutes, flipping the chicken occasionally, or until the chicken is cooked through and tender. Use tongs or a slotted spoon to remove the chicken, and set it on a cutting board or large plate. With two forks, pull the chicken apart into bite-size pieces that resemble shredded chicken.

4. When shredding the chicken, heat the BBQ sauce remaining over medium-high heat in the pan until it's reduced by one-third. Then, gently toss the pulled chicken with the sauce.

Make the Cabbage Slaw:
5. Whisk the yogurt, olive oil, vinegar, salt, and pepper in a large bowl, until it's combined well. Place the green and red cabbage and onion, and toss to coat well with the dressing.
6. To assemble the meal, in each of four bowls place one-quarter of the slaw, the pulled chicken, and the roasted carrots. Garnish the slaw with the black sesame seeds and the entire bowl with the sliced green onions. Serve immediately.

Nutritional Info per Serving
calories: 423, fat: 16g, protein: 34g, carbs: 37g, fiber: 8g, sugar: 23g, sodium: 590mg

Chicken Enchiladas

Prep time: 13 minutes, Cook time: 25 minutes, Serves 6

Ingredients

Cooking oil spray
16 ounces (454 g) mild salsa verde, divided
2 cups cooked, shredded chicken
1 green bell pepper, diced

1 small red onion, diced
12 corn tortillas
1 cup Cheddar cheese, shredded
1 tomato, diced
1 avocado, diced
1 jalapeño, diced

Directions

1. Preheat the oven to 400ºF (205ºC). Coat the inside of a 9-by-13-inch baking dish with cooking spray.
2. Reserve ¼ cup plus 2 tbsps. of salsa verde.
3. Mix together the chicken, bell pepper, onion, and the remaining salsa verde in a large bowl.
4. Spread the ¼ cup of reserved salsa verde evenly on the baking dish.
5. Wrap the tortillas in a damp paper towel. Microwave for 30 seconds to soften.
6. Pour about ⅛ of the chicken mixture in the center of the tortilla. Roll up the tortilla and bake in the baking dish, seam-side down. Repeat with all of the tortillas.
7. Top the rolled tortillas with the remaining 2 tbsps. of salsa verde. Sprinkle with cheese, and cover the baking dish with foil. Bake for 20 minutes, then remove the foil and broil for 1 to 2 minutes.
8. Top with tomato, avocado, and jalapeño before serving!

Nutritional Info per Serving
calories: 568, fat: 22g, protein: 35g, carbs: 47g, fiber: 8g, sugar: 4.6g, sodium: 645mg

Homemade Crispy Baked Wings

Prep time: 12 minutes, Cook time: 30 minutes, Serves 4

Ingredients

1 tsp. garlic powder
1 tsp. paprika
1 tsp. chili powder
½ tsp. salt
½ tsp. ground black pepper

¼ tsp. red pepper flakes (optional)
2 pounds (907 g) chicken wings and drumsticks, separated

Directions

1. Preheat the oven to 400ºF (205ºC).
2. In a large bowl, mix together the garlic powder, paprika, chili powder, salt, pepper, and red pepper flakes, if using.
3. Pat down the wings with a kitchen paper towel, squeeze out any excess liquid and make sure the wings are very dry (very important!).
4. Put the wings in the large bowl with spices. Coat evenly, rubbing in the spices with your hands.
5. Place the wings on a greased cooling rack over a baking sheet in the oven and cook for 30 minutes or until the internal temperature is 165ºF (74ºC).

Nutritional Info per Serving

calories: 429, fat: 24g, protein: 45g, carbs: 1g, fiber: 1.2g, sugar: 0.1g, sodium: 482mg

Easy Pressure Cooker Chicken Tikka Masala

Prep time: 8 minutes, Cook time: 15 minutes, Serves 6

Ingredients

1 yellow onion, diced
3 garlic cloves, minced
1 (14-ounce / 397-g) can diced tomatoes
1 (13½-ounce / 383-g) can full-fat coconut milk
1 tbsp. garam masala
1 tsp. turmeric

1 tsp. fresh ginger, grated
½ tsp. salt
¼ tsp. black pepper
2 to 3 pounds (907 g to 1.4 kg) boneless, skinless chicken thighs
Lime juice and cilantro, for topping (optional)

Directions

1. Place the onion, garlic, diced tomatoes, coconut milk, garam masala, turmeric, ginger, salt, and pepper in a pressure cooker. Blend with an immersion blender.
2. Add the chicken, seal, and run on high for 15 minutes.
3. Once finished, quick release until the pressure subsides.
4. Serve over rice. Top with a squeeze of lime juice and cilantro, if desired.

Nutritional Info per Serving

calories: 317, fat: 20g, protein: 22g, carbs: 5.1g, fiber: 0.8g, sugar: 3.6g, sodium: 523mg

Balsamic Chicken Caprese Bowl

Prep time: 15 minutes, Cook time: 14 minutes, Serves 4

Ingredients

Balsamic Vinaigrette:
2 tbsps. olive oil
3 tbsps. balsamic vinegar
½ tsp. sea salt
¼ tsp. ground black pepper
Chicken:
1 tbsp. olive oil
1½ pounds (680 g) boneless, skinless chicken breasts
⅛ tsp. garlic powder

½ tsp. sea salt
¼ tsp. ground black pepper
Bowl:
4 medium zucchinis, spiralized
2 cups cherry tomatoes, halved
1 cup diced fresh mozzarella
8 basil leaves, for garnish

Directions

Make the Vinaigrette:
1. Combine the balsamic vinegar, olive oil, salt, and pepper in a small mixing bowl. Bring the ingredients together with a whisk or a fork, until the dressing is emulsified.

Make the Chicken:
2. In a large skillet, heat the olive oil over medium-high heat. Sprinkle the chicken with the salt, pepper, and garlic powder. Cook the chicken in the pan for about 4 to 6 minutes on each side, until golden brown and cooked through. Then take the chicken from the heat, leaving behind any remaining oil. Let the chicken to sit for 5 minutes, then slice it, and keep it aside.

Make the Bowl:
3. Place the zucchinis to the same pan you used to cook the chicken. Sauté the zucchinis over medium-high heat for about 2 to 3 minutes, until it's tender, but not mushy.
4. Combine the mozzarella and tomatoes in a medium bowl. Slice the basil leaves.
5. To assemble the bowls, begin with a layer of the zucchinis, topped with the sliced chicken and then the cheese-tomato mixture. Pour the balsamic vinaigrette over the top and sprinkle with the basil. Enjoy!

Nutritional Info per Serving

calories: 363, fat: 15g, protein: 48g, carbs: 7g, fiber: 2g, sugar: 5g, sodium: 565mg

Breaded Chicken Tenders

Prep time: 5 minutes, Cook time: 30 minutes, Serves 4 to 6

Ingredients

1 tbsp. extra-virgin olive oil or olive oil spray
4 boneless, skinless chicken breasts, washed and cut into tenders
2 large eggs, beaten
¾ cup gluten-free bread crumbs
½ cup spelt flour
1 tbsp. Dijon mustard
½ tsp. Himalayan salt
Spice it up:
1 tsp. oregano

Directions

1. Preheat the oven to 400ºF (205ºC). Line a baking sheet with parchment paper and keep aside.
2. Use a paper towel to pat the chicken dry. Rub all over with the salt and mustard.
3. Place the flour in one shallow dish, the eggs in another, and the bread crumbs in a third. Dip both sides of each tender into the flour, then the eggs, then the bread crumbs, finally putting them on the baking sheet.
4. Scatter oregano on top of each of the tenders, if desired, then spray olive oil on top.
5. Bake for 30 minutes, flipping once halfway through the cook time.
6. Serve hot.

Nutritional Info per Serving

calories: 339, fat: 10g, protein: 34g, carbs: 26g, fiber: 1g, sugar: 1g, sodium: 439mg

Curried Chicken

Prep time: 8 minutes, Cook time: 9½ hours, Serves 5

Ingredients

10 (4-ounce / 113-g) boneless, skinless chicken thighs
4 large tomatoes, seeded and chopped
⅔ cup canned coconut milk
½ cup plain Greek yogurt
⅓ cup lemon juice
2 onions, chopped
8 garlic cloves, sliced
5 tsps. curry powder
3 tbsps. cornstarch
2 tbsps. grated fresh ginger root

Directions

1. Mix the yogurt, lemon juice, curry powder, and ginger root in a medium bowl. Place the chicken and stir to coat well. Let stand for about 15 minutes while you make the other ingredients.
2. Mix the tomatoes, onions, and garlic in a 6-quart slow cooker.
3. Place the chicken-yogurt mixture to the slow cooker. Cover the slow cooker and cook on low for 7 to 9 hours, or until the chicken registers 165ºF (74ºC) on a food thermometer.
4. Mix the coconut milk and cornstarch in a small bowl. Stir the mixture into the slow cooker.
5. Cover and cook on low for an additional 15 to 20 minutes, or until the sauce has thickened. Serve warm.

Nutritional Info per Serving

calories: 295, fat: 15g, protein: 30g, carbs: 12g, fiber: 2g, sugar: 5g, sodium: 124mg

Lemon-flavored Greek Chicken Skewers

Prep time: 12 minutes, Cook time: 10 minutes, Serves 4

Ingredients

2 tbsps. olive oil
⅓ cup plain unsweetened Greek yogurt
Juice and zest of 1 large lemon
3 to 4 garlic cloves, minced
1 tbsp. oregano
¼ tsp. salt
¼ tsp. pepper
1½ pounds (680 g) chicken breast, cubed
1 zucchini, sliced
1 small red onion, cut into a 1-inch dice
1 red bell pepper, cut into a 1-inch dice

Directions

1. Whisk together the olive oil, yogurt, lemon juice, lemon zest, garlic, oregano, salt, and pepper in a large bowl.
2. Add the cubed chicken and half of the yogurt mixture into a freezer bag. Press out the air and seal the bag. Massage or shake the bag to coat evenly. Refrigerate for 30 minutes. Reserve the remaining marinade for basting.
3. Preheat the grill to medium heat.
4. Thread 5 or 6 wooden or metal skewers with the chicken, zucchini, red onion, and bell pepper. Discard the marinade you used for the raw chicken.
5. Place the skewers on grill (If using wooden skewers be sure to soak them in water for 30 minutes), turning often and basting with the reserved marinade. Cook for 10 minutes, or until chicken is cooked through, or the internal temperature reaches 165ºF (74ºC).

Nutritional Info per Serving

calories: 284, fat: 11g, protein: 36g, carbs: 9g, fiber: 1.7g, sugar: 1.6g, sodium: 436mg

BBQ Chicken Pita Pizzas

Prep time: 7 minutes, Cook time: 23 minutes, Serves 4

Ingredients

Clean BBQ Sauce:
1 tbsp. olive oil
1 (8-ounce / 227-g) can no-salt tomato sauce
2 cloves garlic, minced
2 tbsps. raw honey
2 tbsps. tomato paste
2 tbsps. molasses
1 tbsp. apple cider vinegar
½ tsp. granulated onion
¼ tsp. sea salt
¼ tsp. ground black pepper
Pizza:

1 tbsp. olive oil
1 large boneless, skinless chicken breast
4 whole wheat pita breads
3 ounces (85 g) fresh Mozzarella, sliced
¼ red onion, thinly sliced
¼ cup chopped fresh cilantro (optional)
¼ tsp. paprika
⅛ tsp. garlic powder
½ tsp. sea salt
¼ tsp. ground black pepper

Directions

1. Preheat the oven to 350ºF (180ºC), and carefully line a baking sheet with parchment paper.
2. To make the BBQ sauce, in a saucepan over medium-high heat, heat the olive oil, then place the garlic. Cook for about 1 minute, until the garlic is fragrant, then pour in the tomato sauce, tomato paste, honey, molasses, vinegar, granulated onion, salt, and pepper, and stir to combine well. Sauté, stirring constantly, for about 6 to 8 minutes, until the sauce is heated through and beginning to thicken. Take the sauce from the heat, and keep it aside.
3. For the chicken, in a small mixing bowl, combine the paprika, salt, pepper, and garlic powder and stir well. Sprinkle the chicken breast liberally with this spice blend.
4. In a large skillet over medium-high heat, heat the olive oil. Place the chicken breast to the skillet, and sauté for about 4 to 6 minutes per side, until it's cooked through and browned on both sides. Then take the chicken from the heat, and cut it into small, bite-size pieces. Keep aside.
5. To assemble the pizza, spread out the pita breads on the prepared baking sheet. (You may need to bake two pizzas at a time or use two baking sheets to avoid crowding the pizzas.) Coat about 2 tbsps. of the BBQ sauce over each of the pitas, leaving about ¼ inch around the edge for the crust. Refrigerate the remaining BBQ sauce in an airtight container for up to 5 days.
6. Place the chicken, Mozzarella, and then the onion over the BBQ sauce on each pita.
7. Bake the pizzas for about 6 to 8 minutes, until the edges of the crust turn golden brown and the cheese is melted and bubbly. Take the pizzas from the oven, cut into quarters, and garnish with the cilantro, if desired. Enjoy!

Nutritional Info per Serving
calories: 352, fat: 14g, protein: 21g, carbs: 36g, fiber: 3g, sugar: 19g, sodium: 737mg

Lemon Herb Chicken Meatballs

Prep time: 18 minutes, Cook time: 20 minutes, Serves 4

Ingredients

¼ cup whole-wheat bread crumbs
¼ cup milk
¼ cup loosely packed fresh parsley, finely chopped
3 tbsps. yellow onion, finely minced
2 tbsps. celery, finely minced
2 tbsps. lemon juice, freshly squeezed
1 tbsp. coconut aminos

1 tbsp. finely garlic, minced
1½ tsps. fresh ginger, peeled and minced
¼ tsp. salt
¼ tsp. black pepper, freshly ground
1 large egg, beaten
1 pound (454 g) chicken, ground
1 tbsp. extra-virgin olive oil

Directions

1. Preheat the oven to 400ºF (205ºC).
2. In a small bowl, stir together the bread crumbs and milk and let it soak.
3. In a large bowl, add the parsley, onion, celery, lemon juice, coconut aminos, garlic, ginger, salt, and pepper. Mix well.
4. Add the cracked egg in the milk mixture. Mix until well incorporated. Add the ground chicken and gently fold the ingredients together until cohesive. Be careful not to overmix. Roll the mixture into about 16 (1½-inch) meatballs.
5. In a large oven-safe skillet or Dutch oven, heat the oil over medium-high heat. Carefully add the meatballs and cook until brown, 3 to 5 minutes per side.
6. Place the skillet in the oven. Bake the meatballs for 10 minutes, or until they reach an internal temperature of 165ºF (74ºC).
7. Evenly divide the meatballs among one half of 4 large two-compartment glass meal-prep containers with tight-fitting lids. Fill the remaining compartment with your favorite side or salad. Cover and refrigerate.

Nutritional Info per Serving (4 meatballs)
calories: 261, fat: 14g, protein: 22g, carbs: 10g, fiber: 0.9g, sugar: 4g, sodium: 302mg

Peachy Chicken Picante

Prep time: 11 minutes, Cook time: 43 minutes, Serves 4

Ingredients
1 tbsp. ghee or butter
1 red onion, diced
3 garlic cloves, minced
1 jalapeño, seeded and diced
4 peaches, chopped
1 (14½-ounce / 411-g) can diced tomatoes
1 tbsp. honey
½ tsp. salt
½ tsp. pepper
¼ tsp. red pepper flakes (optional)
1 pound (454 g) chicken breast

Directions
1. Preheat the oven to 400ºF (205ºC).
2. In a large, oven-safe skillet, heat the ghee over medium heat. Add the onion and sauté for 3 to 5 minutes, or until softened. Add the garlic, jalapeño, and peaches. Sauté for 2 to 3 minutes more.
3. Add the tomatoes, honey, salt, pepper, and red pepper flakes (if using) and simmer for 5 minutes. Add the chicken. Spoon or brush the sauce over the chicken to ensure it completely coated with sauce. Place the skillet in the oven and cook for 30 minutes, or until internal temperature of the chicken reaches 165ºF (74ºC).

Nutritional Info per Serving
calories: 234, fat: 5g, protein: 24g, carbs: 22g, fiber: 3g, sugar: 18g, sodium: 703mg

Keto Egg Roll in a Bowl

Prep time: 11 minutes, Cook time: 12 minutes, Serves 4

Ingredients
2 tbsps. sesame oil, divided
1 pound (454 g) ground chicken
1 small sweet onion, diced
3 garlic cloves, minced
2 large carrots, diced
½ small head cabbage, shredded
2 large eggs, beaten
1 tsp. ginger, freshly grated
1 tbsp. rice vinegar
3 tbsps. soy sauce
1 to 2 tsps. Sriracha (optional)
Sliced green onions (optional)

Directions
1. Heat 1 tbsp. of oil over medium heat in a large skillet. Add the chicken and cook until fully browned, about 8 minutes.
2. Add the remaining oil along with the onion, garlic, carrots, and cabbage Sauté for 3 to 4 minutes.

3. Make a well in the center of the skillet and add the eggs. Let the eggs sit over low heat for 20 to 30 seconds, then scramble until done and incorporate them into the rest of the mixture.
4. Add the ginger, rice vinegar, and soy sauce, and combine.
5. Remove from the heat and top with Sriracha and green onions.

Nutritional Info per Serving
calories: 352, fat: 21g, protein: 26g, carbs: 12g, fiber: 4g, sugar: 7g, sodium: 511mg

Spinach Artichoke Pinwheels

Prep time: 9 minutes, Cook time: 35 minutes, Serves 8

Ingredients
Cooking oil spray
1 tbsp. olive oil
4 garlic cloves, minced
1 (14-ounce / 397-g) can artichoke hearts, drained and chopped
8 cups baby spinach
2 ounces (57 g) cream cheese
½ cup Cheddar cheese, shredded
½ cup Parmesan cheese, grated
1 tsp. salt
½ tsp. pepper
4 (4-ounce / 113-g) chicken breasts

Directions
1. Preheat the oven to 400ºF (205ºC). Coat the inside baking dish with cooking oil spray.
2. Heat the oil over medium heat in a large skillet. Add the garlic and cook for 3 minutes.
3. Stir in the artichokes and spinach until spinach starts to wilt. Remove from the heat and combine the cream cheese, Cheddar cheese, Parmesan. Season with salt and pepper.
4. Unroll the chicken breasts (don't cut all the way through). Place between 2 sheets of parchment paper and pound with a mallet (or rolling pin) until about ½-to ¼-inch thick.
5. Stuff ¼ of the spinach-artichoke mixture in each butterflied chicken breast and roll lengthwise. Place the chicken breast in the prepared baking dish, seam-side down. Bake for 25 to 30 minutes, or until the chicken is cooked to internal temperature of 165ºF (74ºC).
6. Remove from the oven, and cool for 5 minutes, then slice into pinwheels and serve over cauliflower rice or a salad, if desired

Nutritional Info per Serving
calories: 183, fat: 9g, protein: 18g, carbs: 5g, fiber: 4g, sugar: 0.9g, sodium: 625mg

Homemade Crispy Baked Wings, page 56

Lemon-flavored Greek Chicken Skewers, page 57

Oven Chicken Thighs with Paprika, page 54

Sheet-Pan Chicken Fajitas, page 62

Avocado Chicken Salad Sandwich

Prep time: 8 minutes, Cook time: 0 minutes, Serves 2

Ingredients

Avocado Chicken Salad:
1 cup cooked shredded chicken breast
1 avocado, diced
½ Granny Smith apple, cored and finely diced
¼ cup finely diced red onion
½ tbsp. no-sugar-added dried cranberries
1 tsp. freshly squeezed

lemon juice
⅛ tsp. garlic powder
¼ tsp. sea salt
¼ tsp. ground black pepper

Sandwiches:
4 slices whole-grain bread or whole-wheat pita bread
1 large tomato, sliced
6 leaves butter lettuce
¼ cup microgreens

Directions

1. In a medium mixing bowl, mash the avocado until it is mostly pureed. Place the chicken, apple, lemon juice, onion, cranberries, salt, pepper, and garlic powder, and combine together well.
2. On each of 2 slices of bread, spread half of the lettuce, tomato, and microgreens. Top with half of the chicken salad and remaining slices of bread. Serve right away.

Nutritional Info per Serving
calories: 472, fat: 20g, protein: 32g, carbs: 44g, fiber: 12g, sugar: 9g, sodium: 543mg

Homemade Braised Chicken Marsala

Prep time: 11 minutes, Cook time: 50 minutes, Serves 4

Ingredients

1½ pounds (680 g) boneless, skinless chicken thighs
1 pound (454 g) cremini mushrooms, stemmed, cut into ¼-inch slices
2 tsps. garlic, minced
1 tbsp. lemon juice,

freshly squeezed
1 tsp. dried parsley
½ tsp. salt
¼ tsp. black pepper, freshly ground
¾ cup Marsala wine
3 tbsps. butter

Directions

1. Preheat the oven to 325ºF (165ºC).
2. Arrange the chicken thighs in a single layer in a baking dish. Place the mushrooms and garlic on the top and drizzle with lemon juice. Sprinkle with

parsley, salt, and pepper.
3. Pour the Marsala wine over the surface. Place dabs of the butter across the chicken and mushrooms, evenly spaced.
4. Bake for 50 minutes, or until the chicken reaches an internal temperature of 165ºF (74ºC).
5. Evenly portion the chicken thighs and mushroom sauce into one half of 4 large two-compartment glass containers with lids. Fill the remaining compartment with your favorite side or salad. Cover and refrigerate.

Nutritional Info per Serving
calories: 374, fat: 18g, protein: 30g, carbs: 11g, fiber: 1.3g, sugar: 7g, sodium: 484mg

Chicken Broccoli Dijon Rice

Prep time: 14 minutes, Cook time: 24 minutes, Serves 4

Ingredients

1 tbsp. extra-virgin olive oil
1 cup brown rice
3 cups chicken broth
2 tbsps. Dijon mustard
½ tsp. salt
½ tsp. turmeric, ground
½ tsp. Italian seasoning
¼ tsp. black pepper, freshly ground

¼ tsp. red pepper flakes (optional)
12 ounces (340 g) broccoli florets, cut into bite-size pieces
2 tsps. garlic, minced
1 pound (454 g) boneless, skinless chicken breast, cut into 1-inch pieces

Directions

1. In a Dutch oven or other deep pot or pan with a lid. Warm the oil over medium heat.
2. Add the rice and toast until golden brown, stirring frequently, for about 2 minutes.
3. Pour in the chicken broth. Stir in the Dijon, salt, turmeric, Italian seasoning, black pepper, and red pepper flakes (if using). Turn the heat to medium-high and bring to a boil.
4. Stir in the broccoli florets and garlic. Lower the heat, cover the pot, and simmer for 5 minutes.
5. Add the chicken, stir well. Cover the pot, and simmer for 15 more minutes, or until the chicken reaches an internal temperature of 165ºF (74ºC) and the rice is tender.
6. Evenly portion the chicken, broccoli, and rice into 4 large single-compartment glass meal-prep containers with tight-fitting lids.

Nutritional Info per Serving
calories: 367, fat: 10g, protein: 31g, carbs: 40g, fiber: 6g, sugar: 3g, sodium: 482mg

Sheet-Pan Chicken Fajitas

Prep time: 6 minutes, Cook time: 30 minutes, Serves 4 to 6

Ingredients
1½ to 2 pounds (680 to 907 g) chicken breast, sliced
3 bell peppers (assorted colors), sliced
1 red onion, sliced
1 tbsp. avocado oil
1 tbsp. taco seasoning

Directions
1. Preheat the oven to 400ºF (205ºC). Line a baking sheet with parchment paper.
2. Mix together all of the ingredients in a large bowl until evenly coated.
3. Pour the chicken mixture on the baking sheet in a layer. Bake for 30 minutes or until the chicken is cooked through.

Nutritional Info per Serving
calories: 241, fat: 6g, protein: 34g, carbs: 9g, fiber: 1.7g, sugar: 4g, sodium: 442mg

Delicious Chicken Marsala

Prep time: 9 minutes, Cook time: 25 minutes, Serves 4 to 6

Ingredients
1 to 1½ pounds (454 to 680 g) chicken breasts
½ tsp. salt
¼ tsp. pepper
3 tbsps. cornstarch, divided
2 tbsps. butter
8 ounces (227 g) white button mushrooms, sliced
¼ cup diced yellow onion
3 garlic cloves, minced
½ cup Marsala wine
½ cup chicken or beef broth
2 tbsps. parsley, fresh
Salt
Pepper

Directions
1. Place the chicken, salt, pepper, and 2 tbsps. of the cornstarch in a large freezer bag and seal. Shake or massage the bag to better coat the chicken.
2. In a large skillet, heat the butter over medium-high heat. Remove the chicken from the bag and shake off any extra cornstarch. Place the chicken in the skillet and cook for 2 to 3 minutes until brown-colored per side. Transfer the chicken to a plate.
3. Add the mushrooms to the skillet and sauté for 2 to 3 minutes. Add the onion and garlic and sauté for 1 to 2 minutes.
4. Pour in the wine, broth, and remaining tbsp. of cornstarch. Stir, scraping up any brown bits from the sides and bottom of the skillet. Bring to a boil.
5. Reduce the heat to medium and return the chicken to the skillet. Cover and simmer for 15 minutes, or until the chicken is cooked through and the sauce has thickened.
6. Garnish with the parsley and season with the salt and pepper to taste before serving.

Nutritional Info per Serving
calories: 254, fat: 8g, protein: 24g, carbs: 12g, fiber: 0.7g, sugar: 1.8g, sodium: 602mg

Savory Chicken Bruschetta Pasta

Prep time: 13 minutes, Cook time: 16 minutes, Serves 4

Ingredients
Pasta and Tomatoes:
8 ounces (227 g) angel hair pasta
2 cups tomatoes, diced
⅓ cup fresh basil, thinly sliced
¼ cup red onion, finely chopped
3 garlic cloves, minced
1 tbsp. balsamic vinegar
1 tbsp. olive oil
¼ tsp. salt
¼ tsp. pepper
Chicken:
1½ pounds (680 g) chicken breast, sliced
2 tbsps. olive oil, divided
½ tsp. dried basil
½ tsp. salt
¼ tsp. pepper
Fresh basil leaves, Parmesan cheese, red pepper flakes, for topping (optional)

Directions
Make the Pasta and Tomatoes:
1. Bring salted water to boil over high heat. Add the pasta and cook according to the package instructions. When the pasta is cooked, drain.
2. Meanwhile, in a medium bowl, toss together the tomatoes, basil, onion, garlic, vinegar, oil, salt, and pepper.
Make the Chicken:
3. Combine the chicken with 1 tbsp. of the oil, basil, salt, and pepper in a medium bowl.
4. In a large skillet, heat the remaining 1 tbsp. olive oil over medium heat. Add the chicken and sauté until cooked through.
5. Add tomato mixture to skillet with chicken and cook for 3 minutes. Add the pasta to the skillet and fold the ingredients together gently with tongs.
6. Top with basil, Parmesan, and red pepper flakes, if desired.

Nutritional Info per Serving
calories: 487, fat: 15g, protein: 41g, carbs: 48g, fiber: 2.6g, sugar: 2.8g, sodium: 517mg

Barbecue Chicken

Prep time: 6 minutes, Cook time: 7 hours, Serves 4

Ingredients

8 (6-ounce / 170-g) boneless, skinless chicken breasts
2 (8-ounce / 227-g) BPA-free cans no-salt-added tomato sauce
⅓ cup mustard
2 onions, minced
8 garlic cloves, minced
3 tbsps. molasses
2 tbsps. lemon juice
1 tbsp. chili powder
2 tsps. paprika
¼ tsp. cayenne pepper

Directions

1. Mix the tomato sauce, onions, garlic, mustard, lemon juice, molasses, chili powder, paprika, and cayenne in a 6-quart slow cooker.
2. Place the chicken and move the chicken around in the sauce with tongs to coat. Cover the slow cooker and cook on low for 5 to 7 hours, or until the chicken registers 165ºF (74ºC) on a food thermometer. Serve warm.

Nutritional Info per Serving

calories: 231, fat: 4g, protein: 35g, carbs: 16g, fiber: 2g, sugar: 10g, sodium: 490mg

Easy Baked Chicken

Prep time: 12 minutes, Cook time: 15 minutes, Serves 4

Ingredients

1½ tsps. extra-virgin olive oil, divided
1 pound (454 g) chicken breast, cut into 1-inch strips
½ tsp. salt
½ tsp. lemon juice, freshly squeezed
⅛ tsp. black pepper, freshly ground

Directions

1. Preheat the oven to 400ºF (205ºC). Line a baking sheet with foil and brush with 1 tsp. of oil.
2. In a large bowl, place the remaining ½ tsp. of oil, chicken, salt, lemon juice, and pepper. Toss well to coat thoroughly. Transfer the chicken to the prepared baking sheet and spread into a single layer.
3. Bake for 15 minutes, or until the chicken reaches an internal temperature of 165ºF (74ºC).
4. Evenly portion the chicken breast into 4 wells of large compartment glass containers with tight-fitting lids. Fill the remaining compartments with your favorite sides and salads. Cover and refrigerate.

Nutritional Info per Serving

calories: 152, fat: 6g, protein: 23g, carbs: 0.3g, fiber: 0.2g, sugar: 0.3g, sodium: 381mg

Mediterranean Chicken and Quinoa Bowl with Cucumber Dressing

Prep time: 12 minutes, Cook time: 17 minutes, Serves 4

Ingredients

Mediterranean Chicken and Quinoa Bowl:
1 tbsp. olive oil
1 pound (454 g) boneless, skinless chicken breasts
4 cups roughly chopped romaine lettuce leaves
1 large cucumber, sliced into half moons
2 cups cooked quinoa
1 cup grape tomatoes, halved
1 avocado, diced
½ cup crumbled feta cheese
½ red onion, sliced
⅓ cup sliced Kalamata olives
½ tsp. sea salt
½ tsp. ground black pepper
Cucumber Dressing:
1 cup peeled and diced cucumber
½ cup plain full-fat Greek yogurt
1 clove garlic
2 tbsps. unsweetened almond milk
2 tbsps. freshly squeezed lemon juice
1 tbsp. tahini
1 tbsp. hemp seed hearts
1 tsp. chopped fresh dill
¼ tsp. sea salt
¼ tsp. ground black pepper

Directions

Make the Chicken:
1. In a skillet over medium-high heat, heat the olive oil. Rub the chicken on both sides with the salt and pepper. Place the chicken to the hot oil, and cook for 4 to 6 minutes per side, until it is golden brown on both sides and cooked through. Then take it from the heat, and let rest for 5 minutes. Cut it into bite-size slices and keep aside.

Make the Dressing:
2. Combine the yogurt, cucumber, tahini, hemp seed hearts, almond milk, garlic, salt, pepper, lemon juice, and dill in a food processor or blender. Blend until smooth.

Make the Bowl:
3. Spread a layer of quinoa at the bottom of the bowl. In small piles on top of the quinoa, place the chicken, lettuce, tomatoes, cucumber, onion, avocado, olives, and feta cheese. Drizzle with the dressing and serve immediately.

Nutritional Info per Serving

calories: 517, fat: 23g, protein: 39g, carbs: 42g, fiber: 10g, sugar: 13g, sodium: 495mg

Classic Chicken Provençal

Prep time: 16 minutes, Cook time: 9 hours, Serves 10

Ingredients

3 pounds (1.4 kg) boneless, skinless chicken thighs
4 large tomatoes, seeded and chopped
3 bulbs fennel, cored and sliced
2 red bell peppers, stemmed, seeded, and chopped
¼ cup sliced black Greek olives
2 onions, chopped
6 garlic cloves, minced
4 sprigs fresh thyme
1 bay leaf
2 tbsps. lemon juice

Directions

1. Mix all of the ingredients in a 6-quart slow cooker. Cover the slow cooker and cook on low for 7 to 9 hours, or until the chicken registers 165ºF (74ºC) on a food thermometer.
2. Remove the thyme stems and bay leaf and discard. Serve warm.

Nutritional Info per Serving

calories: 302, fat: 14g, protein: 34g, carbs: 13g, fiber: 4g, sugar: 7g, sodium: 187mg

Jerk Chicken Thigh

Prep time: 13 minutes, Cook time: 9 hours, Serves 6

Ingredients

10 (4-ounce / 113-g) boneless, skinless chicken thighs
3 onions, chopped
6 garlic cloves, minced
½ cup freshly squeezed orange juice
3 tbsps. grated fresh ginger root
2 tbsps. honey
1 tbsp. chili powder
1 tsp. ground red chili
½ tsp. ground cloves
¼ tsp. ground allspice

Directions

1. Cut slashes across the chicken thighs so the flavorings can permeate.
2. Mix the honey, ginger root, ground chili, chili powder, cloves, and allspice in a small bowl. Gently rub this mixture into the chicken. Allow the chicken to stand while you make the vegetables.
3. Place the onions and garlic in a 6-quart slow cooker. Then top with the chicken. Add the orange juice over all. Cover the slow cooker and cook on low for 7 to 9 hours, or until a food thermometer registers 165ºF (74ºC). Serve warm.

Nutritional Info per Serving

calories: 184, fat: 3g, protein: 30g, carbs: 11g, fiber: 1g, sugar: 7g, sodium: 316mg

Chicken Breast with Artichokes

Prep time: 8 minutes, Cook time: 6 hours, Serves 4 to 6

Ingredients

8 (6-ounce / 170-g) boneless, skinless chicken breasts
2 (14-ounce / 397-g) BPA-free cans no-salt-added artichoke hearts, drained
2 red bell peppers, stemmed, seeded, and chopped
2 leeks, chopped
1 cup chicken stock
½ cup chopped flat-leaf parsley
3 garlic cloves, minced
2 tbsps. lemon juice
1 tsp. dried basil leaves

Directions

1. Layer the leeks, garlic, artichoke hearts, bell peppers, chicken, stock, lemon juice, and basil in a 6-quart slow cooker. Cover the slow cooker and cook on low for 4 to 6 hours, or until the chicken registers 165ºF (74ºC) on a food thermometer.
2. Garnish with the parsley and serve warm.

Nutritional Info per Serving

calories: 200, fat: 4g, protein: 36g, carbs: 7g, fiber: 3g, sugar: 2g, sodium: 372mg

Thai Chicken with Greens and Peppers

Prep time: 10 minutes, Cook time: 8 hours, Serves 6 to 8

Ingredients

2 (16-ounce / 454-g) packages prepared collard greens
10 (4-ounce / 113-g) boneless, skinless chicken thighs
2 cups chopped kale
2 red chili peppers, minced
2 onions, chopped
1 cup canned coconut milk
1 cup chicken stock
6 garlic cloves, minced
1 lemongrass stalk
3 tbsps. freshly squeezed lime juice

Directions

1. Mix the greens and kale and top with the onions, garlic, chili peppers, lemongrass, and chicken in a 6-quart slow cooker. Pour in the chicken stock and coconut milk over all.
2. Cover the slow cooker and cook on low for 6 to 8 hours, or until the chicken registers 165ºF (74ºC) on a food thermometer and the greens are soft.

3. Remove the lemongrass and discard. Gently stir in the lime juice and serve warm.

Nutritional Info per Serving
calories: 338, fat: 17g, protein: 33g, carbs: 15g, fiber: 7g, sugar: 3g, sodium: 173mg

Classic Jambalaya

Prep time: 20 minutes, Cook time: 9½ hours, Serves 6 to 8

Ingredients
1½ pounds (680 g) raw shrimp, shelled and deveined
10 (4-ounce / 113-g) boneless, skinless chicken thighs, cut into 2-inch pieces
5 celery stalks, sliced
2 jalapeño peppers, minced
2 green bell peppers, stemmed, seeded, and chopped
2 cups chicken stock
2 onions, chopped
6 garlic cloves, minced
1 tbsp. Cajun seasoning
¼ tsp. cayenne pepper

Directions
1. Mix the chicken, onions, garlic, jalapeños, bell peppers, celery, chicken stock, Cajun seasoning, and cayenne in a 6-quart slow cooker. Cover the slow cooker and cook on low for 7 to 9 hours, or until the chicken registers 165ºF (74ºC) on a food thermometer.
2. Stir in the shrimp. Cover and cook for an additional 30 to 40 minutes, or until the shrimp are curled and pink. Serve warm.

Nutritional Info per Serving
calories: 417, fat: 20g, protein: 34g, carbs: 27g, fiber: 3g, sugar: 3g, sodium: 385mg

Honey Chicken

Prep time: 17 minutes, Cook time: 8 hours, Serves 8 to 10

Ingredients
2 pounds (907 g) skinless chicken drumsticks
2 pounds (907 g) skinless chicken thighs
1 onion, chopped
3 garlic cloves, minced
2 cups chicken stock, divided
4 scallions, cut on the bias
2 tbsps. honey
2 tbsps. grated fresh ginger root
2 tbsps. miso paste
2 tbsps. toasted sesame seeds

Directions
1. Mix the onion, garlic, and ginger root in a 6-quart slow cooker. Place the chicken drumsticks and thighs on top.
2. Mix ½ cup of the chicken stock with the honey and miso paste in a medium bowl, and whisk to blend. Pour in the remaining 1½ cups of the chicken stock and mix until well blended, then add this mixture into the slow cooker.
3. Cover the slow cooker and cook on low for 7 to 8 hours, or until the chicken registers 165ºF (74ºC) on a food thermometer.
4. Garnish with the sesame seeds and scallions and serve warm.

Nutritional Info per Serving
calories: 405, fat: 19g, protein: 48g, carbs: 10g, fiber: 1g, sugar: 7g, sodium: 529mg

Lemony Chicken Breast with Capers

Prep time: 9 minutes, Cook time: 9 minutes, Serves 4

Ingredients
2 tbsps. extra-virgin olive oil
1 pound (454 g) boneless, skinless chicken breast, thinly sliced
¼ cup water
Juice of 1 large lemon
3 tbsps. almond flour
2 tbsps. capers
1 tbsp. fresh oregano, chopped (optional)
½ tsp. Himalayan salt
Freshly ground black pepper (optional)

Directions
1. Add the almond flour on a shallow plate. Keep aside.
2. Pound the chicken on both sides, season with salt, and dip each side into the almond flour. Pat off the extra flour.
3. In a large, nonstick sauté pan or skillet, heat the olive oil over medium heat.
4. Place the chicken and sauté on one side for 3 minutes, then flip. Cover and cook for 2 minutes, then squeeze lemon all over the chicken, and place the capers and ¼ cup water. Cover and reduce the heat to low.
5. When the water evaporates, flip the meat once again, cook for about 1 minute, and turn off the heat.
6. Squeeze extra lemon juice on top as well as some freshly ground black pepper, if desired. Add fresh oregano as a finishing touch (if using). Enjoy!

Nutritional Info per Serving
calories: 227, fat: 12g, protein: 27g, carbs: 2g, fiber: 1g, sugar: 0g, sodium: 298mg

Chapter 6: Pork, Beef and Lamb

Mustard Beef Brisket

Prep time: 15 minutes, Cook time: 11 hours, Serves 12

Ingredients

1 (3-pound / 1.4-kg) grass-fed beef brisket, trimmed
2 (8-ounce / 227-g) BPA-free cans no-salt-added tomato sauce
⅓ cup natural mustard
3 onions, chopped
8 garlic cloves, minced
3 tbsps. honey
2 tsps. paprika
1 tsp. dried marjoram leaves
1 tsp. dried oregano leaves
½ tsp. cayenne pepper

Directions

1. Mix the onions and garlic in a 6-quart slow cooker.
2. In a small bowl, mix the oregano, marjoram, paprika, and cayenne. Gently rub this mixture into the beef brisket.
3. Mix the tomato sauce, mustard, and honey until well combined in another small bowl.
4. Place the beef on the onions and garlic in the slow cooker. Add the tomato mixture over all.
5. Cover the slow cooker and cook on low for 8 to 11 hours, or until the beef is very soft.
6. Slice or shred the beef and serve it on buns.

Nutritional Info per Serving

calories: 303, fat: 10g, protein: 37g, carbs: 18g, fiber: 2g, sugar: 12g, sodium: 277mg

Baked Hawaiian Pork Kebabs

Prep time: 24 minutes, Cook time: 15 minutes, Serves 6 to 8

Ingredients

⅓ cup soy sauce
1 tbsp. honey
½ tsp. paprika
½ tsp. garlic powder
½ tsp. onion powder
¼ tsp. cumin
¼ tsp. salt
¼ tsp. pepper
2 pounds (907 g) boneless pork loin, chopped
Cooking oil spray
2 bell peppers, chopped
1 pineapple, cored and chopped
1 yellow onion, chopped

Directions

1. In a large freezer bag or baking dish, combine the soy sauce, honey, paprika, garlic powder, onion powder, cumin, salt, and pepper. Mix well.
2. Add the pork, coating evenly with the sauce. Marinate for 20 minutes or up to 2 hours.
3. Preheat the grill to medium and coat with spray.
4. Remove the pork from the marinade. Discard the marinade.
5. Assemble the kebabs. Divide the pork, peppers, pineapple, and onion evenly among 6 skewers.
6. Grill the kebabs for 12 to 15 minutes.

Nutritional Info per Serving

calories: 286, fat: 10g, protein: 27g, carbs: 18g, fiber: 2g, sugar: 14g, sodium: 632mg

Healthy Beef Stroganoff

Prep time: 15 minutes, Cook time: 9½ hours, Serves 6 to 8

Ingredients

2½ pounds (1.1 kg) grass-fed chuck shoulder roast, trimmed of fat and cut into 2-inch cubes
5 large carrots, sliced
2 cups sliced cremini mushrooms
1½ cups sour cream
2 cups beef stock
2 onions, chopped
8 garlic cloves, sliced
1 bay leaf
3 tbsps. mustard
3 tbsps. cornstarch
1 tsp. dried marjoram

Directions

1. Mix the onions, mushrooms, carrots, garlic, and beef in a 6-quart slow cooker.
2. Mix the beef stock and mustard in a medium bowl. Place the bay leaf and marjoram and pour into the slow cooker.
3. Cover the slow cooker and cook on low for 7 to 9 hours, or until the beef is very soft.
4. In a medium bowl, combine the sour cream and cornstarch. Pour 1 cup of the liquid from the slow cooker and whisk until blended well.
5. Place the sour cream mixture to the slow cooker. Cover and cook on low for 20 to 30 minutes more, or until the liquid has thickened. Discard the bay leaf and serve warm.

Nutritional Info per Serving

calories: 503, fat: 33g, protein: 32g, carbs: 15g, fiber: 2g, sugar: 6g, sodium: 246mg

Apple, Brie and Onion Burger

Prep time: 6 minutes, Cook time: 30 minutes, Serves 4

Ingredients

1 tbsp. olive oil
2 onions, peeled and sliced
¼ tsp. salt, plus more for seasoning
¼ tsp. pepper, plus more for seasoning

1 pound (454 g) lean ground beef
1 apple, cored and sliced
4 ounces (113 g) Brie, sliced
4 hamburger buns

Directions

1. In a large skillet, heat the oil over medium heat.
2. Add the onions. Cook for 20 minutes until caramelized, stirring frequently. Stir in the salt and pepper.
3. Mix the onion and beef, then form the beef mixture into four patties and season with salt and pepper.
4. Grill the patties for about 5 minutes each side.
5. During the last minute of grilling, top with the apple slices and Brie slices on each patty and continue until the Brie is slightly melted.
6. Place the patties on the burger buns and serve right now!

Nutritional Info per Serving

calories: 502, fat: 20g, protein: 31g, carbs: 42g, fiber: 2.7g, sugar: 4g, sodium: 657mg

Skillet Pepper Steak

Prep time: 24 minutes, Cook time: 14 minutes, Serves 4

Ingredients

¼ cup soy sauce
¼ cup water
2 tsps. maple syrup
1 tbsp. cornstarch
½ tsp. black pepper
1 pound (454 g) flank steak, cut into ¼-to ½-inch slices
2 tbsps. avocado oil, divided
2 bell peppers, sliced into

strips
1 yellow onion, sliced into strips
3 garlic cloves, minced
1-inch piece of fresh ginger, peeled and minced
Red pepper flakes (optional)
Cooked rice

Directions

1. In a small baking dish or large freezer bag, add the steal along with the soy sauce, water, maple syrup, cornstarch, and pepper. Let marinate in the fridge for 20 minutes (or longer, if possible).
2. In a large skillet over medium heat, heat 1 tbsp. of

the oil until it glistens.
3. Add the peppers and onion, and stir until softened, about 8 minutes. Transfer the vegetables to a medium bowl.
4. Heat the remaining tbsp. of oil in the skillet. Add the garlic and ginger and sauté for one minute.
5. Remove the steak from the marinade and cook until browned on each side, about 2 minutes per side.
6. Add the cooked peppers and onions to the skillet to combine.
7. Garnish with red pepper flakes, if using, and serve over rice.

Nutritional Info per Serving

calories: 308, fat: 14g, protein: 24g, carbs: 16g, fiber: 3g, sugar: 3.5g, sodium: 635mg

Taco Pasta

Prep time: 12 minutes, Cook time: 20 minutes, Serves 6

Ingredients

1 tbsp. olive oil
1 small red onion, diced
3 garlic cloves, minced
1 pound (454 g) lean ground beef
1 tbsp. taco seasoning
2 tbsps. tomato paste
1 bell pepper, diced
1 (15-ounce / 425-g) can black beans, drained and rinsed
1 (14½-ounce / 411-g) can diced tomatoes

3 cups chicken broth
8 ounces (227 g) elbow macaroni
1 cup Cheddar cheese, shredded
Juice of 1 lime
2 tbsps. cilantro, chopped
1 jalapeño, seeded and diced
Avocado, cheese, jalapeños, lime wedges, sour cream, for topping (optional)

Directions

1. In a large stockpot, heat the oil over medium heat. Add the onion and garlic and sauté for 2 minutes, or until the onion softens.
2. Add the ground beef and cook until brown, 5 to 7 minutes. Stir in the taco seasoning, tomato paste, and bell pepper.
3. Add the black beans, diced tomatoes, and broth and bring to a slow boil.
4. Add the macaroni and cook for 8 to 10 minutes or until the pasta is done.
5. Stir in the cheese and top with the lime juice, cilantro, and diced jalapeño. Serve with your favorite toppings.

Nutritional Info per Serving

calories: 425, fat: 14g, protein: 29g, carbs: 47g, fiber: 5.7g, sugar: 4g, sodium: 782mg

Fried Pork Cauliflower Rice

Prep time: 8 minutes, Cook time: 20 minutes, Serves 4

Ingredients
2 tbsps. sesame oil, divided
2 large eggs, beaten
3 garlic cloves, minced
1 small red onion, minced
1 carrot, diced
1 pound (454 g) ground pork
½ tsp. salt
¼ tsp. black pepper
½ cup peas, frozen
1 medium head cauliflower, riced
¼ cup soy sauce
1 to 2 tsps. Sriracha (optional)
3 green onions, thinly sliced

Directions
1. In a large skillet, heat 1 tbsp. of sesame oil over medium heat. Add the eggs and sit for 20 to 30 seconds. Scramble, stir the eggs and cook through. Remove from the skillet and set aside.
2. Put the remaining oil in skillet. Add the garlic, onion, and carrot, and sauté until the onion softens, about 3 minutes.
3. Add the pork, salt, and pepper to the skillet, and sauté until no longer pink, about 8 minutes.
4. Stir in the peas and cauliflower rice. Sauté until the cauliflower is slightly softened, 3 to 5 minutes.
5. Mix in the soy sauce and Sriracha, if using.
6. Fold in the eggs and top with green onions.

Nutritional Info per Serving
calories: 456, fat: 32g, protein: 26g, carbs: 15g, fiber: 5g, sugar: 3g, sodium: 754mg

Delicious Lamb Kofta Kebabs

Prep time: 13 minutes, Cook time: 10 minutes, Serves 4

Ingredients
Lamb Kofta:
1 pound (454 g) ground lamb
1 small onion, chopped
3 garlic cloves, chopped
2 tbsps. fresh mint, finely chopped
1 tsp. cumin
1 tsp. salt
½ tsp. cinnamon
¼ tsp. turmeric
¼ tsp. black pepper
Mint Yogurt:
½ cup plain unsweetened Greek yogurt
¼ cup feta, crumbled
2 tbsps. mint, finely chopped
1 tbsp. lemon
Salt
Pepper

Directions
Make the Lamb Kofta:
1. Mix all of the ingredients for lamb kofta in a blender until no big chunks of onion remain.
2. Form into 4 equal balls and flatten to create long ovals. Place the lamb ovals on a dish and refrigerate, covered, for at least 15 minutes.
3. Preheat a grill to medium high.
4. Thread the lamb removed from the fridge with skewers lengthwise (about 2 per skewer). Grill for 5 to 6 minutes, then flip over and grill until the lamb is cooked through, for about 5 minutes.
Make the Mint Yogurt:
5. In a small bowl, whisk together all of the ingredients. Serve alongside the lamb.

Nutritional Info per Serving
calories: 394, fat: 30g, protein: 21g, carbs: 4.6g, fiber: 1.2g, sugar: 1.8g, sodium: 725mg

Asian Lettuce Wraps

Prep time: 9 minutes, Cook time: 15 minutes, Serves 4

Ingredients
Hoisin Sauce:
¼ cup soy sauce
2 tbsps. peanut butter
1 tbsp. maple syrup
2 tsps. apple cider vinegar
2 tsps. sesame oil
1 tsp. Sriracha
1 garlic clove, minced
Salt
Pepper
Wraps:
2 tsps. sesame oil
1 tsp. fresh ginger, minced
3 garlic cloves, minced
1 pound (454 g) pork, ground
1 large carrot, julienne
4 green onions (greens and whites), chopped
4 large lettuce leaves (romaine, butter, or iceberg)
¼ cup unsalted roasted peanuts, chopped

Directions
Make the Hoisin Sauce:
1. Whisk together all of the ingredients.
Make the Wraps:
2. In a large skillet, heat the oil over medium heat. Add the ginger and garlic and cook for 2 minutes.
3. Add the pork and cook until no longer pink, 5 to 6 minutes.
4. Add the carrot and green onion and cook for 2 to 3 minutes more, or until the vegetables have softened.
5. Do not turn off the heat and stir in the hoisin sauce, cooking until sauce thickens, 3 to 4 minutes. Remove from the heat.
6. Divide the pork into 8 lettuce wraps. Top with chopped peanuts.

Nutritional Info per Serving (2 wraps)
calories: 463, fat: 35g, protein: 23g, carbs: 11g, fiber: 1.8g, sugar: 4.6g, sodium: 654mg

Flank Steak Fajita and Sweet Potato Nachos

Prep time: 17 minutes, Cook time: 48 minutes, Serves 4

Ingredients

Steak:
2 tbsps. olive oil, divided
1 pound (454 g) flank steak
⅓ cup freshly squeezed lime juice
¼ cup no-sugar-added pineapple juice
¼ cup chopped fresh cilantro
2 tbsps. low-sodium soy sauce
1 clove garlic, minced
1 tsp. ground cumin
½ tsp. crushed red pepper flakes

Sweet Potato Chips:
1 tbsp. olive oil
2 large sweet potatoes
1 tsp. paprika
¼ tsp. garlic powder
½ tsp. sea salt
¼ tsp. ground black pepper

Fajita Bell Peppers:
1 white onion, sliced
1 red bell pepper, sliced
1 green bell pepper, sliced
1 poblano chile, sliced
¼ tsp. cayenne pepper
1 tsp. sea salt
½ tsp. ground black pepper

Nacho Toppings:
1 avocado, diced
½ cup black beans
½ cup shredded Jack cheese
½ jalapeño pepper, seeded and sliced
3 tbsps. plain full-fat Greek yogurt
2 tbsps. chopped fresh cilantro

Directions

Make the Steak:
1. Place the steak, lime juice, pineapple juice, soy sauce, 1 tbsp. of the olive oil, the garlic, cumin, crushed red pepper flakes, and cilantro in a large resealable bag or refrigerator-safe storage container. Seal the bag tightly to ensure no leakage, and then marinate the steak in the refrigerator for at least 20 minutes, or up to 8 hours.
2. Make the sweet potato chips when the steak is marinating. Preheat your oven to 400ºF (205ºC), and carefully line a rimmed baking sheet with parchment paper.
3. Use either a mandoline or a sharp knife to slice the sweet potatoes into ¼-inch slices. Add the sliced potatoes, olive oil, paprika, salt, garlic powder, and black pepper in a large bowl, and toss to coat evenly. Arrange the slices on the baking sheet, taking care not to overcrowd them as much as possible. Bake the potatoes for about 15 minutes, gently flip them, and bake for an additional 12 to 15 minutes, or until the sweet potato chips are browned and crispy around the edges and starting to curl upward. Take the potatoes from the oven, and reduce the temperature to 350ºF (180ºC).
4. In a large skillet over medium-high heat, heat the remaining 1 tbsp. of the olive oil for the steak. Place the steak, and cook for about 6 to 8 minutes per side, until golden brown on all sides, but not completely cooked through. Take the steak from the heat, slice it into strips, and keep aside.

Make the fajita Veggies:
5. In the pan you cooked the steak, quickly toss the poblano chile, onion, red and green bell peppers, salt, black pepper, and cayenne pepper for about 3 to 4 minutes, until the veggies just begin to soften, but are not entirely tender.

Make the Nachos:
6. Place the beans over the sweet potato chips on the baking sheet. Then put the fajita veggies, steak, and the cheese.
7. Cook the nachos in the oven, uncovered, for 6 to 8 minutes, or until the cheese has melted and the beans have been heated through.
8. Top the nachos with the avocado, jalapeño, cilantro, and a dollop of Greek yogurt. Enjoy!

Nutritional Info per Serving
calories: 575, fat: 28g, protein: 37g, carbs: 45g, fiber: 10g, sugar: 9g, sodium: 839mg

Thai Beef Roast and Veggies

Prep time: 14 minutes, Cook time: 10 hours, Serves 10

Ingredients

2½ pounds (1.1 kg) grass-fed beef sirloin roast, cut into 2-inch pieces
3 large tomatoes, seeded and chopped
3 large carrots, shredded
3 onions, chopped
1 cup canned coconut
milk
¾ cup peanut butter
6 garlic cloves, minced
½ cup beef stock
1 small red chili pepper, minced
2 tbsps. grated fresh ginger root
3 tbsps. lime juice

Directions

1. Mix the onions, garlic, carrots, ginger root, and tomatoes in a 6-quart slow cooker.
2. In a medium bowl, mix the coconut milk, peanut butter, chili pepper, lime juice, and beef stock until blended well.
3. Place the roast on top of the vegetables in the slow cooker and pour the peanut sauce over all.
4. Cover the slow cooker and cook on low for 8 to 10 hours, or until the beef is very soft. Serve warm.

Nutritional Info per Serving
calories: 530, fat: 35g, protein: 36g, carbs: 18g, fiber: 5g, sugar: 8g, sodium: 225mg

Pork Chops and Carrot

Prep time: 20 minutes, Cook time: 8 hours, Serves 8

Ingredients

8 (5-ounce / 142-g) pork chops
4 large carrots, peeled and cut into chunks
½ cup chicken stock
2 onions, chopped
3 garlic cloves, minced
3 tbsps. grated fresh ginger root
3 tbsps. honey
½ tsp. ground ginger
½ tsp. salt
⅛ tsp. freshly ground black pepper

Directions

1. Mix the onions, garlic, and carrots in a 6-quart slow cooker. Place the pork chops on top.
2. Mix the ginger root, honey, stock, ginger, salt, and pepper in a small bowl. Pour into the slow cooker.
3. Cover the slow cooker and cook on low for 6 to 8 hours, or until the pork is very soft. Serve warm.

Nutritional Info per Serving

calories: 241, fat: 6g, protein: 32g, carbs: 15g, fiber: 6g, sugar: 11g, sodium: 267mg

Classic Moroccan Beef in Lettuce Cups

Prep time: 21 minutes, Cook time: 9 hours, Serves 10

Ingredients

3 pounds (1.4 kg) grass-fed beef sirloin roast
1 (14-ounce / 397-g) BPA-free can no-salt-added diced tomatoes, undrained
20 butter lettuce leaves
4 radishes, thinly sliced
1 cup grated carrot
½ cup pomegranate seeds
½ cup beef stock
¼ cup tomato paste
4 garlic cloves, cut into slivers
1 tsp. ground cinnamon
1 tsp. ground cumin

Directions

1. Use a fork to poke holes in the sirloin roast and insert the slivers of garlic. Place the roast into a 6-quart slow cooker.
2. Mix the beef stock, tomatoes, tomato paste, cumin, and cinnamon until well blended in a medium bowl. Pour the mixture over the roast.
3. Cover the slow cooker and cook on low for 7 to 9 hours or until the beef is soft.
4. Remove the beef from the slow cooker and use two forks to shred. In a large serving bowl, mix the beef with about 1 cup of the liquid from the slow cooker.
5. Serve the beef mixture with the remaining ingredients.

Nutritional Info per Serving

calories: 376, fat: 21g, protein: 35g, carbs: 9g, fiber: 2g, sugar: 5g, sodium: 141mg

Pork Tenderloin

Prep time: 13 minutes, Cook time: 50 minutes, Serves 8

Ingredients

¼ cup sun-dried tomatoes
2 pounds (907 g) pork tenderloin, trimmed
Salt
Pepper
2 tbsps. olive oil, divided
4 garlic cloves, minced
2 shallots, diced
4 ounces (113 g) goat cheese
5 ounces (142 g) baby spinach

Directions

1. Preheat the oven to 400ºF (205ºC).
2. Boil water in a kettle and pour the hot water over the sun-dried tomatoes. Sit for 10 minutes or until ready to use. Drain and chop before using.
3. Prepare the pork tenderloin by trimming off any excess fat. Cut a slit down the center of tenderloin so it can unrolled. Note not cut completely through. Open it up and place it between two sheets of parchment paper or plastic wrap. Pound the pork with meat mallet until it is ½-inch thick.
4. Season each side of the pork generously with salt and pepper.
5. In a large cast iron or oven-safe skillet, heat the oil over medium heat. Add the garlic and shallots. Sauté for 3 to 5 minutes.
6. Add the goat cheese, spinach, and sun-dried tomatoes and sauté until the spinach is wilted. Remove from the heat and add salt and pepper.
7. Spread filling over the middle of the pork tenderloin, then roll it up and wrap with kitchen twine in 3 or 4 places.
8. Heat the remaining tbsp. of oil over medium heat with the same skillet. When hot, add the pork and brown on all sides.
9. Transfer the skillet to the oven and cook for 40 minutes.

Nutritional Info per Serving

calories: 223, fat: 9g, protein: 27g, carbs: 4g, fiber: 1.3g, sugar: 0.8g, sodium: 227mg

Feta Lamb Burgers

Prep time: 15 minutes, Cook time: 10 minutes, Serves 4

Ingredients

⅓ cup sun-dried tomatoes
Cooking oil spray
1 pound (454 g) ground lamb
⅓ cup feta cheese, crumbled
1 tbsp. tomato paste
½ tsp. cumin
½ tsp. salt
¼ tsp. pepper

Directions

1. In a medium bowl, cover sun-dried tomatoes with boiling water and soak until softened, for 10 to 15 minutes. Drain and dice.
2. Preheat the grill to medium. Lightly coat the grill with spray.
3. Combine all of the ingredients and form 4 evenly shaped patties.
4. Grill about 5 minutes per side, until the internal temperature reads 145ºF (63ºC).

Nutritional Info per Serving
calories: 368, fat: 28g, protein: 20g, carbs: 5g, fiber: 1.3g, sugar: 2.1g, sodium: 617mg

Apples-Onions Pork Chops

Prep time: 4 minutes, Cook time: 30 minutes, Serves 4

Ingredients

1 tbsp. olive oil
4 pork chops, boneless
1 tsp. salt
1 tsp. cinnamon
¼ tsp. black pepper
3 apples, cored and sliced
1 sweet onion, sliced
½ cup broth
½ cup apple cider
1 tbsp. Dijon mustard
Salt
Pepper

Directions

1. Preheat the oven to 400ºF (205ºC).
2. In a large skillet, heat the oil over medium-high heat.
3. Season the pork chops with the salt, cinnamon, and pepper, then add them to the skillet. Cook for 4 to 5 minutes per side. Transfer the pork chops to a platter.
4. Add the apples, the onion and extra oil, if needed to the skillet. Sauté until softened, 3 to 4 minutes.
5. Pour in the broth and apple cider. Stir in the mustard and simmer for 5 minutes until the liquid is reduced by half.
6. Return the pork chops and any juices that have collected on the plate to the skillet. Place the skillet in the oven. Cook for 15 minutes until the pork is cooked through. Season with salt and pepper as desired.

Nutritional Info per Serving
calories: 263, fat: 8g, protein: 21g, carbs: 20g, fiber: 2g, sugar: 17g, sodium: 751mg

Greek Lamb Bowls with Turmeric Cauliflower Rice and Cucumber Salsa

Prep time: 12 minutes, Cook time: 13 minutes, Serves 4

Ingredients

Cucumber Salsa:
1 small red onion, chopped
1 cucumber, chopped
1 red bell pepper, chopped
Juice of 1 lemon
1 tsp. apple cider vinegar
Salt
Pepper
Turmeric Cauliflower Rice:
1 tbsp. olive oil
1 head cauliflower, stem removed and riced
½ tsp. turmeric
Salt
Pepper
Lamb Bowls:
1 tsp. salt
1 tsp. oregano
½ tsp. black pepper
½ tsp. garlic powder
¼ tsp. turmeric
1 pound (454 g) ground lamb
1 tbsp. tomato paste
½ cup hummus of choice
½ cup feta cheese, crumbled
Tzatziki

Directions

Make the Cucumber Salsa:
1. In a large bowl, mix all of the ingredients together and cover.

Make the Turmeric Cauliflower Rice:
2. In a large skillet, heat the olive oil over medium heat. Add the cauliflower and cook for 5 minutes, or until the cauliflower is cooked down and tender.
3. Season with the turmeric, salt, and pepper..

Make the Lamb Bowls:
4. In a small bowl, mix together the salt, oregano, pepper, garlic powder, and turmeric.
5. In a larger skillet over medium heat, combine the lamb and the spice mixture and cook, stirring occasionally, until the lamb no longer pink.
6. Mix the tomato paste into the lamb.
7. Divide the cauliflower rice, lamb mixture, hummus, cucumber salsa, and feta evenly among four bowls. Top each bowl with 2 tbsps. of tzatziki.

Nutritional Info per Serving
calories: 605, fat: 42g, protein: 31g, carbs: 27g, fiber: 7.7g, sugar: 5g, sodium: 712mg

Homemade Beef Tacos in Lettuce, page 76

Apple, Brie and Onion Burger, page 68

Garlic-Herb Steak, page 74

Baked Hawaiian Pork Kebabs, page 67

Garlic-Herb Steak

Prep time: 3 minutes, Cook time: 7 minutes, Serves 4

Ingredients

2 (8-ounce / 227-g) New York strip or rib-eye steaks, trimmed of excess fat	½ tsp. pepper
	1 tsp. thyme
	1 tsp. rosemary
1 tsp. salt	1 tbsp. butter or ghee
	4 garlic cloves, minced

Directions

1. Season both sides of steak with salt, pepper, thyme, and rosemary.
2. In a large skillet, heat the butter over medium-high heat. Add the garlic and sauté for 1 minute.
3. Add the seasoned steaks and sear 3 minutes per side. Reduce to medium heat and cook, flipping frequently until internal temperature reaches 135ºF (57ºC).
4. Remove from the heat and rest for 5 minutes before serving and slicing.

Nutritional Info per Serving

calories: 251, fat: 9g, protein: 33g, carbs: 2.1g, fiber: 0.1g, sugar: 0.3g, sodium: 635mg

Beef and Mushroom Lo Mein

Prep time: 20 minutes, Cook time: 10½ hours, Serves 10

Ingredients

2 pounds (907 g) grass-fed beef chuck roast, cut into 2-inch pieces	2 onions, chopped
	1 jalapeño pepper, minced
1 (8-ounce / 227-g) package whole-wheat spaghetti pasta, broken in half	4 garlic cloves, minced
	2 tbsps. honey
	2 tbsps. low-sodium soy sauce
2 cups shiitake mushrooms, sliced	1 tbsp. grated fresh ginger root
3 cups beef stock	

Directions

1. Mix the onions, mushrooms, garlic, ginger root, and jalapeño pepper in a 6-quart slow cooker. Place the beef cubes and gently stir.
2. In a medium bowl, mix the soy sauce, beef stock, and honey until well combined. Pour the mixture into the slow cooker.
3. Cover the slow cooker and cook on low for 8 to 10 hours, or until the beef is very tender.
4. Turn the slow cooker to high heat. Place the pasta and stir slowly, making sure all of the spaghetti is covered with liquid.

---

5. Cook on high for about 20 to 30 minutes, or until the pasta is soft. Serve hot.

Nutritional Info per Serving

calories: 355, fat: 14g, protein: 28g, carbs: 33g, fiber: 4g, sugar: 8g, sodium: 294mg

French Dip Sandwiches

Prep time: 13 minutes, Cook time: 2 hours 10 minutes, Serves 8 to 10

Ingredients

3 pounds (1.4 kg) beef rump roast, fat trimmed	sliced
	1 cup dry red wine
1 tsp. salt	2 cups beef broth
½ tsp. pepper	8 rolls
2 tbsps. olive oil	8 slices Swiss cheese
2 medium yellow onions,	

Directions

1. Cut the beef into large chunks, season with salt and pepper.
2. Turn a pressure cooker to sauté and pour in the oil. When the oil is hot, place the meat in the pressure cooker and sear on all sides until golden brown on the outside, 3 to 4 minutes.
3. Transfer the pork from the pressure cooker to a clean platter.
4. Put the onions in the pressure cooker and sauté until they start to turn translucent, for 3 to 5 minutes. Add the wine and stir, scraping up any brown bits on the sides or the bottom of the pressure cooker. Simmer for 1 to 2 minutes.
5. Pour the beef broth and return the beef and any juice on the platter back into the slow cooker.
6. Turn off the sauté function, close the top, and seal it (making sure the vent is closed) and turn on high for 90 minutes.
7. Wait for 90 minutes and allow the pressure cooker to naturally release pressure for 20 to 25 minutes.
8. Open the vent and finish depressurizing manually.
9. Transfer the beef to a cutting board. Shred the beef with two forks.
10. Reserve the onions and liquid for dipping.
11. Evenly distribute the beef among the 8 rolls, top with the cheese, and place the sandwiches on a baking sheet. Put the sandwiches under the broiler for 2 to 3 minutes until the cheese is melted.
12. Serve the sandwiches with the reserved broth for dipping.

Nutritional Info per Serving

calories: 567, fat: 26g, protein: 38g, carbs: 32g, fiber: 0.9g, sugar: 3.8g, sodium: 618mg

Lemony Pork Chops

Prep time: 18 minutes, Cook time: 8 hours, Serves 4

Ingredients

8 (5-ounce / 142-g) bone-in pork loin chops
2 leeks, chopped
2 red bell peppers, stemmed, seeded, and chopped
1 cup chicken stock
⅓ cup lemon juice
8 garlic cloves, sliced
1 tsp. dried thyme leaves
½ tsp. salt

Directions

1. Mix the leeks, garlic, and red bell peppers in a 6-quart slow cooker. Top with the pork chops.
2. In a small bowl, mix the chicken stock, thyme, lemon juice, and salt. Pour the mixture over the pork.
3. Cover the slow cooker and cook on low for 7 to 8 hours, or until the chops register at least 145ºF (63ºC) on a food thermometer. Serve warm.

Nutritional Info per Serving

calories: 269, fat: 13g, protein: 30g, carbs: 6g, fiber: 1g, sugar: 2g, sodium: 249mg

Pork Loin with Apricots

Prep time: 17 minutes, Cook time: 9 hours, Serves 8 to 10

Ingredients

1 (3-pound / 1.4-kg) boneless pork loin
1 cup dried apricots
1 cup dried pears, sliced
1 cup apricot nectar
2 leeks, sliced
½ cup golden raisins
½ tsp. salt
1 tsp. dried thyme leaves

Directions

1. Add the leeks, apricots, pears, and raisins in a 6-quart slow cooker. Place the pork on top. Scatter the pork with the salt and thyme.
2. Pour the apricot nectar around the pork, over the fruit.
3. Cover the slow cooker and cook on low for 7 to 9 hours, or until the pork registers at least 150ºF (66ºC) on a food thermometer. Serve warm.

Nutritional Info per Serving

calories: 370, fat: 7g, protein: 40g, carbs: 38g, fiber: 4g, sugar: 10g, sodium: 239mg

Thai Pork and Mushroom with Peanut Sauce

Prep time: 22 minutes, Cook time: 9 hours, Serves 8

Ingredients

1 (3-pound / 1.4-kg) boneless pork loin roast
2 cups chopped portabello mushrooms
1 cup chopped unsalted peanuts
1 cup peanut butter
1 cup chicken stock
2 onions, chopped
4 garlic cloves, minced
1 small dried red chili pepper, sliced
2 tbsps. apple cider vinegar
¼ tsp. cayenne pepper

Directions

1. Mix the onions, mushrooms, garlic, chili pepper, and cayenne pepper in a 6-quart slow cooker.
2. In a medium bowl, mix the chicken stock, peanut butter, and vinegar and mix until well blended.
3. Put the pork roast on top of the vegetables in the slow cooker. Pour the peanut butter sauce over all.
4. Cover the slow cooker and cook on low for 7 to 9 hours, or until the pork is very tender.
5. Scatter with peanuts and serve warm.

Nutritional Info per Serving

calories: 664, fat: 44g, protein: 54g, carbs: 19g, fiber: 4g, sugar: 6g, sodium: 232mg

Curried Pork Chop with Bell Peppers

Prep time: 11 minutes, Cook time: 8 hours, Serves 4 to 6

Ingredients

8 (5½-ounce / 156-g) bone-in pork loin chops
2 red bell peppers, stemmed, seeded, and chopped
2 yellow bell peppers, stemmed, seeded, and chopped
2 onions, chopped
1 cup chicken stock
4 garlic cloves, minced
1 tbsp. curry powder
1 tbsp. grated fresh ginger root
½ tsp. salt

Directions

1. Mix the onions, garlic, and bell peppers in a slow cooker. Put the pork chops to the slow cooker, nestling them into the vegetables.
2. Mix the salt, curry powder, ginger root, and chicken stock in a small bowl, and pour the mixture into the slow cooker.
3. Cover the slow cooker and cook on low for 7 to 8 hours, or until the pork chops are soft. Serve warm.

Nutritional Info per Serving

calories: 306, fat: 14g, protein: 34g, carbs: 10g, fiber: 2g, sugar: 3g, sodium: 268mg

Homemade Beef Tacos in Lettuce

Prep time: 6 minutes, Cook time: 17 minutes, Serves 4

Ingredients

1 tbsp. olive oil
1 pound (454 g) lean ground beef
1 tbsp. tomato paste
1 tbsp. taco seasoning
¼ tsp. black pepper
1 yellow onion, chopped
3 small bell peppers, chopped
Lettuce, for serving

Directions

1. In a large skillet, heat the oil over medium heat, add the ground beef. Cook until light brown, 5 to 7 minutes.
2. Add the tomato paste, taco seasoning, and pepper. Reduce to low heat and add the onion and bell peppers. Cook for 5 to 10 minutes until well combined.
3. Serve over lettuce wraps with toppings of your choice.

Nutritional Info per Serving

calories: 227, fat: 11g, protein: 23g, carbs: 6.6g, fiber: 2.1g, sugar: 2.8g, sodium: 268mg

Roast Pork with Red Cabbage

Prep time: 20 minutes, Cook time: 9 hours, Serves 6 to 8

Ingredients

1 (3-pound / 1.4-kg) pork loin roast
1 large head red cabbage, chopped
2 medium pears, peeled and chopped
2 red onions, chopped
1 cup chicken stock
¼ cup apple cider vinegar
4 garlic cloves, minced
3 tbsps. honey
1 tsp. dried thyme leaves
½ tsp. salt

Directions

1. Mix the cabbage, onions, pears, and garlic in a 6-quart slow cooker.
2. In a small bowl, mix the vinegar, honey, chicken stock, thyme, and salt, and pour the mixture into the slow cooker.
3. Place the pork on top, nestling the meat into the vegetables.
4. Cover the slow cooker and cook on low for 7 to 9 hours, or until the pork is soft. Enjoy!

Nutritional Info per Serving

calories: 365, fat: 14g, protein: 38g, carbs: 21g, fiber: 3g, sugar: 14g, sodium: 263mg

Moroccan Beef Tagine

Prep time: 15 minutes, Cook time: 10 hours, Serves 8 to 10

Ingredients

1 (3-pound / 1.4-kg) grass-fed beef sirloin roast, cut into 2-inch pieces
3 carrots, cut into chunks
1 cup chopped dates
2 jalapeño peppers, minced
2 onions, chopped
1 cup beef stock
6 garlic cloves, minced
2 tbsps. honey
2 tsps. ground cumin
1 tsp. ground turmeric

Directions

1. Mix the onions, garlic, jalapeño peppers, carrots, and dates in a 6-quart slow cooker. Place the beef on top.
2. In a small bowl, mix the beef stock, honey, cumin, and turmeric until combined well. Pour the mixture into the slow cooker.
3. Cover the slow cooker and cook on low for 8 to 10 hours, or until the beef is soft. Enjoy!

Nutritional Info per Serving

calories: 452, fat: 21g, protein: 35g, carbs: 29g, fiber: 4g, sugar: 22g, sodium: 154mg

Savory Pot Roast and Potato

Prep time: 13 minutes, Cook time: 10 hours, Serves 10

Ingredients

1 (3-pound / 1.4-kg) grass-fed chuck shoulder roast or tri-tip roast
8 Yukon Gold potatoes, cut into chunks
4 large carrots, peeled and cut into chunks
2 onions, chopped
1 leek, sliced
1 cup beef stock
8 garlic cloves, sliced
1 tsp. dried marjoram
½ tsp. salt
¼ tsp. freshly ground black pepper

Directions

1. Mix the potatoes, carrots, onions, leek, and garlic in a 6-quart slow cooker.
2. Put the beef on top of the vegetables and scatter with the marjoram, salt, and pepper.
3. Add the beef stock into the slow cooker.
4. Cover the slow cooker and cook on low for 8 to 10 hours, or until the beef is very soft. Serve the beef with the vegetables.

Nutritional Info per Serving

calories: 567, fat: 31g, protein: 37g, carbs: 36g, fiber: 4g, sugar: 5g, sodium: 301mg

Garlic-Parmesan Pork and Potato

Prep time: 23 minutes, Cook time: 9 hours, Serves 12

Ingredients

1 (3-pound / 1.4-kg) boneless pork loin
2 pounds (907 g) small creamer potatoes, rinsed
4 large carrots, cut into chunks
1 cup chicken stock

½ cup grated Parmesan cheese
1 onion, chopped
12 garlic cloves, divided
1 tsp. dried marjoram leaves

Directions

1. Mix the potatoes, carrots, and onions in a 6-quart slow cooker. Mince 6 of the garlic cloves and place them to the vegetables.
2. Slice the remaining 6 garlic cloves into slivers. Use a sharp knife to poke holes in the pork loin and put a garlic sliver into each hole.
3. Arrange the pork loin on the vegetables in the slow cooker.
4. Add the chicken stock over all and scatter with the marjoram.
5. Cover the slow cooker and cook on low for 7 to 9 hours, or until the pork is tender.
6. Sprinkle with the Parmesan cheese and serve warm.

Nutritional Info per Serving

calories: 393, fat: 11g, protein: 45g, carbs: 27g, fiber: 3g, sugar: 5g, sodium: 404mg

Beef and Bean Burrito Casserole with Cheese

Prep time: 12 minutes, Cook time: 7 hours, Serves 8

Ingredients

1½ pounds (680 g) grass-fed lean ground beef
1 (16-ounce / 454-g) BPA-free can no-salt-added vegetarian refried beans
1 (15-ounce / 425-g) BPA-free can no-salt-added black beans, drained and rinsed
8 corn tortillas

2 cups shredded white Cheddar cheese
2 jalapeño peppers, minced
2 onions, chopped
4 garlic cloves, minced
1 tbsp. chili powder
1 tsp. dried oregano

Directions

1. In a large saucepan over medium-high heat, cook the beef, onions, and garlic for 8 to 10 minutes, stirring to break up the meat. Drain well.
2. Place the refried beans, black beans, jalapeño peppers, chili powder, and oregano to the beef mixture.
3. Layer the beef mixture with the tortillas and shredded cheese in a 6-quart slow cooker.
4. Cover the slow cooker and cook on low for 5 to 7 hours, or until the tortillas have softened. Serve warm.

Nutritional Info per Serving

calories: 553, fat: 28g, protein: 39g, carbs: 34g, fiber: 8g, sugar: 4g, sodium: 517mg

Beef Chili Bean

Prep time: 16 minutes, Cook time: 10 hours, Serves 7

Ingredients

2½ pounds (1.1 kg) sirloin tip, cut into 2-inch cubes

2 cups dried beans, rinsed and drained

4 large tomatoes, seeded and chopped

1 (6-ounce / 170-g) BPA-free can tomato paste

2 jalapeño peppers, minced

2 onions, chopped

6 garlic cloves, minced

11 cups vegetable broth

2 tbsps. chili powder

1 tsp. ground cumin

Directions

1. Mix all of the ingredients in a 6-quart slow cooker. Cover the slow cooker and cook on low for 8 to 10 hours, or until the beans are soft. Serve warm.

Nutritional Info per Serving

calories: 459, fat: 10g, protein: 45g, carbs: 47g, fiber: 14g, sugar: 10g, sodium: 290mg

Chapter 7: Fish and Seafood

White Fish and Spinach Risotto

Prep time: 7 minutes, Cook time: 5 hours, Serves 4

Ingredients

2 cups short-grain brown rice

8 ounces (227 g) cremini mushrooms, sliced

6 (5-ounce / 142-g) tilapia fillets

2 cups baby spinach leaves

½ cup grated Parmesan cheese

6 cups vegetable broth or fish stock

2 onions, chopped

5 garlic cloves, minced

2 tbsps. unsalted butter

1 tsp. dried thyme leaves

Directions

1. Mix the mushrooms, onions, garlic, rice, thyme, and vegetable broth in a 6-quart slow cooker. Cover the slow cooker and cook on low for 3 to 4 hours, or until the rice is soft.
2. Place the fish on top of the rice. Cover and cook for 25 to 35 minutes more, or until the fish flakes when tested with a fork.
3. Gently place the fish into the risotto. Then put the baby spinach leaves.
4. Stir in the butter and cheese. Cover and allow to cook on low for 10 minutes, then serve warm.

Nutritional Info per Serving
calories: 469, fat: 12g, protein: 34g, carbs: 61g, fiber: 5g, sugar: 2g, sodium: 346mg

Salmon Vegetables Chowder

Prep time: 15 minutes, Cook time: 8½ hours, Serves 8 to 10

Ingredients

2 pounds (907 g) skinless salmon fillets

6 medium Yukon Gold potatoes, cut into 2-inch pieces

4 large carrots, sliced

2 cups sliced cremini mushrooms

1½ cups shredded Swiss cheese

1 cup whole milk

8 cups vegetable broth or fish stock

4 shallots, minced

3 garlic cloves, minced

2 tsps. dried dill weed

Directions

1. Mix the potatoes, carrots, mushrooms, shallots, garlic, vegetable broth, and dill weed in a 6-quart slow cooker. Cover the slow cooker and cook on low for 6 to 8 hours, or until the vegetables are soft.
2. Place the salmon fillets to the slow cooker. Cover and cook on low for an additional 20 to 30 minutes, or until the salmon flakes when tested with a fork.
3. Gently stir the chowder to break up the salmon.
4. Pour in the milk and Swiss cheese and cover. Let the chowder sit for 10 minutes to let the cheese melt. Stir in the chowder and serve warm.

Nutritional Info per Serving
calories: 453, fat: 20g, protein: 34g, carbs: 31g, fiber: 3g, sugar: 6g, sodium: 252mg

Salmon, Mushroom and Barley Bake

Prep time: 9 minutes, Cook time: 8½ hours, Serves 4 to 6

Ingredients

6 (5-ounce / 142-g) salmon fillets

2 cups hulled barley, rinsed

1 (8-ounce / 227-g) package cremini mushrooms, sliced

2 fennel bulbs, cored and chopped

2 red bell peppers, stemmed, seeded, and chopped

⅓ cup grated Parmesan cheese

5 cups vegetable broth

4 garlic cloves, minced

1 tsp. dried tarragon leaves

⅛ tsp. freshly ground black pepper

Directions

1. Mix the barley, fennel, bell peppers, garlic, mushrooms, vegetable broth, tarragon, and pepper in a 6-quart slow cooker. Cover the slow cooker and cook on low for 7 to 8 hours, or until the barley has absorbed most of the liquid and is soft, and the vegetables are soft too.
2. Arrange the salmon fillets on top of the barley mixture. Cover and cook on low for 20 to 40 minutes more, or until the salmon flakes when tested with a fork.
3. Stir in the Parmesan cheese, breaking up the salmon, and serve warm.

Nutritional Info per Serving
calories: 609, fat: 20g, protein: 49g, carbs: 55g, fiber: 13g, sugar: 4g, sodium: 441mg

Sweet Potato and Salmon Cakes

Prep time: 7 minutes, Cook time: 10 minutes, Serves 4

Ingredients

2 (5-ounce / 142-g) cans salmon packed in water, drained
1 small sweet potato, peeled, cooked, and mashed
1 large egg
2 garlic cloves, minced
2 green onions (greens and whites), minced
2 tbsps. flax meal, plus more to thicken as needed
1 tbsp. Dijon mustard
½ tsp. paprika
½ tsp. salt
¼ tsp. pepper
Juice of 1 lemon
2 tbsps. avocado oil

Directions

1. Mix together all of the ingredients except the avocado oil in a medium bowl. Add more flax meal as needed to bind the mixture.
2. Heat the oil over medium heat in a large skillet until glistening.
3. Divide the salmon mixture into 8 equal portions and form them into patties. Working in batches, place the patties in the skillet for 3 to 4 minutes per side or until golden brown on outside.

Nutritional Info per Serving

calories: 226, fat: 12g, protein: 13g, carbs: 10g, fiber: 2g, sugar: 2.2g, sodium: 457mg

Linguine with Clams

Prep time: 7 minutes, Cook time: 19 minutes, Serves 4

Ingredients

12 ounces (340 g) linguine or spaghetti
½ cup dry white wine (or reserved pasta water)
2 tbsps. ghee or butter
2 shallots, minced
4 garlic cloves, minced
2 (6½-ounce / 184-g) cans chopped clams,
drained and juice reserved
1 tbsp. cornstarch (optional)
¼ cup parsley, chopped
¼ cup Parmesan, grated
Salt
Pepper

Directions

1. Add salt to water and bring to boil over high heat. Add the pasta and cook according to the package instructions. If you are using pasta water instead of wine, reserve ½ cup, then drain the pasta.
2. Using the same large pot (pasta removed), heat the ghee over medium heat until melted.
3. Add the shallots and cook for 2 minutes, then add the garlic and cook for 1 minute more.
4. Pour in the wine and stir, scraping up any brown bits from the sides and the bottom of the pot.
5. Whisk in the reserved clam juice and cornstarch, simmering for 5 minutes. Add the linguine, clams, and parsley to the pot. Simmer for an additional 5 minutes.
6. Remove from the heat and add the grated Parmesan. Season with salt and pepper to taste.

Nutritional Info per Serving

calories: 452, fat: 10g, protein: 23g, carbs: 65g, fiber: 3.1g, sugar: 1.7g, sodium: 167mg

Watermelon Salsa with Honey-Lime Salmon

Prep time: 8 minutes, Cook time: 15 minutes, Serves 4

Ingredients

Salmon:
4 (6-ounce / 170-g) salmon fillets, skin on
1 tbsp. olive oil
2 tsps. honey
½ tsp. salt
¼ tsp. pepper
1 lime, cut into 4 slices
Watermelon Salsa:
2 cups seedless watermelon, diced
¼ cup red onion, diced
1 jalapeño, seeded and diced
2 tbsps. cilantro, chopped
½ tsp. salt
¼ tsp. pepper
Juice of 1 lime

Directions

Make the Salmon:
1. Preheat the oven to 400ºF (205ºC) and line with four large torn-off foil sheets.
2. Place each salmon fillet, skin-side down, onto a piece of foil.
3. Whisk together the oil, honey, salt, and pepper. Drizzle the honey mixture over the salmon with a spoon and spread it on each fillet evenly with the back of a spoon. Place a slice of lime on each fillet and close foil around salmon making a packet.
4. Bake the salmon packets on middle rack of the oven for 12 to 15 minutes or until fish easily flakes when tested with a fork. Open the packets carefully to avoid a steam burn.
Make the Watermelon Salsa:
5. Combine all of the ingredients for the watermelon salsa in a medium bowl. Mix well.
6. When the salmon is done, open the packets carefully and scoop ¼ of salsa onto each fillet.

Nutritional Info per Serving

calories: 501, fat: 21g, protein: 61g, carbs: 11g, fiber: 1.4g, sugar: 7g, sodium: 687mg

Shrimp and Grits with Tomato

Prep time: 16 minutes, Cook time: 7½ hours, Serves 9

Ingredients
2 pounds (907 g) raw shrimp, peeled and deveined
2½ cups stone-ground grits
4 large tomatoes, seeded and chopped
2 green bell peppers, stemmed, seeded, and chopped
1½ cups shredded Cheddar cheese
8 cups chicken stock or vegetable broth
2 onions, chopped
5 garlic cloves, minced
1 bay leaf
1 tsp. Old Bay Seasoning

Directions
1. Mix the grits, onions, garlic, tomatoes, bell peppers, chicken stock, bay leaf, and seasoning in a 6-quart slow cooker. Cover the slow cooker and cook on low for 5 to 7 hours, or until the grits are soft and most of the liquid is absorbed.
2. Place the shrimp and stir. Cover and cook on low for 30 to 40 minutes more, or until the shrimp are curled and pink.
3. Stir in the cheese and serve warm.

Nutritional Info per Serving
calories: 415, fat: 10g, protein: 33g, carbs: 51g, fiber: 5g, sugar: 5g, sodium: 415mg

Salmon and Veggies Ratatouille

Prep time: 20 minutes, Cook time: 7½ hours, Serves 8

Ingredients
2 tbsps. olive oil
2 pounds (907 g) salmon fillets
5 large tomatoes, seeded and chopped
2 eggplants, peeled and chopped
2 cups sliced button mushrooms
2 red bell peppers, stemmed, seeded, and chopped
2 onions, chopped
5 garlic cloves, minced
1 tsp. dried herbes de Provence

Directions
1. Mix the eggplants, tomatoes, mushrooms, onions, bell peppers, garlic, olive oil, and herbes de Provence in a 6-quart slow cooker. Cover the slow cooker and cook on low for 6 to 7 hours, or until the vegetables are soft.
2. Place the salmon to the slow cooker. Cover and cook on low for another 30 to 40 minutes, or until the salmon flakes when tested with a fork.
3. Gently toss the salmon into the vegetables and serve

warm.

Nutritional Info per Serving
calories: 342, fat: 16g, protein: 32g, carbs: 18g, fiber: 7g, sugar: 10g, sodium: 218mg

Coated Fish Sticks with Tartar Sauce

Prep time: 6 minutes, Cook time: 12 to 14 minutes, Serves 6

Ingredients
Fish Sticks:
2 pounds (907 g) skinless cod fillet
¼ tsp. sea salt
¼ tsp. ground black pepper
Coating:
2 eggs
1 cup almond flour
⅔ cup chickpea flour (aka garbanzo bean flour)
½ tsp. garlic powder
½ tsp. sea salt
Tartar Sauce:
¼ cup plain full-fat Greek yogurt
1 tbsp. Dijon mustard
1 tbsp. finely diced dill pickles
1 tsp. freshly squeezed lemon juice
½ tsp. chopped fresh dill
⅛ tsp. garlic powder
⅛ tsp. sea salt

Directions
1. For the fish sticks, preheat the oven to 400ºF (205ºC), and carefully line a rimmed baking sheet with parchment paper.
2. Slice the cod into four 2 × 3-inch long slices to make the sticks. Sprinkle the fish with the salt and pepper.
3. For the coating, you'll need three shallow bowls. In the first bowl, combine the salt and chickpea flour. Beat the eggs in the second bowl. Mix the almond flour and garlic powder in the third bowl. Dredge each cod piece in the chickpea flour mixture to coat fully. Dip it into the egg, then the almond flour mixture. It is useful to use one hand for the wet dipping and the other hand for the dry dipping, so your fingers don't get coated.
4. Arrange the cod about 2 inches apart on the prepared baking sheet, and bake for about 12 to 14 minutes, or until the cod is cooked through and flaky. Gently flip the sticks halfway through the baking time.
5. Prepare the tartar sauce when the fish is baking. In a medium mixing bowl, stir together the yogurt, mustard, pickles, lemon juice, dill, salt, and garlic powder. Serve immediately.

Nutritional Info per Serving
calories: 371, fat: 6g, protein: 44g, carbs: 32g, fiber: 3g, sugar: 3g, sodium: 823mg

Carrot Mélange with Poached Trout

Prep time: 15 minutes, Cook time: 9½ hours, Serves 8

Ingredients
6 (5-ounce / 142-g) trout fillets
4 large orange carrots, peeled and sliced
3 purple carrots, peeled and sliced
3 yellow carrots, peeled and sliced
½ cup vegetable broth or fish stock
2 onions, chopped
4 garlic cloves, minced
1 bay leaf
1 tsp. dried marjoram leaves
½ tsp. salt

Directions
1. Mix the carrots, onions, garlic, vegetable broth, marjoram, bay leaf, and salt in a 6-quart slow cooker. Cover the slow cooker and cook on low for 7 to 9 hours, or until the carrots are soft.
2. Remove the bay leaf and discard.
3. Place the trout fillets to the slow cooker. Cover and cook on low for another 20 to 30 minutes, or until the fish flakes when tested with a fork. Enjoy!

Nutritional Info per Serving
calories: 263, fat: 9g, protein: 28g, carbs: 19g, fiber: 5g, sugar: 9g, sodium: 357mg

Spring Shrimp Rolls

Prep time: 12 minutes, Cook time: 0 minutes, Serves 8

Ingredients
Peanut Sauce:
¾ cup peanut butter
⅓ cup soy sauce
⅓ cup water (plus more to thin)
3 tbsps. maple syrup
1 tsp. sesame oil
1 tbsp. Sriracha
Juice of 2 limes
Pinch red pepper flakes
Pinch sesame seeds
Spring Rolls:
1 pound (454 g)
cooked shrimp, halved lengthwise
8 butter lettuce leaves, shredded
2 large carrots, julienned
2 avocados, diced
1 cucumber, thinly sliced
1 red bell pepper, thinly sliced
Fresh basil leaves
Warm water
16 rice paper wraps

Directions
Make the Peanut Sauce:
1. Whisk together all of the ingredients in a small bowl for the sauce.
Make the Spring Rolls:
2. Fill a large shallow bowl with warm water. Dip the

rice paper wraps into bowl one at a time. Let it sit for 5 to 10 seconds and make sure the entire paper is moistened.
3. Remove and place on a clean, flat surface (a cutting board or a plate). Fill each wrap with the ingredients you desire.
4. Start with end closest to you and fold the sides of the wrap toward the middle, until the filling is rolled up inside the spring roll. Repeat for each wrap.
5. Serve with the peanut sauce for dipping.

Nutritional Info per Serving
calories: 375, fat: 19g, protein: 20g, carbs: 17g, fiber: 7g, sugar: 8g, sodium: 558mg

Easy Baked Fish and Chips

Prep time: 12 minutes, Cook time: 25 minutes, Serves 4

Ingredients
Chips:
2 large sweet potatoes, cut into wedges
1 tbsp. olive oil
Salt
Pepper
Fish:
½ cup flour
¼ tsp. salt
¼ tsp. pepper
1 large egg
¼ cup milk
1 cup old-fashioned oats
½ tbsp. garlic powder
¼ tbsp. paprika
1 tsp. cayenne
1 pound (454 g) cod or haddock, cut into 8 to 10 thin fillets
Malt vinegar

Directions
Make the Chips:
1. Preheat the oven to 450ºF (235ºC). Line a baking sheet with aluminum foil.
2. Combine the sweet potatoes, olive oil, salt, and pepper in a large bowl. Place the potatoes on the baking sheet in a single layer. Bake for 20 minutes. Remove from the oven.
Make the Fish:
3. Line a second baking sheet with aluminum foil.
4. Take out three large bowls. In the first bowl, mix together the flour, salt, and pepper. In the second bowl, combine the egg and milk. In the third bowl, whisk the oats, garlic powder, paprika, and cayenne.
5. Dredge each fillet in the flour mixture, dip into the egg mixture, and coat with the oat mixture. Place each fillet on the baking sheet.
6. Bake for 4 to 5 minutes on each side, or until the internal temperature is 145ºF (63ºC).
7. Serve the fish and chips with malt vinegar.

Nutritional Info per Serving
calories: 392, fat: 7g, protein: 33g, carbs: 42g, fiber: 7g, sugar: 3.6g, sodium: 276mg

Baked Fish Sticks

Prep time: 6 minutes, Cook time: 16 minutes, Serves 4

Ingredients

1 pound (454 g) cod, flounder, or other white fish, cut into ½-inch sticks
½ tsp. salt
¼ tsp. pepper
½ cup tapioca flour
2 eggs, beaten
1 cup almond flour
¼ cup Parmesan cheese, grated
1 tsp. paprika
1 tsp. garlic powder
½ tsp. salt
¼ tsp. black pepper

Directions

1. Preheat the oven to 425ºF (220ºC). Line a baking sheet with parchment paper.
2. Pat the fish dry with kitchen paper towels. Season with salt and pepper.
3. Put the tapioca flour on a plate and the cracked eggs into a small bowl.
4. Combine the almond flour, Parmesan, paprika, garlic powder, salt, and pepper in a large bowl.
5. Dip the fish sticks first in tapioca flour, shaking any excess back onto the plate. Dip the floured fish stick in egg, roll it in the almond flour mixture and place on the baking sheet. Repeat this process for each fish stick.
6. Bake for 8 minutes. Turn the fish sticks over and bake for 8 minutes more, or until the fish is tested an internal temperature of 145ºF (63ºC).

Nutritional Info per Serving
calories: 407, fat: 17g, protein: 35g, carbs: 18g, fiber: 2.8g, sugar: 0.8g, sodium: 542mg

Maple Cedar Plank Salmon

Prep time: 13 minutes, Cook time: 25 minutes, Serves 4

Ingredients

1 to 2 cedar planks
¼ cup maple syrup
2 tbsps. lemon juice
1 tbsp. Dijon mustard
1 tbsp. soy sauce
½ tsp. garlic powder
1 tsp. paprika
4 (6-ounce / 170-g) salmon fillets, cleaned and deboned
¼ tsp. salt
¼ tsp. pepper
Lemon juice, freshly squeezed

Directions

1. Soak the cedar planks for at least 1 hour prior to grilling. Place the planks in a baking dish and cover with water. They will float, so weigh them down with something like a teapot or a heavy bowl to keep submerged.
2. Heat a large saucepan over medium heat. Whisk together the maple syrup, lemon juice, mustard, soy sauce, garlic powder, and paprika and bring to a boil. When the sauce thickens, after 3 to 5 minutes. Remove the sauce from the heat.
3. Heat the grill to medium-high when the cedar plank has fully soaked.
4. Rub the salmon fillets with salt and pepper and place them skin-side down on the cedar plank.
5. Brush the salmon fillets with the maple glaze.
6. Place the cedar plank with the salmon on the grill. Cook for 15 to 20 minutes or until internal temperature reaches 145ºF (63ºC).

Nutritional Info per Serving
calories: 476, fat: 17g, protein: 58g, carbs: 14g, fiber: 0.2g, sugar: 12g, sodium: 586mg

Baked Cod Fillets in Mushroom-Tomato Sauce

Prep time: 5 minutes, Cook time: 25 minutes, Serves 2

Ingredients

1 tbsp. extra-virgin olive oil, plus more for serving
2 codfish fillets, washed and patted dry
1½ cups shiitake mushrooms, chopped
¾ cup crushed tomatoes
2 garlic cloves, minced
1 tbsp. fresh oregano, chopped
½ tsp. Himalayan salt
Freshly ground black pepper

Directions

1. Preheat the oven to 400ºF (205ºC). Line a small baking sheet with parchment paper and keep aside.
2. In a small, nonstick sauté pan or skillet, heat the olive oil over medium heat. Place the shiitake mushrooms and cook for 2 minutes, then place the garlic and salt.
3. Put the crushed tomatoes and continue cooking for about 5 minutes, until the sauce is reduced by one-third. Toss in the oregano.
4. Spread the cod fillets on the prepared baking sheet and ladle some of the mushroom tomato mixture over each. Pour any leftover sauce to the baking sheet.
5. Bake for 20 minutes, until fish is cooked through.
6. Place some black pepper and a drizzle of olive oil before serving.

Nutritional Info per Serving
calories: 209, fat: 8g, protein: 28g, carbs: 6g, fiber: 3g, sugar: 3g, sodium: 518mg

Salmon, Mushroom and Barley Bake, page 80

Sweet Potato and Salmon Cakes, page 81

Traditional Mediterranean Fish in Parchment, page 87

Spicy and Classic Shrimp Tacos, page 88

Codfish Risotto

Prep time: 7 minutes, Cook time: 20 minutes, Serves 4

Ingredients

2 tbsps. extra-virgin olive oil

1 pound (454 g) codfish fillets, washed and patted dry, cut into small rectangles

1 cup Arborio rice, washed and drained

2 leeks, white parts only, thinly sliced (optional)

½ medium yellow onion, thinly sliced

2 cups water

2 garlic cloves, minced

¼ tsp. saffron, plus more as needed

½ tsp. Himalayan salt

Freshly ground black pepper (optional)

Directions

1. In a large sauté pan or skillet, heat the olive oil over medium heat. Place the leeks, onion, and garlic. Cook until the onion is translucent.
2. Put the rice, salt, and saffron. Stir to combine well.
3. Create small pockets in the rice and insert the fish.
4. Pour in the water, cover, reduce the heat to low, and cook for about 20 minutes. Most of the liquid will evaporate.
5. Place some more saffron and black pepper, if desired. Serve hot.

Nutritional Info per Serving

calories: 513, fat: 11g, protein: 32g, carbs: 68g, fiber: 4g, sugar: 3g, sodium: 353mg

Baked Salmon and Asparagus

Prep time: 4 minutes, Cook time: 25 minutes, Serves 4

Ingredients

1 tbsp. extra-virgin olive oil

4 salmon fillets

2 bunches asparagus (about 24 pieces), woody ends cut off

1 tbsp. sesame seeds

1 tbsp. freshly grated Parmesan cheese

¼ tsp. garlic powder

¾ tsp. Himalayan salt, divided

Freshly ground black pepper (optional)

Directions

1. Preheat the oven to 400ºF (205ºC). Carefully line 2 baking sheets or dishes with parchment paper (one for asparagus and one for salmon).
2. Spread the salmon fillets on a prepared baking sheet and scatter with ½ tsp. of salt and sesame seeds.
3. Bake for about 12 to 15 minutes, then remove from the oven and allow it to rest while you prepare the asparagus.
4. Place asparagus to the other baking sheet, scatter with the remaining ¼ tsp. of salt and garlic powder. Drizzle with the olive oil and toss with hands until evenly coated.
5. Bake for about 10 minutes, until tender.
6. In the last 2 minutes of baking, place the Parmesan cheese on top.
7. Season with black pepper before serving, if desired. Serve the salmon surrounded by asparagus. Enjoy!

Nutritional Info per Serving

calories: 269, fat: 14g, protein: 31g, carbs: 4g, fiber: 2g, sugar: 2g, sodium: 262mg

Garlicky Cilantro Grilled Shrimp

Prep time: 13 minutes, Cook time: 7 minutes, Serves 4

Ingredients

3 garlic cloves, peeled

1 scallion, sliced, white and green parts

½ cup fresh parsley

½ cup fresh cilantro

2 tbsps. lime juice, freshly squeezed

½ tsp. fresh ginger, peeled and minced

½ tsp. salt

¼ tsp. black pepper, freshly ground

⅛ tsp. cayenne pepper (optional)

1 tbsp. avocado oil

1 pound (454 g) large raw shrimp, peeled and deveined

Directions

1. Preheat a grill to high heat. Soak 5 wooden skewers in water to prevent burning once grilled.
2. In a food processor, add the garlic, scallion, parsley, cilantro, lime juice, ginger, salt, black pepper, and cayenne (if using). Pulse on high in 30-second intervals until the smooth. With the food processor running, slowly drizzle in the oil.
3. Tread 4 or 5 shrimp onto each soaked wooden skewer, creating a "C" shape, to ensure even cooking. Brush the shrimp with half the cilantro sauce, the other half for serving.
4. Gently lay the skewers on the grill and cook for 2 to 3 minutes. Flip and grill for 1 to 2 minutes, until the shrimp are pink and opaque. Remove from the heat and take the shrimp off the skewers.
5. Portion 4 or 5 shrimp into one half of 4 large two-compartment glass meal-prep containers with tight-fitting lids. Top with the reserved cilantro sauce. Fill the remaining compartment with your favorite side or salad. Cover and refrigerate.

Nutritional Info per Serving

calories: 114, fat: 5g, protein: 16g, carbs: 3g, fiber: 1.2g, sugar: 0.2g, sodium: 424mg

Traditional Mediterranean Fish in Parchment

Prep time: 4 minutes, Cook time: 20 minutes, Serves 4

Ingredients

1 yellow onion, sliced
4 (6-ounce / 170-g) cod fillets
1 pint cherry or grape tomatoes, halved
2 tbsps. capers
1 lemon, cut into 4 slices
2 tbsps. olive oil
4 garlic cloves, minced
¼ cup feta cheese, crumbled

Directions

1. Preheat the oven to 450ºF (235ºC) and line with four large torn-off parchment paper sheets.
2. Place ¼ of the onion and a fish fillet on top of the onions on every sheet.
3. Top each fish fillet with ¼ of the tomatoes, ¼ of the capers, and 1 slice of lemon. Drizzle the olive oil over each fillet. Sprinkle ¼ of the garlic and ¼ of the feta cheese on each fillet.
4. Fold the parchment paper to form a pouch. Bake for 15 to 20 minutes or until fish flakes when tested with a fork. Let rest 5 minutes. Carefully open the packet to avoid a steam burn.

Nutritional Info per Serving

calories: 264, fat: 10g, protein: 32g, carbs: 9g, fiber: 2.5g, sugar: 3.2g, sodium: 348mg

Authentic Shrimp Saganaki

Prep time: 15 minutes, Cook time: 13 to 18 minutes, Serves 2

Ingredients

1 tbsp. extra-virgin olive oil
1 pound (454 g) shrimp, cleaned
1 (13-ounce / 369-g) can whole peeled tomatoes (with liquid), mashed or chopped small
1 (13-ounce / 369-g) can
tomato purée
3 garlic cloves, chopped
2 or 3 tbsps. feta
1 tbsp. fresh basil, chopped
½ tsp. oregano
½ tsp. Himalayan salt
Freshly ground black pepper (optional)

Directions

1. Combine the shrimp, garlic, and olive oil in a bowl. Stir and marinate for about 15 minutes.
2. In another bowl, add the tomato purée, tomatoes, basil, oregano, and salt. Mix well and keep aside.
3. Preheat the oven to 425ºF (220ºC).
4. Heat a cast-iron skillet over high heat. Toss in the shrimp when the skillet is very hot. Flash-fry for 3 minutes on each side, leaving the shrimp half cooked, just until they turn pink.
5. Take the shrimp to a baking dish, then pour in the tomato mixture. Scatter feta on top and season with black pepper, if desired.
6. Bake for 10 to 15 minutes, until the cheese is bubbly.
7. Serve plain or over some jasmine or brown rice.

Nutritional Info per Serving

calories: 359, fat: 12g, protein: 51g, carbs: 15g, fiber: 7g, sugar: 6g, sodium: 512mg

Baked Salmon with Dill and Scallion Pesto

Prep time: 16 minutes, Cook time: 25 minutes, Serves 4

Ingredients

¼ cup extra-virgin olive oil, plus 1 tsp.
1 cup fresh parsley leaves
¼ cup chopped scallions, white and green parts
1 tbsp. fresh dill
1 garlic clove, peeled
2 tbsps. Parmesan,
freshly grated
1 tbsp. lemon juice, freshly squeezed
1 pound (454 g) wild-caught salmon fillets, cut into 4 pieces
½ tsp. salt
¼ tsp. black pepper, freshly ground

Directions

1. Preheat the oven to 350ºF (180ºC). Line a large baking sheet with foil. Brush it with 1 tsp. of oil.
2. In a food processor, ass the parsley, scallions, dill, garlic, Parmesan, and lemon juice. Process on high speed in 30-second intervals until smooth. Do not stop the food processor and slowly drizzle in the remaining ¼ cup of oil.
3. Place the salmon fillets on the prepared baking sheet, skin side-down. Sprinkle with salt and pepper. Brush the dill pesto over each piece of salmon to coat.
4. Bake for 20 to 25 minutes, or until the salmon reaches an internal temperature of 130ºF (54ºC) or 145ºF (63ºC).
5. Place a salmon fillet in one half of 4 large two-compartment glass meal-prep containers with tight-fitting lids. Add cooked brown rice or any side or salad of your choice in the remaining compartment. Cover and refrigerate.

Nutritional Info per Serving

calories: 283, fat: 18g, protein: 23g, carbs: 3g, fiber: 1.3g, sugar: 3g, sodium: 505mg

Spicy and Classic Shrimp Tacos

Prep time: 6 minutes, Cook time: 5 minutes, Serves 4

Ingredients

1 pound (454 g) shrimp, peeled and deveined
2 tbsps. avocado oil, divided
3 garlic cloves, minced
1 tbsp. taco seasoning
Juice of ½ lime
8 hard taco shells
Avocado lettuce, red onion, and tomato, for topping (optional)

Directions

1. Combine the shrimp, 1 tbsp. avocado oil, garlic, and Taco Seasoning in a medium bowl. Toss to coat the shrimp with the oil and seasonings.
2. Heat the remaining oil in a large skillet over medium heat.
3. When the oil is hot, add the shrimps and sauté for 3 to 4 minutes, flipping once until the shrimps turn pink and opaque.
4. Add a squeeze of the fresh lime juice over the shrimp. Fill the hard taco shells with the shrimp and your choice of toppings.

Nutritional Info per Serving

calories: 315, fat: 14g, protein: 24g, carbs: 18g, fiber: 3.5g, sugar: 0.3g, sodium: 285mg

Tuna and Spinach Burgers

Prep time: 4 minutes, Cook time: 7 minutes, Serves 2 to 4

Ingredients

2 tbsps. extra-virgin olive oil
1 (8½-ounce / 241-g) can tuna in water, drained
½ cup cornmeal (polenta)
½ cup baby spinach, chopped
1 scallion, chopped (green and white parts)
1 tbsp. Dijon mustard
½ tsp. Himalayan salt
¼ tsp. freshly ground black pepper

Directions

1. Combine the tuna, mustard, scallion, spinach, cornmeal, salt, and pepper in a small bowl. Mix well.
2. Shape the mixture into 2 large or 4 small patties. Keep aside.
3. In a nonstick sauté pan or skillet, heat the olive oil over medium heat. Put the burgers and pan-fry on one side for about 3 to 4 minutes, then flip and leave them for 3 minutes more.
4. Take the burgers onto a plate lined with a paper towel to soak up some of the excess olive oil. Enjoy!

Nutritional Info per Serving

calories: 319, fat: 16g, protein: 22g, carbs: 24g, fiber: 3g, sugar: 0g, sodium: 510mg

Mushroom Shrimp Scampi

Prep time: 22 minutes, Cook time: 7½ hours, Serves 8 to 10

Ingredients

2 tbsps. butter
2 pounds (907 g) raw shrimp, shelled and deveined
1 pound (454 g) cremini mushrooms, sliced
2 leeks, chopped
1 cup fish stock
¼ cup freshly squeezed lemon juice
2 onions, chopped
8 garlic cloves, minced
1 tsp. dried basil leaves

Directions

1. Mix the mushrooms, onions, leeks, garlic, fish stock, lemon juice, and basil in a 6-quart slow cooker. Cover the slow cooker and cook on low for 5 to 7 hours, or until the vegetables are soft.
2. Gently stir in the shrimp. Cover and cook on high for 30 to 40 minutes, or until the shrimp are curled and pink.
3. Stir in the butter. Cover and allow to stand for about 10 minutes, then serve.

Nutritional Info per Serving

calories: 158, fat: 4g, protein: 22g, carbs: 10g, fiber: 2g, sugar: 3g, sodium: 275mg

Lemon-Pepper Ghee Grilled Clams

Prep time: 8 minutes, Cook time: 8 to 10 minutes, Serves 8

Ingredients

½ cup ghee, melted
Zest and juice of 1 lemon
¼ tsp. pepper
2 pounds (907 g)
littleneck clams, scrubbed clean
Pinch sea salt

Directions

1. Preheat the grill to medium.
2. Meanwhile, in a small saucepan, warm the ghee, lemon zest, lemon juice, and pepper over low heat and whisk to combine. Reduce the heat to low until the clams are ready to eat.
3. Place the clams directly on the grill. Cook for 8 to 10 minutes without turning. When the clams have

opened, they can be removed from the grill and transferred to a medium bowl. Discard clams that do not open.
4. Pour lemon-pepper ghee over the clams, sprinkle with salt before serving.

Nutritional Info per Serving
calories: 152, fat: 13g, protein: 7g, carbs: 2g, fiber: 0.3g, sugar: 0.2g, sodium: 26mg

Quick Grilled Ahi Tuna

Prep time: 15 minutes, Cook time: 5 minutes, Serves 2

Ingredients
Marinade:
1 tbsp. sesame oil
2 tbsps. soy sauce
1 tbsp. rice vinegar

Tuna:
2 (6-ounce / 170-g) ahi tuna steaks
Sesame seeds (optional)

Directions
1. Preheat the grill to the highest setting.
2. To make the marinade: Whisk together the soy sauce, sesame oil, and rice vinegar in a small bowl.
3. To make the tuna: Wash the tuna steaks and pat them dry with a paper towel. Place the steaks to a bowl, and put the marinade on top. Rub the steaks on both sides to coat well. Leave at room temperature for 15 minutes.
4. Grill the steaks for about 3 minutes on one side and 2 minutes on the other. The steaks will be seared on the outside and pink on the inside.
5. Slice thin with a fork and serve alongside a large green salad of your choice.Garnish with some sesame seeds, if desired.

Nutritional Info per Serving
calories: 256, fat: 8g, protein: 43g, carbs: 1g, fiber: 0g, sugar: 0g, sodium: 455mg

Marinara Shrimp with Zoodles

Prep time: 16 minutes, Cook time: 18 minutes, Serves 2 to 3

Ingredients
1 tbsp. extra-virgin olive oil
1 pound (454 g) shrimp, cleaned
4 medium green zucchinis, spiralized
Juice of ½ lemon

½ cup marinara sauce
1 tbsp. freshly grated Parmesan cheese
Spice it up:
¼ tsp. garlic powder
Red pepper flakes, for garnish

Directions
1. Preheat the grill to the highest setting. Coat with olive oil if needed.
2. Toss the shrimp with the olive oil, garlic powder (if using), and lemon juice in a bowl. Marinate for 10 minutes.
3. Grill the shrimp on one side for about 3 minutes, then flip and cook for another 3 minutes. Turn off the heat and keep aside.
4. Bring the marinara sauce to a boil in a small sauté pan or skillet. Place the spiralized zucchinis and cook for 3 minutes, until tender. Scatter with the Parmesan cheese, toss, and turn off the heat.
5. Serve zoodles with shrimp on top on individual plates. Sprinkle with red pepper flakes if you like it spicy.

Nutritional Info per Serving
calories: 315, fat: 11g, protein: 37g, carbs: 19g, fiber: 5g, sugar: 5g, sodium: 353mg

Tropical White Fish Ceviche

Prep time: 18 minutes, Cook time: 0 minutes, Serves 6

Ingredients
½ pound (227 g) white fish (mahi-mahi, cod, tilapia, haddock, etc.), finely chopped
Juice of 3 to 4 limes
Juice of 1 orange
1 mango, diced
1 small bell pepper, diced
1 avocado, diced

1 jalapeño, seeded and diced
¼ cup thinly sliced red onion
2 tbsps. cilantro, chopped
½ tsp. salt
½ tsp. pepper
1 sliced cucumber or tortilla chips, for serving

Directions
1. Place the white fish in a shallow bowl and cover with lime juice and orange juice.
2. Cover and chill for 1 to 2 hours, or until fish no longer looks raw when cut into.
3. Meanwhile, in a large bowl, add the mango, bell pepper, avocado, jalapeño, red onion, cilantro, salt, and pepper. Stir gently and refrigerate in a covered container.
4. After the fish has been done, add the fish to larger bowl of vegetables and season with additional salt and pepper, if desired.
5. Serve with cucumber slices or tortilla chips of your choice.

Nutritional Info per Serving
calories: 142, fat: 4g, protein: 9g, carbs: 10g, fiber: 2.7g, sugar: 7g, sodium: 234mg

Blackened Fish

Prep time: 3 minutes, Cook time: 8 minutes, Serves 4

Ingredients
2 tsps. paprika
1 tsp. cayenne pepper
1 tsp. dry mustard
1 tsp. garlic powder
½ tsp. cumin

½ tsp. pepper
½ tsp. salt
1½ pounds (680 g) white fish, patted dry and sliced into 4 even-size fillets
2 tbsps. olive oil

Directions
1. Add the paprika, cayenne, dry mustard, garlic powder, cumin, pepper, and salt in a small bowl. Mix until well combined.
2. Rub the spice mixture over the fish fillets.
3. Heat the oil over medium heat in a large skillet. Add the fish and cook for 3 to 4 minutes per side or until cooked through.

Nutritional Info per Serving
calories: 251, fat: 8g, protein: 36g, carbs: 0.7g, fiber: 0.2g, sugar: 0.3g, sodium: 427mg

Parmesan Salmon with Root Vegetables

Prep time: 12 minutes, Cook time: 9 hours, Serves 6

Ingredients
4 large carrots, sliced
4 Yukon Gold potatoes, cubed
2 sweet potatoes, peeled and cubed
6 (5-ounce / 142-g) salmon fillets
⅓ cup grated Parmesan cheese

2 onions, chopped
3 garlic cloves, minced
⅓ cup vegetable broth or fish stock
1 tsp. dried thyme leaves
½ tsp. salt

Directions
1. Mix carrots, sweet potatoes, Yukon Gold potatoes, onions, garlic, vegetable broth, thyme, and salt in a 6-quart slow cooker. Cover the slow cooker and cook on low for 7 to 9 hours, or until the vegetables are soft.
2. Place the salmon fillets and scatter each with some of the cheese. Cover and cook on low for another 30 to 40 minutes, or until the salmon flakes when tested with a fork. Serve warm.

Nutritional Info per Serving
calories: 491, fat: 19g, protein: 42g, carbs: 38g, fiber: 5g, sugar: 8g, sodium: 560mg

Chapter 8: Salads

Tuscan Tuna and Bean Salad

Prep time: 6 minutes, Cook time: 0 minutes, Serves 4

Ingredients

1 (15-ounce / 425-g) can white kidney beans, drained and rinsed	cubed
	½ small red onion, sliced
2 (5-ounce / 142-g) cans tuna packed in oil	Zest of 1 lemon
	Juice of 1 lemon
4 cups baby spinach	Sea salt
1 tomato, diced	Freshly ground black pepper
1 avocado, pitted and	

Directions

1. Add all the ingredients in a large bowl. Gently toss the ingredients together with two wooden spoons, ensuring they are mixed together evenly.
2. Divide the salad equally among 4 bowls. Serve right away.

Nutritional Info per Serving

calories: 320, fat: 14g, protein: 27g, carbs: 24g, fiber: 9g, sugar: 4g, sodium: 418mg

Green Bean and Chickpea Salad Bowl

Prep time: 8 minutes, Cook time: 5 minutes, Serves 4

Ingredients

2 tbsps. olive oil	1 cup walnuts, chopped
1 pound (454 g) green beans, ends trimmed	4 cups water
	2 tbsps. lemon juice
½ pound (227 g) radishes, halved and sliced thinly	2 tbsps. plain Greek yogurt
	1 tbsp. Dijon mustard
1 small head Bibb lettuce, washed and rinsed	Sea salt
	Freshly ground black pepper
1 cup canned chickpeas, drained	

Directions

1. In a large pot over high heat, bring the water to a boil. Place the beans and cook for about 4 to 5 minutes, until just soft. Drain the beans well and allow to cool.
2. Fill 4 bowls about three-fourths full with the Bibb lettuce.
3. Spread the green beans, chickpeas, radishes, and walnuts on top of each bowl.
4. Whisk together the lemon juice, mustard, yogurt, and oil in a bowl. Sprinkle with salt and pepper.
5. Drizzle the salad bowls with the dressing and serve.

Nutritional Info per Serving

calories: 353, fat: 28g, protein: 10g, carbs: 21g, fiber: 8g, sugar: 4g, sodium: 274mg

Skirt Steak and Kale Salad Bowl

Prep time: 6 minutes, Cook time: 18 minutes, Serves 4

Ingredients

5 to 7 tbsps. extra-virgin olive oil, divided	seeds
	1 garlic clove, minced
1 pound (454 g) skirt steak, trimmed and halved crosswise	4 tbsps. freshly squeezed orange juice
	2 tbsps. shallots, finely chopped
2 cups kale, chopped	
¼ cup red onion, thinly sliced	1 tbsp. Dijon mustard
	¼ tsp. sea salt
¼ cup shredded carrot	¼ tsp. freshly ground black pepper
¼ cup pomegranate	

Directions

1. In a cast-iron skillet, heat 1 to 2 tbsps. olive oil over medium-high heat. Put the steak in the skillet and do not move it for about 5 minutes. Turn it once, and cook for an additional 3 minutes for medium-rare. Depending on the size of your pan, you may need to cook your steak halves separately.
2. Take the steak to a cutting board and allow to rest, loosely covered with foil, for about 5 minutes.
3. Divide the kale equally among 4 bowls. Place the red onion and shredded carrot.
4. Thinly slice the steak on the diagonal, across the grain, and spread over the salad bowls.
5. Add the orange juice, 4 tbsps. olive oil, mustard, shallots, garlic, salt, and pepper in a blender. Blend until smooth.
6. Pour the dressing over salad and sprinkle with pomegranate seeds. Serve immediately.

Nutritional Info per Serving

calories: 356, fat: 22g, protein: 35g, carbs: 7g, fiber: 1g, sugar: 4g, sodium: 495mg

Hearty 7-Layer Taco Salad

Prep time: 15 minutes, Cook time: 10 minutes, Serves 4

Ingredients
Salad:
1 tbsp. olive oil
2 (15-ounce / 425-g) cans no-salt-added black beans drained and rinsed
3 cups romaine lettuce, chopped
2 cups cooked quinoa
2 cups fresh or frozen corn kernels
2 (2¼-ounce / 64-g) cans sliced black olives, drained
2 avocados, diced
1 cup grape tomatoes, halved
½ tsp. chili powder
¼ tsp. paprika
½ tsp. sea salt
¼ tsp. ground black pepper

Taco Ranch Dressing:
½ cup plain full-fat Greek yogurt
¼ cup unsweetened almond milk
1 tbsp. freshly squeezed lime juice
1 tsp. onion powder
½ tsp. ground cumin
½ tsp. paprika
¼ tsp. ground black pepper
¼ tsp. coconut sugar
¼ tsp. dried oregano
¼ tsp. dried dill
¼ tsp. garlic powder
⅛ tsp. cayenne pepper
¼ tsp. sea salt

Directions
Make the Salad:
1. In a large nonstick skillet, heat the oil over medium-high heat. Place the corn, chili powder, salt, pepper, and paprika, and cook for about 8 to 10 minutes, or until the corn begins to brown, stirring occasionally. Keep aside the corn to cool.
2. In a deep, clear glass bowl, place the quinoa, followed by a layer of the lettuce, then the black beans, then the pan-roasted corn, then the tomatoes, then the avocados and the olives. For each layer, begin by putting the food around the perimeter of the bowl to define the layer, and then fill the middle with the rest.

Make the Dressing:
3. In a medium bowl, whisk together well the yogurt, milk, lime juice, dill, garlic powder, onion powder, coconut sugar, salt, cumin, paprika, oregano, black pepper, and cayenne.
4. Pour the dressing over the salad.
5. Alternatively, you could stack this salad in a 1-quart Mason jar, beginning with the salad dressing, then the tomatoes, black beans, quinoa, corn, olives, avocado, and finally place the lettuce to the very top. Once you are ready to eat the salad, pour it into a large mixing bowl, and toss to coat evenly with the dressing. Enjoy!

Nutritional Info per Serving
calories: 477, fat: 23g, protein: 13g, carbs: 61g, fiber: 16g, sugar: 10g, sodium: 518mg

Greek Kale and Quinoa Salad

Prep time: 13 minutes, Cook time: 30 minutes, Serves 4

Ingredients
Salad:
1 tsp. olive oil
1 (15-ounce / 425-g) can no-salt-added chickpeas, drained and rinsed
3 cups chopped kale
2 cups water
1 cup quinoa
1 cup cherry tomatoes, halved
1 cup peeled and diced cucumber
¾ cup Kalamata olives, halved
⅓ cup finely diced red onion
¼ cup crumbled feta, plus more for garnish

Greek Dressing:
¼ cup olive oil
1 clove garlic, minced
1 tbsp. red wine vinegar
1 tbsp. Dijon mustard
2 tsps. freshly squeezed lemon juice
1 tsp. raw honey
¼ tsp. dried oregano
¼ tsp. sea salt

Directions
Make the Salad:
1. Rinse the quinoa in a fine-mesh sieve to remove any debris and dirt. In a medium saucepan over medium-high heat, cook the quinoa for about 6 to 8 minutes, tossing constantly, to toast the quinoa. It's well done when the quinoa is no longer wet and starts to pop and turns golden brown.
2. Pour the water to the pan, bring it to a boil, and then reduce the heat to a simmer. Cook for 15 to 20 minutes, covered, until all of the liquid is absorbed and the quinoa has doubled in size. Then, fluff the quinoa with a fork, and let it cool.
3. Place the kale to a large mixing bowl, and drizzle it with the olive oil. Use your hands to massage the kale with the olive oil for about 2 to 3 minutes to soften the kale.
4. Place the tomatoes, cucumber, olives, chickpeas, onion, feta, and 1½ cups of the cooked quinoa, and toss well.

Make the Greek Dressing:
5. Combine the olive oil, red wine vinegar, mustard, lemon juice, oregano, garlic, honey, and salt in a small bowl, and whisk together vigorously until emulsified. Pour the dressing over the salad, and toss once more to coat well.
6. Garnish with feta cheese, and serve right away.

Nutritional Info per Serving
calories: 496, fat: 24g, protein: 16g, carbs: 57g, fiber: 11g, sugar: 8g, sodium: 478mg

Orange Beet Arugula Salad

Prep time: 5 minutes, Cook time: 30 minutes, Serves 6

Ingredients
Salad:
4 beets, peeled and chopped
⅔ cup walnuts, chopped
3 ounces (85 g) feta, crumbled
1 orange, peeled and sliced in rounds
4 cups arugula
Dressing:
¼ cup olive oil
2 tbsps. balsamic vinegar
1 tbsp. honey
Salt
Pepper

Directions
1. Preheat the oven to 400ºF (205ºC). Line a baking sheet with parchment paper.
2. Spread the beets on the baking sheet in a single layer. Bake for 30 minutes.
3. Meanwhile, whisk together all of the ingredients in a small bowl for dressing.
4. In a large bowl, mix together the walnuts, feta, orange, arugula, and cooked beets.
5. Transfer the dressing to the salad and toss. Note not to let all of the beets, oranges, and walnuts sink to the bottom.

Nutritional Info per Serving
calories: 254, fat: 22g, protein: 5.4g, carbs: 13g, fiber: 2.6g, sugar: 9g, sodium: 207mg

Healthy Rainbow Salad

Prep time: 9 minutes, Cook time: 0 minutes, Serves 4

Ingredients
Sesame-Ginger Peanut Dressing:
1 tbsp. toasted sesame oil
2 tbsps. natural peanut butter
1 tbsp. low-sodium soy sauce
2 tsps. freshly squeezed lime juice
2 tsps. raw honey
½ tsp. crushed red pepper flakes
1 tsp. minced ginger
Hot water
Salad:
2 cups finely chopped kale leaves
2 cups finely chopped red cabbage
1 cup frozen shelled edamame, thawed
1 cup shredded carrots
¾ cup roughly chopped fresh cilantro
½ yellow bell pepper, thinly sliced
⅓ cup thinly sliced green onions
⅓ cup toasted, slivered raw almonds

Directions

1. In a blender, add the sesame oil, peanut butter, honey, soy sauce, lime juice, crushed red pepper flakes, and ginger. Blend on high until completely pureed. If the dressing is too thick, pour in 1 tbsp. of hot water at a time and blend again, until the dressing is thin enough to toss with the salad.
2. Add the kale, red cabbage, carrots, bell pepper, almonds, cilantro, green onions, and edamame to a large bowl, and toss to combine well.
3. Drizzle the salad with the dressing, and toss the salad to coat. Serve immediately.

Nutritional Info per Serving
calories: 217, fat: 13g, protein: 10g, carbs: 19g, fiber: 6g, sugar: 9g, sodium: 184mg

Roasted Red Pepper and Parsley Salad

Prep time: 2 minutes, Cook time: 30 minutes, Serves 3

Ingredients
2 tbsps. extra-virgin olive oil
6 long red peppers, washed and patted dry
1 tbsp. white wine
vinegar
1 tbsp. fresh parsley, chopped, for garnish
¼ tsp. Himalayan salt, plus more as needed

Directions
1. Turn on the broiler and let it preheat while you cook the peppers.
2. Line a baking sheet with parchment paper and place the peppers in a single layer, skin-side up.
3. Broil the peppers on one side for about 5 minutes, until the skin starts bubbling. Gently flip the peppers and broil on the other side.
4. Keep turning until all sides of the pepper are brown and the skin is lifted up. This should take about 15 to 20 minutes, depending on your oven.
5. Remove the peppers from the oven and cover the baking sheet with a kitchen towel. Let stand for about 10 minutes.
6. Peel the skin off the peppers and put them flat on a serving plate.
7. Drizzle with the vinegar, oil, and salt. Use clean hands to toss gently so the dressing is evenly applied.
8. Scatter with a little salt and parsley.
9. Serve immediately or refrigerate for 15 minutes to cool further.

Nutritional Info per Serving
calories: 186, fat: 10g, protein: 3g, carbs: 21g, fiber: 7g, sugar: 4g, sodium: 118mg

Roasted Beet and Pistachio Salad

Prep time: 5 minutes, Cook time: 30 minutes, Serves 4

Ingredients

3 tbsps. extra-virgin olive oil, divided
4 medium beets, quartered
¼ cup pistachios, chopped
¼ cup goat cheese, crumbled
2 tbsps. rice vinegar
¼ tsp. Himalayan salt

Directions

1. Preheat the oven to 400ºF (205ºC).
2. Mix 2 tbsps. of olive oil with the rice vinegar and salt in a bowl. Keep aside.
3. Line a baking sheet with parchment paper. Gently toss the beets with the remaining tbsp. of olive oil and place on the baking sheet.
4. Cover with another sheet of parchment paper and bake for 25 to 30 minutes, until the beets are tender.
5. Allow the beets to cool and take them to a bowl.
6. Toss the beets in the olive oil dressing and transfer to a serving plate.
7. Put goat cheese and pistachios on top. Enjoy!

Nutritional Info per Serving

calories: 188, fat: 15g, protein: 4g, carbs: 10g, fiber: 3g, sugar: 6g, sodium: 175mg

Traditional Mexican Street Corn Salad

Prep time: 3 minutes, Cook time: 0 minutes, Serves 6

Ingredients

Salad:
3 cups corn kernels, fresh or frozen
2 medium vine-ripened tomatoes, diced
1 medium avocado, diced
1 red bell pepper, diced
½ cup red onion, chopped
Dressing:
2 tbsps. plain
unsweetened Greek yogurt
½ cup crumbled Cotija cheese
2 tbsps. lime juice (juice of 1 to 2 limes)
2 tbsps. cilantro
½ tsp. paprika
¼ tsp. salt
¼ tsp. pepper
¼ tsp. garlic powder
¼ tsp. cumin

Directions

Make the Salad:

1. In a large bowl, combine the corn, tomatoes, avocado, bell pepper, and onion.

Make the Dressing:

2. In a small bowl, combine the yogurt, cheese, lime juice, cilantro, paprika, salt, pepper, garlic powder, and cumin.
3. Toss the yogurt dressing with the corn salad to coat evenly.
4. Serve immediately or chill in a sealed container for 3 to 4 days.

Nutritional Info per Serving

calories: 185, fat: 8g, protein: 8g, carbs: 21g, fiber: 4.5g, sugar: 6g, sodium: 214mg

Vietnamese Cabbage and Carrot Noodle Salad

Prep time: 12 minutes, Cook time: 5 minutes, Serves 4

Ingredients

3 tbsps. extra-virgin olive oil
4 cups Chinese cabbage, shredded
3 carrots, cut into strips
1 seedless cucumber, cut into strips
1 jalapeño, thinly sliced
¾ cup chopped fresh cilantro
¾ cup rice vinegar
¼ cup peanuts
1½ tbsps. organic maple syrup
¼ tsp. salt

Directions

1. In a large saucepan over high heat, bring the vinegar, maple syrup, and salt to a boil.
2. Put the carrot noodles in the pan, take the mixture back to a boil, then reduce the heat to low. Cover and cook for about 90 seconds to 2 minutes.
3. Place the cucumber and jalapeño to the pan, stirring to combine well. Turn the mixture from the heat and cover. Let it stand, covered, for about 2 hours, stirring occasionally.
4. Once the vegetables have pickled, remove and reserve 3 tbsps. of the pickling liquid, then drain the rest liquid.
5. Whisk together the olive oil and the pickling liquid to make a dressing in a small bowl.
6. Place the shredded cabbage and dressing to a large bowl. Toss to coat evenly.
7. Divide the cabbage equally among 4 bowls. Place the pickled vegetables, cilantro, and peanuts on top. Serve right away.

Nutritional Info per Serving

calories: 191, fat: 15g, protein: 4g, carbs: 11g, fiber: 2g, sugar: 7g, sodium: 162mg

Greek Kale and Quinoa Salad, page 93

Avocado Cucumber Feta Salad, page 99

Fresh Cucumber and Tomato Salad Bowl, page 98

Vietnamese Cabbage and Carrot Noodle Salad, page 95

Tasteful Quinoa Tabbouleh

Prep time: 8 minutes, Cook time: 15 minutes, Serves 8

Ingredients
1 cup quinoa, uncooked
2 cups water
8 ounces (227 g) cherry tomatoes, quartered
1 cucumber, chopped
1 cup chopped roasted red peppers
4 ounces (113 g) feta cheese, crumbled
½ cup red onion, diced
Juice of 1 lemon
1 tbsp. olive oil
¼ cup parsley fresh, chopped
Salt
Pepper

Directions
1. Place the quinoa and water in a medium saucepan and bring to a boil. Reduce the heat to low, cover, and cook for 15 minutes, or until all of the water has been absorbed. Mash up with a fork.
2. Combine the cooked quinoa with the remaining ingredients in a large bowl and mix well.
3. Chill in the fridge until ready to serve.

Nutritional Info per Serving
calories: 162, fat: 7g, protein: 5g, carbs: 20g, fiber: 5g, sugar: 4g, sodium: 226mg

Healthy Greek Salad Bowl

Prep time: 9 minutes, Cook time: 0 minutes, Serves 2

Ingredients
2 tbsps. extra-virgin olive oil, for drizzling
2 cups romaine lettuce, chopped
1 cucumber, sliced
½ cup pepperoncini peppers
½ cup cherry tomatoes, halved
¼ cup Kalamata olives, pitted and sliced
½ red onion, chopped
1 tsp. fresh oregano, chopped
Sea salt
Freshly ground black pepper

Directions
1. Combine the lettuce, cucumber, red onion, tomatoes, peppers, and olives in a large bowl.
2. Scatter with the oregano and season with salt and black pepper.
3. Pour in the olive oil and toss gently to coat well.
4. Divide the salad equally between 2 bowls and serve immediately.

Nutritional Info per Serving
calories: 181, fat: 15g, protein: 2g, carbs: 11g, fiber: 3g, sugar: 5g, sodium: 211mg

Quick Chopped Caprese Salad

Prep time: 6 minutes, Cook time: 10 minutes, Serves 8

Ingredients
10 vine-ripened tomatoes, chopped
8 ounces (227 g) buffalo mozzarella, chopped
½ cup basil, chopped
½ tsp. salt
¼ tsp. pepper
2 tsps. olive oil
½ cup balsamic vinegar
2 tbsps. honey

Directions
1. In a large bowl, combine the tomatoes, mozzarella, basil, salt, and pepper. Drizzle with the olive oil.
2. Heat a small saucepan over medium-high heat, add and cook the balsamic vinegar and honey until simmering. Reduce the heat to low and simmer for 5 to 10 minutes, or until thickened. Cool for 5 minutes.
3. Drop the balsamic glaze over the salad and chill before serving.

Nutritional Info per Serving
calories: 128, fat: 6g, protein: 8g, carbs: 13g, fiber: 1.7g, sugar: 8g, sodium: 195mg

Baked Acorn Squash and Arugula Salad

Prep time: 5 minutes, Cook time: 0 minutes, Serves 2 to 3

Ingredients
Extra-virgin olive oil, for coating squash
4 cups arugula
1 medium acorn squash, cut into rounds
½ cup Brussels sprouts, shaved or thinly sliced
⅓ cup pomegranate seeds
¼ cup pumpkin seeds

Directions
1. Preheat the oven to 400ºF (205ºC).
2. Line a baking sheet with parchment paper. Arrange the acorn squash on the baking sheet and slowly toss with olive oil to coat well. Place in a single layer and bake for about 20 to 25 minutes, until squash is tender.
3. Meanwhile, combine the arugula, Brussels sprouts, pomegranate, and pumpkin seeds in a bowl, and toss with the dressing of choice.
4. Place acorn squash on top and drizzle additional dressing on top. Enjoy!

Nutritional Info per Serving
calories: 351, fat: 22g, protein: 8g, carbs: 34g, fiber: 7g, sugar: 5g, sodium: 352mg

Apple & Cranberry Slaw

Prep time: 20 minutes, Cook time: 0 minutes, Serves 8

Ingredients
2 apples, cored and julienne
½ head green cabbage, sliced thinly
2 carrots, shredded
½ red onion, sliced thinly
1 cup cranberries, dried
1 cup almonds, sliced
1 cup plain unsweetened Greek yogurt
1 tbsp. olive oil
1 tbsp. apple cider vinegar
1 tbsp. honey
½ tsp. salt
¼ tsp. pepper

Directions
1. In a large bowl, combine all of the ingredients. Refrigerate in a covered container for at least 1 hour before serving.

Nutritional Info per Serving
calories: 215, fat: 9g, protein: 6g, carbs: 28g, fiber: 6g, sugar: 14g, sodium: 192mg

Asian Vegetables Salad Bowl

Prep time: 9 minutes, Cook time: 0 minutes, Serves 4

Ingredients
½ tsp. sesame oil
1 cup kale, chopped
1 red cabbage, cored and chopped
1 carrot, julienned
½ cup cashews, chopped
½ cup chopped fresh cilantro
2 red bell peppers, sliced
2 scallions, sliced
2 tbsps. sesame seeds
1 tsp. natural peanut butter
1 tsp. tamari
½ tsp. freshly squeezed lime juice
½ tsp. rice vinegar

Directions
1. Toss the kale, red cabbage, bell peppers, carrot, cilantro, and scallions in a large bowl.
2. Whisk together the peanut butter, tamari, rice vinegar, sesame oil, and lime juice in a small bowl.
3. Pour the peanut sauce over the salad and toss gently to coat well. Divide the salad equally among 4 bowls. Garnish with the cashews and sesame seeds. Serve immediately.

Nutritional Info per Serving
calories: 159, fat: 11g, protein: 5g, carbs: 12g, fiber: 3g, sugar: 4g, sodium: 130mg

Fresh Cucumber and Tomato Salad Bowl

Prep time: 6 minutes, Cook time: 0 minutes, Serves 2

Ingredients
2 tbsps. extra-virgin olive oil
1 seedless cucumber, sliced
1 medium tomato, diced
1 cup kale, chopped
¼ cup pecans, chopped
¼ cup fresh basil leaves, chopped
2 tbsps. red wine vinegar
2 tbsps. goat cheese

Directions
1. In a large bowl, combine the kale, cucumber, tomato, basil, olive oil, and vinegar. Toss to combine well.
2. Divide the salad equally between 2 bowls. Top with the goat cheese and pecans. Serve immediately.

Nutritional Info per Serving
calories: 269, fat: 24g, protein: 6g, carbs: 6g, fiber: 2g, sugar: 2g, sodium: 137mg

Caprese Salad Quinoa Bowl

Prep time: 10 minutes, Cook time: 0 minutes, Serves 2

Ingredients
1 cup cooked quinoa, cooled completely
4 ounces (113 g) baby spinach
1 cup fresh basil, roughly chopped
2 tbsps. extra-virgin olive oil
1 tbsp. lemon juice, freshly squeezed
1 cup cherry tomatoes, diced
6 ounces (170 g) fresh mozzarella, diced
1 tsp. balsamic glaze

Directions
1. In a large bowl, place the spinach and basil.
2. In a small bowl, whisk the oil and lemon juice to combine. Portion the dressing evenly into 2 stainless-steel salad dressing containers.
3. Evenly divide the greens into 2 large glass meal-prep containers with lids. Top with the cooked quinoa, diced tomatoes, and mozzarella. Drizzle each with ½ tsp. of balsamic glaze. Cover and refrigerate.

Nutritional Info per Serving
calories: 532, fat: 32g, protein: 21g, carbs: 28g, fiber: 4g, sugar: 7g, sodium: 67mg

Tuna and Carrot Salad

Prep time: 6 minutes, Cook time: 0 minutes, Serves 2

Ingredients

1 (8½-ounce / 241-g) can tuna packed in olive oil
⅓ cup shredded carrots
⅓ cup parsley, chopped
2 scallions, chopped (green and white parts)
1 tbsp. Dijon mustard
Whole-grain toast (optional)
Avocado slices (optional)
¼ tsp. Himalayan salt

Directions

1. Combine the tuna with all the oil from the can, carrots, parsley, scallions, Dijon mustard, and salt in a medium bowl. Mix well.
2. Serve over whole-grain toast with avocado slices on top, if desired.

Nutritional Info per Serving

calories: 205, fat: 8g, protein: 27g, carbs: 4g, fiber: 2g, sugar: 0g, sodium: 315mg

Classic Mediterranean Wheat Berry Salad

Prep time: 22 minutes, Cook time: 0 minutes, Serves 4

Ingredients

2 cups cooked wheat berries
2 medium cucumbers, cut into ½-inch dice
1 cup grape tomatoes, halved
¼ cup paper-thin red onion slices
½ tsp. sea salt
¼ tsp. black pepper, freshly ground
1 tbsp. loosely packed chopped fresh basil
1 tbsp. loosely packed chopped fresh parsley
1 tsp. loosely packed chopped fresh oregano
1 tsp. garlic, minced
1 tbsp. red wine vinegar
2 tsps. extra-virgin olive oil
⅛ tsp. red pepper flakes (optional)
½ cup crumbled feta cheese

Directions

1. In a large bowl, combine the cucumbers, tomatoes, red onion, salt, and pepper and toss well to combine. Sit for 10 minutes.
2. Add the basil, parsley, oregano, garlic, vinegar, oil, and red pepper flakes (if using) to the cucumber mixture. Stir until well combined.
3. Stir in the cooked wheat berries and feta cheese. Let it rest for 5 minutes to marinate.
4. Evenly portion the salad into 4 glass meal-prep containers with lids. Cover and refrigerate.

Nutritional Info per Serving

calories: 152, fat: 8g, protein: 7g, carbs: 17g, fiber: 4g, sugar: 3g, sodium: 554mg

Avocado Cucumber Feta Salad

Prep time: 4 minutes, Cook time: 0 minutes, Serves 4

Ingredients

2 avocados, chopped
2 English cucumbers, chopped
4 ounces (113 g) feta cheese, crumbled
1 tbsp. olive oil
2 tbsps. lemon juice
½ tsp. salt
¼ tsp. pepper
Pinch red pepper flakes (optional)

Directions

1. In a large bowl, mix all of the ingredients. Chill until ready to enjoy.

Nutritional Info per Serving

calories: 275, fat: 22g, protein: 7g, carbs: 13g, fiber: 5.5g, sugar: 3g, sodium: 621mg

Arugula Watermelon and Avocado Salad

Prep time: 5 minutes, Cook time: 0 minutes, Serves 1 to 2

Ingredients

2 tbsps. extra-virgin olive oil
4 cups arugula
½ cup watermelon, cubed
¼ avocado, sliced
¼ cup goat cheese, crumbled
1 tbsp. balsamic vinegar
⅛ tsp. sea salt (optional)

Directions

1. Toss the arugula and olive oil in a bowl.
2. Add the watermelon, avocado, goat cheese, and salt (if using), and toss gently.
3. Pour balsamic vinegar on top and serve right away.

Nutritional Info per Serving

calories: 462, fat: 41g, protein: 10g, carbs: 17g, fiber: 6g, sugar: 9g, sodium: 158mg

Chapter 9: Soup and Stew

Chicken and Carrot Barley Stew

Prep time: 17 minutes, Cook time: 10 hours, Serves 10

Ingredients

10 boneless, skinless chicken thighs, cut into 2-inch pieces
4 large carrots, sliced
2 cups baby spinach leaves
1½ cups frozen corn
1¼ cups hulled barley
8 cups chicken stock
2 onions, chopped
4 garlic cloves, minced
1 sprig fresh rosemary
1 tsp. dried thyme leaves

Directions

1. Mix the onions, garlic, carrots, and barley. Top with the chicken and corn in a 6-quart slow cooker.
2. Add the chicken stock over all and place the rosemary and thyme leaves.
3. Cover the slow cooker and cook on low for 8 to 10 hours, or until the chicken is cooked to 165ºF (74ºC) and the barley is soft.
4. Remove the rosemary stem and discard. Toss in the spinach leaves. Cover and allow to for 5 minutes, then serve.

Nutritional Info per Serving
calories: 430, fat: 13g, protein: 35g, carbs: 44g, fiber: 8g, sugar: 11g, sodium: 501mg

Nourishing Chicken Tortilla Soup

Prep time: 12 minutes, Cook time: 6 to 8 hours, Serves 8

Ingredients

1½ to 2 pounds (680 to 907 g) chicken breast
4 cups chicken broth
1 yellow onion, diced
2 jalapeño peppers, seeded and diced
1 green bell pepper, chopped
2 chipotle peppers (from a can of chipotles in adobo) with ½ tbsp. adobo sauce, puréed
1 (15-ounce / 425-g) can black beans, drained and rinsed
1 (16-ounce / 454-g) bag frozen corn kernels
1 (14-ounce / 397-g) can tomatoes, diced
1½ tbsps. taco seasoning
8 corn tortillas, sliced thinly (for garnish)
1 avocado, sliced (for garnish)

Directions

1. In a slow cooker, place all of the ingredients, except the optional toppings. Cook on low for 6 to 8 hours (or on high for 4 to 6 hours).
2. Remove from the pot. Shred the chicken breast with two forks, then place it back in the soup and stir. Serve with sliced corn tortilla strips or avocado slices of your choice.

Nutritional Info per Serving
calories: 295, fat: 6g, protein: 24g, carbs: 37g, fiber: 8g, sugar: 5g, sodium: 634mg

Creamy Mushroom Soup

Prep time: 8 minutes, Cook time: 36 minutes, Serves 6

Ingredients

2 tbsps. extra-virgin olive oil, divided
1 small sweet onion, chopped
4 garlic cloves, minced
24 ounces (680 g) mushrooms, washed and sliced
1½ cups vegetable broth (or water)
1½ cups milk
1 tsp. salt
1 tbsp. rosemary, fresh
1 tsp. parsley, dried
¼ tsp. black pepper, ground

Directions

1. In a large stockpot, heat the oil over medium heat. Add the onion and sauté for 3 minutes. Toss the garlic and sauté for additional 3 minutes, or until the onion becomes translucent.
2. Add the mushrooms and stir to coat in olive oil. Sauté for 5 minutes or until the soup turns brown because of the mushroom.
3. Reserve 1 cup of mushrooms.
4. Add the broth and the milk, salt, rosemary, parsley, and pepper. Increase the heat to high and whisk constantly while the liquid boils. Now, reduce the heat to low and simmer for 15 minutes.
5. Purée the soup with an immersion blender. Alternatively, pour the soup into a blender and purée, then return the puréed soup to the pot.
6. Pour the reserved mushrooms back to pot, and simmer for 10 minutes, stirring every few minutes.

Nutritional Info per Serving
calories: 115, fat: 6g, protein: 5g, carbs: 8g, fiber: 1.8g, sugar: 7.2g, sodium: 655mg

Easy Minestrone

Prep time: 10 minutes, Cook time: 30 minutes, Serves 4

Ingredients

1 tbsp. olive oil
1 yellow onion, chopped
1 large carrot, chopped
1 celery stalk, chopped
4 garlic cloves, minced
4 cups vegetable broth
¼ cup tomato paste
1 (28-ounce / 794-g) can tomatoes, diced
1 (15-ounce / 425-g) can

cannellini beans, drained and rinsed
2 cups spinach, chopped
2 tsps. oregano
1 tsp. thyme
Salt
Pepper
Parmesan, freshly grated
4 cups cooked pasta (optional)

Directions

1. Heat the oil over medium heat in a large stockpot. Add the onion, carrot, and celery and sauté for 3 to 5 minutes.
2. Add the garlic and sauté for additional 1 minute.
3. Pour in the vegetable broth, then add the tomato paste, diced tomatoes, and beans. Bring to a simmer.
4. Stir in the spinach, oregano, thyme, salt, and pepper. Reduce to the heat to low, cooking for 20 minutes.
5. Add the Parmesan and cooked pasta, if needed.

Nutritional Info per Serving

calories: 252, fat: 5.2g, protein: 12g, carbs: 41g, fiber: 11g, sugar: 12g, sodium: 624mg

Wild Rice and Mushroom Soup

Prep time: 11 minutes, Cook time: 1 hour, Serves 6

Ingredients

1 tbsp. extra-virgin olive oil
1 pound (454 g) mixed mushrooms, chopped
1 cup wild rice
2 carrots, sliced
2 celery stalks, sliced
1 yellow onion, diced

6 cups organic vegetable broth
1 tbsp. red wine vinegar
1 tsp. dried oregano
1 tsp. dried thyme
¼ tsp. sea salt
¼ tsp. freshly ground black pepper

Directions

1. In a large pot, heat the olive oil over medium heat. Place the onion and cook for about 5 to 8 minutes, until tender and translucent.
2. Put the carrots and celery to the pot and sauté for another 2 minutes, stirring constantly. Add the mushrooms and sauté for 10 minutes more, stirring constantly, until they reduce in size (they lose a lot of water while they cook).
3. Pour in the vegetable broth, rice, thyme, oregano, salt, and pepper to the pot. Raise the heat to high and bring to a boil. Then lower the heat, cover the pot, and allow to simmer for 30 minutes. Stir in the red wine vinegar and let simmer for an additional 10 minutes.
4. Divide the soup equally among 6 bowls and serve immediately.

Nutritional Info per Serving

calories: 360, fat: 3g, protein: 11g, carbs: 79g, fiber: 11g, sugar: 5g, sodium: 215mg

Rustic White Bean and Tomato Soup

Prep time: 7 minutes, Cook time: 30 minutes, Serves 4 to 6

Ingredients

1 tbsp. olive oil
1 (28 ounce / 794-g) can diced tomatoes
1 (15-ounce / 425-g) can white beans, rinsed and drained
2 potatoes, diced
2 carrots, diced
4 to 5 kale leaves, stemmed, roughly chopped
2 celery stalks, trimmed

and diced
1 large leek, rinsed and sliced
6 to 8 cups vegetable broth
1 small onion, diced
2 garlic cloves, chopped
2 sprigs fresh thyme
3 tbsps. tomato paste
Sea salt
Freshly ground black pepper

Directions

1. In a large pot, heat the olive oil over medium heat. Place the onion and cook for 3 to 4 minutes, until tender and translucent. Put the carrots, celery, and leek and sauté for another 5 minutes, stirring constantly. Add the garlic and cook for another 30 seconds, being careful not to let it burn.
2. Pour in the tomato paste and stir well. Put the beans, diced tomatoes, thyme, broth, and potatoes. Sprinkle with salt and pepper. Raise the heat to high and bring to a boil. Turn the heat and allow to simmer for about 15 to 20 minutes, or until the potatoes are soft.
3. Stir in the chopped kale and allow to cook for another 5 minutes or until the kale is wilted.
4. Divide the soup equally among 4 bowls and serve immediately.

Nutritional Info per Serving

calories: 161, fat: 3g, protein: 4g, carbs: 32g, fiber: 7g, sugar: 10g, sodium: 347mg

Wild Rice, Mushroom and Carrot Soup

Prep time: 16 minutes, Cook time: 9 hours, Serves 10 to 12

Ingredients

1½ cups wild rice, rinsed and drained
4 carrots, peeled and sliced
2 cups sliced cremini mushrooms
2 cups chopped kale
2 cups frozen corn
1 leek, chopped
2 onions, chopped
5 garlic cloves, sliced
8 cups vegetable broth
1 tsp. dried thyme leaves

Directions

1. Mix the wild rice, onions, leek, garlic, mushrooms, carrots, and corn in a 6-quart slow cooker.
2. Add the vegetable broth over all and place the thyme leaves.
3. Cover the slow cooker and cook on low for 7 to 9 hours, or until the vegetables and wild rice are soft.
4. Toss in the kale. Cover and cook on low for 20 minutes more, or until the kale wilts. Serve warm.

Nutritional Info per Serving

calories: 226, fat: 1g, protein: 7g, carbs: 46g, fiber: 5g, sugar: 8g, sodium: 172mg

Sweet Potato and Red Lentil Soup

Prep time: 6 minutes, Cook time: 1 hour, Serves 6

Ingredients

1 tbsp. extra-virgin olive oil
2 sweet potatoes, peeled and diced
2 tomatoes, diced
1 cup red lentils
1 cup kale, chopped
1 yellow onion, diced
6 cups organic vegetable
broth
1½ tsps. ground turmeric
1 tsp. ground cumin
1 tsp. ground coriander
1 tsp. minced fresh ginger
½ tsp. ground cinnamon
¼ tsp. cayenne pepper
Pinch sea salt

Directions

1. In a large pot, heat the olive oil over medium heat. Place the onion and cook for about 5 to 8 minutes, until tender and translucent. Put the tomatoes and ginger to the pot and sauté for 2 minutes more, stirring constantly. Add the sweet potatoes and cook for another 10 minutes.
2. Pour the broth, lentils, turmeric, cinnamon, cumin,

coriander, and cayenne pepper to the pot and sprinkle with the salt. Raise the heat to high and bring to a boil. Then turn the heat to low, cover the pot, and allow simmer for about 30 minutes.
3. Stir in the kale and simmer for about 8 to 10 minutes, until the kale is wilted.
4. Divide the soup equally among 6 bowls and serve immediately.

Nutritional Info per Serving

calories: 167, fat: 3g, protein: 8g, carbs: 28g, fiber: 5g, sugar: 4g, sodium: 262mg

Black Bean and Quinoa Soup

Prep time: 12 minutes, Cook time: 53 minutes, Serves 4

Ingredients

1 tbsp. extra-virgin olive oil
1 (15-ounce / 425-g) can black beans, drained and rinsed
1 cup quinoa, rinsed and drained
1 tomato, diced
1 cup roasted corn
½ avocado, sliced
1 jalapeño, diced
½ yellow onion, diced
6 cups organic vegetable broth
2 cups water
3 garlic cloves, minced
1 tsp. ground cumin
1 tsp. chili powder
½ tsp. ground coriander
¼ tsp. cayenne pepper
¼ tsp. sea salt
¼ tsp. freshly ground black pepper

Directions

1. In a large pot over high heat, bring the quinoa and water to a boil, stirring constantly. Turn the heat to low and let simmer for about 15 to 20 minutes, stirring occasionally. Once the liquid is absorbed and the quinoa is soft, turn off the heat.
2. When the quinoa is cooking, heat the olive oil in a large pot over medium heat. Place the onion and cook for about 5 to 8 minutes, until soft and translucent. Put the garlic and jalapeño to the pot and cook for another 5 minutes.
3. Pour vegetable broth, cumin, chili powder, and coriander to the pot. Raise the heat to high and bring to a boil. Then turn the heat to low and let simmer for about 20 minutes.
4. Stir in the cooked quinoa, black beans, and cayenne pepper. Sprinkle with salt and pepper.
5. Divide the soup equally among 4 bowls and top with the avocado, tomato, and corn. Enjoy!

Nutritional Info per Serving

calories: 435, fat: 11g, protein: 18g, carbs: 70g, fiber: 16g, sugar: 7g, sodium: 281mg

Healthy Veggie Minestrone Soup

Prep time: 6 minutes, Cook time: 32 minutes, Serves 4

Ingredients

3 tbsps. extra-virgin olive oil
1 (13-ounce / 369-g) can chickpeas, rinsed and drained
2 medium green zucchinis, cubed
1 small head broccoli, broken into small, bite-size florets
2½ cups tomato purée
4 cups water
1 large yellow onion, thinly sliced
1 tsp. Himalayan salt
Spice it up:
¾ to 1 tsp. oregano
¾ to 1 tsp. basil

Directions

1. In a medium stockpot, heat the oil over medium heat.
2. Add the onion and cook for 2 minutes.
3. Place the salt, oregano and basil (if using), followed by the broccoli, zucchinis, and chickpeas.
4. Pour in the water and tomato purée. Stir, cover, and cook on low heat for 30 minutes, until the liquid reduces by half and the vegetables are soft.
5. Serve hot.

Nutritional Info per Serving

calories: 313, fat: 13g, protein: 12g, carbs: 42g, fiber: 12g, sugar: 11g, sodium: 576mg

Celery Root and Pear Soup

Prep time: 9 minutes, Cook time: 1 hour, Serves 4

Ingredients

1 tbsp. extra-virgin olive oil, plus additional for garnish
1 pound (454 g) celery root, peeled and diced
1 pear, peeled and cored
1 yellow onion, diced
3 cups water
¾ cup organic vegetable broth
4 tarragon sprigs
2 bay leaves
1 garlic clove, minced
¼ tsp. sea salt
¼ tsp. cayenne pepper
¼ tsp. ground white pepper

Directions

1. In a large pot, heat the olive oil over medium heat. Place the onion and cook for about 5 to 8 minutes, until tender and translucent. Put the celery root and garlic, and sauté for 5 minutes, stirring constantly. Add the pear and sauté for another 3 minutes, stirring constantly.
2. Add vegetable broth, tarragon, bay leaves, cayenne pepper, and white pepper to the pot. Sprinkle with salt. Increase the heat to high and cook, stirring occasionally, until most of the liquid has evaporated.
3. Pour the water to the pot and bring to a boil. Turn the heat to low, cover the pot, and allow to simmer for about 20 to 25 minutes, until the celery root is tender. Remove the bay leaves and tarragon sprigs and discard.
4. With an immersion blender, blend the soup right in the pot until completely smooth. Divide the soup equally among 4 bowls and drizzle with olive oil. Enjoy!

Nutritional Info per Serving

calories: 79, fat: 4g, protein: 1g, carbs: 11g, fiber: 4g, sugar: 5g, sodium: 325mg

Cheesy Broccoli and Carrot Soup

Prep time: 4 minutes, Cook time: 23 minutes, Serves 3

Ingredients

1 small head broccoli, broken into florets
½ head cauliflower, broken into florets
1 small carrot, chopped
1 small yellow onion, cut in half
1 tbsp. Pecorino Romano cheese
6 cups water
1¾ tsps. Himalayan salt
Spice it up:
½ tsp. basil

Directions

1. Combine the broccoli, cauliflower, onion, carrot, salt, basil (if using), and 6 cups water in a medium stockpot.
2. Bring to a boil, then reduce the heat to medium and simmer for about 20 minutes, covered, until the veggies are soft.
3. Drain the water with a colander, reserving 2 cups of cooking liquid.
4. Place the vegetables to a high-speed blender with 1 cup of the reserved liquid. Gently blend to desired consistency, working in batches, if needed. If you like bisque to be on the thinner side, pour in more of the reserved liquid.
5. Take the bisque back in the pot and bring to a boil.
6. Stir in the cheese, then cover and allow soup to rest for about 3 minutes.
7. Serve hot with some high-fiber crackers or a piece of whole-grain toast.

Nutritional Info per Serving

calories: 106, fat: 2g, protein: 7g, carbs: 19g, fiber: 7g, sugar: 6g, sodium: 430mg

15-Bean Soup

Prep time: 11 minutes, Cook time: 6 hours, Serves 8

Ingredients

1 pound (454 g) dried 15-bean mix, rinsed
10 cups vegetable broth
3 celery stalks, cut into ½-inch dice
3 large carrots, cut into ½-inch dice
1 large onion, cut into ½-inch dice
1 large bay leaf
1 tbsp. whole-grain mustard
1 tsp. turmeric, ground
1 tsp. kosher salt
½ tsp. no-salt-added poultry seasoning
½ tsp. fennel seed
¼ tsp. black pepper, freshly ground
⅛ tsp. red pepper flakes (optional)

Directions

1. In a 7-quart slow cooker, combine the beans, vegetable broth, celery, carrots, onion, bay leaf, mustard, turmeric, salt, poultry seasoning, fennel seed, black pepper, and red pepper flakes, if using. Stir to incorporate well.
2. Cover the cooker. Cook for 4 to 6 hours on high heat or for 8 to 10 hours on low, until the beans are cooked through and very tender. Remove the bay leaf.
3. Portion 1½ cups of soup each into 4 glass meal-prep containers or pint-size Mason jars with lids. Portion the leftover soup into individual freezer-safe storage containers with lids. Cover, refrigerate, and freeze.

Nutritional Info per Serving (1½ cups)

calories: 246, fat: 1.1g, protein: 12g, carbs: 43g, fiber: 18g, sugar: 5g, sodium: 323mg

Spinach and Potato Soup

Prep time: 7 minutes, Cook time: 48 minutes, Serves 4

Ingredients

1 tbsp. extra-virgin olive oil, plus additional for garnish
1 potato, peeled and diced
1½ cups spinach, stemmed
1 cup kale, chopped
½ cup chopped fresh parsley
3 cups organic vegetable broth
1 yellow onion, diced
4 scallions, sliced
1 garlic clove, minced
1 tbsp. freshly squeezed lemon juice
¼ tsp. cayenne pepper
¼ tsp. sea salt
¼ tsp. freshly ground black pepper

Directions

1. In a large pot, heat the olive oil over medium heat. Place the yellow onion and cook for about 5 to 8 minutes, until tender and translucent. Add the garlic and potato and sauté for another 10 minutes, stirring constantly.
2. Pour the vegetable broth, spinach, kale, scallions, and parsley to the pot. Sprinkle with salt. Raise the heat to high and bring to a boil. Turn the heat to low, cover the pot, and allow to simmer for 30 minutes.
3. Drizzle the soup with the black pepper, cayenne pepper, and lemon juice.
4. Blend the soup right in the pot with an immersion blender, until completely smooth. Divide the soup equally among 4 bowls and drizzle with olive oil. Serve immediately.

Nutritional Info per Serving

calories: 141, fat: 4g, protein: 4g, carbs: 25g, fiber: 4g, sugar: 4g, sodium: 274mg

Swiss Chard Zucchini and Celery Soup

Prep time: 8 minutes, Cook time: 20 minutes, Serves 2

Ingredients

2 cups Swiss chard, chopped
1 large zucchini, chopped
2 celery stalks, chopped
1 small sweet potato, cut into small (½-inch) cubes
6 cups water
1 tsp. Himalayan salt
Freshly ground black pepper
Spice it up:
¾ to 1 tsp. oregano
¾ to 1 tsp. basil

Directions

1. In a large stockpot, combine the Swiss chard, zucchini, sweet potato, celery, salt, oregano and basil (if using), and 6 cups water.
2. Bring to a boil, reduce the heat to medium, and simmer for about 20 minutes, until tender.
3. Drain the water with a colander, reserving 2 cups of the cooking liquid.
4. Place the vegetables and 2 cups of water to a high-speed blender. Gently blend to desired consistency, working in batches and covering the top with a towel to prevent spattering.
5. Take the soup back in the stockpot and bring to a boil. Season with additional salt, if needed, and black pepper to taste. Serve warm.

Nutritional Info per Serving

calories: 94, fat: 1g, protein: 4g, carbs: 20g, fiber: 5g, sugar: 3g, sodium: 430mg

Carrot, Celery and Barley Soup

Prep time: 11 minutes, Cook time: 9 hours, Serves 6

Ingredients

1 bunch (about 6) large carrots, cut into 2-inch chunks and tops reserved	2 cups bottled unsweetened carrot juice
1½ cups hulled barley	2 onions, chopped
1 large celery root, peeled and cubed	5 garlic cloves, minced
8 cups vegetable broth	1 bay leaf
	2 tbsps. freshly squeezed lemon juice
	1 tsp. dried dill weed

Directions

1. Mix the barley, carrots, celery root, onions, and garlic in a 6-quart slow cooker.
2. Pour in the vegetable broth, carrot juice, dill weed, and bay leaf.
3. Cover the slow cooker and cook on low for 8 to 9 hours, or until the barley and vegetables are soft. Remove the bay leaf and discard.
4. Dice the carrot tops and add 1 cup to the slow cooker. Pour in the lemon juice. Cover and cook on low for 15 minutes more. Serve warm.

Nutritional Info per Serving

calories: 220, fat: 1g, protein: 6g, carbs: 43g, fiber: 9g, sugar: 9g, sodium: 240mg

Lentil Soup with Lemon

Prep time: 7 minutes, Cook time: 22 minutes, Serves 4

Ingredients

1 tbsp. olive oil	1 tsp. curry powder
1 yellow onion, chopped	1 tsp. turmeric
2 celery stalks, chopped	¼ tsp. cayenne
4 garlic cloves, minced	Juice and zest of 1 lemon
4 cups vegetable broth	Salt
2 cups water	Pepper
1½ cups lentils	

Directions

1. Heat the oil over medium heat in a large stockpot. Sauté the onion and celery for 3 minutes. Add the garlic and sauté for 1 minute more, or until fragrant.
2. Combine with the broth, water, lentils, curry powder, turmeric, and cayenne. Boil the soup
3. Reduce the heat to low. Cover and cook for 15 minutes, stirring occasionally, until the lentils are tender.
4. Purée the soup with an immersion blender until smooth. Alternatively, pour batches of the soup into

a blender and process until smooth and repeat after all of the soup is puréed, returning the soup to the pot.

5. Add the lemon juice and zest. Taste and add salt and pepper, if desired.

Nutritional Info per Serving

calories: 302, fat: 5.2g, protein: 18g, carbs: 45g, fiber: 20g, sugar: 4g, sodium: 567mg

Lemon Chicken and Zucchini Soup

Prep time: 8 minutes, Cook time: 68 minutes, Serves 4

Ingredients

1 tbsp. extra-virgin olive oil	1 tbsp. chopped fresh dill
1 cup shredded cooked chicken	1 tbsp. chopped fresh parsley
1 zucchini, diced	1 tbsp. red pepper flakes
½ cup quinoa	1 tbsp. freshly squeezed lemon juice
2 celery stalks, chopped	½ tsp. lemon zest
4 cups chicken stock	½ tsp. sea salt
1 cup water	¼ tsp. freshly ground black pepper
2 scallions, sliced	
2 garlic cloves, minced	

Directions

1. In a large pot over high heat, bring the quinoa and water to a boil, stirring constantly. Turn the heat to low and allow to simmer for about 15 to 20 minutes, stirring occasionally. Once the liquid is absorbed and the quinoa is soft, take the pot from the heat.
2. When the quinoa is cooking, heat the olive oil over medium heat in a large pot. Add the scallions and cook for about 3 to 4 minutes, until soft and tender.
3. Place the celery and garlic to the pot and cook for another 2 minutes, stirring constantly. Add the zucchini, salt, and pepper, and sauté for another 10 minutes, stirring constantly.
4. Pour the chicken stock and lemon zest to the pot. Raise the heat to high and bring to a boil. Turn the heat to low, cover the pot, and let simmer for about 30 minutes.
5. Stir in the cooked quinoa, chicken, parsley, dill and and simmer for an additional 2 minutes. Divide the soup equally among 4 bowls and garnish with the lemon juice and red pepper flakes. Enjoy!

Nutritional Info per Serving

calories: 190, fat: 7g, protein: 15g, carbs: 18g, fiber: 2g, sugar: 2g, sodium: 420mg

Creamy Broccoli and Cauliflower Soup, page 111

Lentil Soup with Lemon, page 106

Rustic White Bean and Tomato Soup, page 102

Sweet Potato and Red Lentil Soup, page 103

Garlic Roasted Tomato Bisque

Prep time: 12 minutes, Cook time: 9 hours, Serves 8 to 10

Ingredients

3 pounds (1.4 kg) tomatoes, quartered
2 onions, chopped
8 cups vegetable broth
1½ cups whole milk
2 shallots, minced

4 garlic cloves, minced
1 tsp. dried dill weed
1 tsp. honey
½ tsp. salt
⅛ tsp. freshly ground black pepper

Directions

1. Mix the tomatoes, onions, shallots, garlic, and salt in a 6-quart slow cooker. Cover the slow cooker and cook on low for 8 hours.
2. Pour the vegetable broth, dill weed, honey, and pepper into the slow cooker. Cover and cook on high for about 50 minutes. Pour in the milk and cook for 10 minutes more.
3. Puree the soup to desired consistency with an immersion blender or a potato masher.

Nutritional Info per Serving
calories: 100, fat: 2g, protein: 4g, carbs: 17g, fiber: 2g, sugar: 10g, sodium: 250mg

French Chicken, Mushroom and Wild Rice Stew

Prep time: 14 minutes, Cook time: 9 hours, Serves 9

Ingredients

10 boneless, skinless chicken thighs, cut into 2-inch pieces
2 (14-ounce / 397-g) BPA-free cans diced tomatoes, undrained
2 cups sliced cremini mushrooms
3 large carrots, sliced

1 cup wild rice, rinsed and drained
2 leeks, chopped
½ cup sliced ripe olives
8 cups vegetable broth
3 garlic cloves, minced
2 tsp. dried herbes de Provence

Directions

1. Mix all the ingredients in a 6-quart slow cooker. Cover the slow cooker and cook on low for 7 to 9 hours, or until the chicken is cooked to 165ºF (74ºC) and the wild rice is soft. Serve warm.

Nutritional Info per Serving
calories: 363, fat: 12g, protein: 32g, carbs: 31g, fiber: 3g, sugar: 5g, sodium: 470mg

Curry Yellow Vegetables

Prep time: 13 minutes, Cook time: 8 hours, Serves 8

Ingredients

4 large carrots, peeled and cut into chunks
2 medium sweet potatoes, peeled and cut into chunks
2 medium zucchinis, cut into 1-inch slices
3 cups broccoli florets
1 (8-ounce / 227-g) package button mushrooms, sliced

2 red bell peppers, stemmed, seeded, and chopped
5 cups vegetable broth
1 cup canned coconut milk
2 onions, chopped
3 garlic cloves, minced
2 to 4 tbsps. yellow curry paste

Directions

1. Mix all the ingredients in a 6-quart slow cooker. Cover the slow cooker and cook on low for 6 to 8 hours, or until the vegetables are soft.
2. Serve over hot cooked brown rice in soup bowls, if you prefer.

Nutritional Info per Serving
calories: 161, fat: 6g, protein: 4g, carbs: 32g, fiber: 6g, sugar: 9g, sodium: 562mg

Pasta Vegetables Stew

Prep time: 9 minutes, Cook time: 7½ hours, Serves 6

Ingredients

1½ cups whole-wheat orzo pasta
6 large tomatoes, seeded and chopped
2 cups sliced cremini mushrooms
2 cups sliced button mushrooms
2 cups chopped yellow

summer squash
2 red bell peppers, stemmed, seeded, and chopped
8 cups vegetable broth
2 onions, chopped
5 garlic cloves, minced
2 tsps. dried Italian seasoning

Directions

1. Mix the onions, garlic, mushrooms, summer squash, bell peppers, tomatoes, vegetable broth, and Italian seasoning in a 6-quart slow cooker. Cover the slow cooker and cook on low for 6 to 7 hours, or until the vegetables are soft.
2. Place the pasta and stir. Cover and cook on low for 20 to 30 minutes more, or until the pasta is tender. Enjoy!

Nutritional Info per Serving
calories: 248, fat: 1g, protein: 11g, carbs: 48g, fiber: 9g, sugar: 10g, sodium: 462mg

Homemade Chicken Stock

Prep time: 7 minutes, Cook time: 10 hours, Makes 14 cups

Ingredients

6 bone-in, skinless chicken thighs
2 large carrots, cut into 2-inch chunks
2 celery stalks, cut into 2-inch pieces
1 onion, cut into 6 wedges
12 cups water
1 bay leaf
1 tsp. peppercorns
½ tsp. salt

Directions

1. Mix all the ingredients in a 6-quart slow cooker. Cover the slow cooker with lid and cook on low for 7 to 10 hours.
2. Use tongs to remove the solids and discard. Strain the stock through cheesecloth into a large bowl.
3. Evenly divide the stock into 2-cup portions and freeze up to 3 months.

Nutritional Info per Serving (½ cup)

calories: 40, fat: 2g, protein: 4g, carbs: 1g, fiber: 0g, sugar: 0g, sodium: 51mg

Authentic Ratatouille Soup

Prep time: 18 minutes, Cook time: 9 hours, Serves 6

Ingredients

2 tbsps. olive oil
6 large tomatoes, seeded and chopped
2 medium eggplants, peeled and chopped
2 red bell peppers, stemmed, seeded, and chopped
1½ cups shredded Swiss cheese
6 cups vegetable broth
2 onions, chopped
4 garlic cloves, minced
2 tsps. herbes de Provence
2 tbsps. cornstarch

Directions

1. Mix the olive oil, onions, garlic, eggplants, bell peppers, tomatoes, vegetable broth, and herbes de Provence in a 6-quart slow cooker. Cover the slow cooker and cook on low for 7 to 9 hours, or until the vegetables are soft.
2. Toss the cheese with the cornstarch in a small bowl. Place the cheese mixture to the slow cooker. Cover and allow to stand for 10 minutes, then stir in the soup and serve warm.

Nutritional Info per Serving

calories: 215, fat: 10g, protein: 9g, carbs: 23g, fiber: 8g, sugar: 11g, sodium: 144mg

Broth

Prep time: 6 minutes, Cook time: 8 hours, Makes 12 cups

Ingredients

2 to 4 pounds (907 g to 1.8 kg) bones (e.g., beef, chicken, pork, oxtail, etc.)
3 to 4 quarts water (depending on size of your slow cooker)
2 tbsps. apple cider vinegar
5 to 6 garlic cloves, smashed
2 to 3 cups assorted vegetables, including scraps and ends (optional)
½ tsp. salt

Directions

1. Place all of the ingredients in a slow cooker and cover the lid. Cook on low for a least 8 hours or up to 24 hours.
2. Pour the broth through a fine-mesh strainer. Cool and store in glass containers. Chill for up to 1 week or freeze until ready to use.

Nutritional Info per Serving (1 cup)

calories: 18, fat: 0.2g, protein: 0.8g, carbs: 3.6g, fiber: 2.1g, sugar: 0.4g, sodium: 150mg

Moroccan Pork and Tomato Stew

Prep time: 19 minutes, Cook time: 9 hours, Serves 10

Ingredients

2 pounds (907 g) sirloin tip, cut into 2-inch pieces
5 large tomatoes, seeded and chopped
2 large sweet potatoes, peeled and cubed
1 cup cooked whole-wheat couscous
⅔ cup chopped dried apricots
⅔ cup golden raisins
2 onions, chopped
3 garlic cloves, minced
9 cups beef stock
2 tsps. curry powder

Directions

1. Mix the sirloin, onions, garlic, sweet potatoes, apricots, raisins, tomatoes, beef stock, and curry powder in a 6-quart slow cooker. Cover the slow cooker and cook on low for 7 to 9 hours, or until the sweet potatoes are soft.
2. Toss in the couscous. Cover and allow to stand for 5 to 10 minutes, or until the couscous has softened.
3. Stir in the stew and serve warm.

Nutritional Info per Serving

calories: 383, fat: 7g, protein: 30g, carbs: 51g, fiber: 7g, sugar: 21g, sodium: 200mg

Lentil and Tomato Barley Soup

Prep time: 10 minutes, Cook time: 7 hours, Serves 6

Ingredients

3 large tomatoes, seeded and chopped
4 large carrots, peeled and sliced
2 cups chopped kale
1½ cups pearl barley
1½ cups Puy lentils
12 cups vegetable broth
2 onions, chopped
1 leek, chopped
4 garlic cloves, minced
1 tsp. dried dill weed

Directions

1. Mix the onions, leek, garlic, carrots, tomatoes, barley, lentils, vegetable broth, and dill weed in a 6-quart slow cooker. Cover the slow cooker and cook on low for 6 to 7 hours, or until the barley and lentils are soft.
2. Toss in the kale. Cover and cook on low for about 15 to 20 minutes, or until the kale wilts. Enjoy!

Nutritional Info per Serving

calories: 347, fat: 2g, protein: 16g, carbs: 66g, fiber: 14g, sugar: 10g, sodium: 250mg

Pork, Sweet Potato and Corn Chowder

Prep time: 22 minutes, Cook time: 8 hours, Serves 12

Ingredients

1 (3-pound / 1.4-kg) pork loin, cut into 1½-inch cubes
4 large sweet potatoes, peeled and cubed
2 cups frozen corn
2 leeks, chopped
8 cups vegetable broth
⅔ cup 2% milk
4 garlic cloves, minced
3 tbsps. grated fresh ginger root
2 tbsps. cornstarch
1 tsp. ground ginger

Directions

1. Mix the pork, leeks, sweet potatoes, corn, garlic, ginger root, ground ginger, and vegetable broth in a 6-quart slow cooker. Cover the slow cooker and cook on low for 6 to 8 hours, or until the sweet potatoes are soft.
2. Whisk the milk and cornstarch until well blended in a small bowl. Stir this mixture into the slow cooker.
3. Cover and cook on low for another 15 to 20 minutes, or until the chowder is thickened. Enjoy!

Nutritional Info per Serving

calories: 382, fat: 8g, protein: 42g, carbs: 33g, fiber: 4g, sugar: 11g, sodium: 414mg

Fresh Watermelon Gazpacho

Prep time: 6 minutes, Cook time: 0 minutes, Serves 4

Ingredients

4 cups watermelon, cubed
1 small red onion, chopped
1 cucumber, chopped
2 tomatoes, chopped
1 red or green bell pepper, chopped
4 garlic cloves, smashed
1 tbsp. apple cider vinegar
Salt
Pepper
Chopped avocado, chopped cilantro, chopped cucumber, chopped tomato, and sliced jalapeño(optional)

Directions

1. In a blender, put all of the ingredients except the optional toppings. Process on high for 30 to 60 seconds, pulsing to incorporate all ingredients evenly.
2. Pour the gazpacho into a large bowl, cover, and cool for 30 minutes before serving.
3. Top with any vegetables of your choice.

Nutritional Info per Serving

calories: 86, fat: 0.7g, protein: 3.1g, carbs: 22g, fiber: 3.2g, sugar: 12g, sodium: 13mg

Italian Chickpea and Carrot Soup

Prep time: 20 minutes, Cook time: 6 hours, Serves 7

Ingredients

2 (15-ounce / 425-g) BPA-free cans no-salt-added chickpeas, drained and rinsed
2 (14-ounce / 397-g) BPA-free cans diced tomatoes, undrained
4 carrots, peeled and cut into chunks
2 medium parsley roots, peeled and sliced
2 onions, chopped
3 garlic cloves, minced
6 cups vegetable broth
1 tsp. dried basil leaves
¼ tsp. freshly ground black pepper

Directions

1. Layer all the ingredients in a 6-quart slow cooker. Cover the slow cooker and cook on low for 5 to 6 hours, or until the vegetables are soft.
2. Stir in the soup and top with pesto, if desired. Serve warm.

Nutritional Info per Serving

calories: 154, fat: 2g, protein: 6g, carbs: 30g, fiber: 6g, sugar: 10g, sodium: 469mg

Easy Beef Stock

Prep time: 12 minutes, Cook time: 13 hours, Makes 14 cups

Ingredients
4 pounds (1.8 kg) beef bones

3 carrots, cut into 2-inch chunks

2 onions, cut into 8 wedges each

2 celery stalks, cut into 2-inch pieces

3 garlic cloves, peeled and smashed

12 cups water

1 bay leaf

1 tbsp. freshly squeezed lemon juice

1 tsp. black peppercorns

1 tsp. salt

Directions
1. Brown the beef bones before you make the stock, for the richest flavor. Bake at 375ºF (190ºC) for 30 to 40 minutes in a large roasting pan, until they are browned.
2. Add the bones and remaining ingredients in a 6-quart slow cooker. Cover the slow cooker with the lid and cook on low for 9 to 12 hours, or until the stock is a rich brown color.
3. Use tongs to remove the solids and discard. Strain the stock through cheesecloth into a large bowl.
4. Evenly divide the stock into 2-cup portions and freeze up to 3 months.

Nutritional Info per Serving (½ cup)
calories: 80, fat: 5g, protein: 7g, carbs: 2g, fiber: 0g, sugar: 1g, sodium: 183mg

Bone Broth

Prep time: 14 minutes, Cook time: 10½ hours, Makes 16 cups

Ingredients
4 pounds (1.8 kg) beef bones

14 cups water

4 carrots, chopped

2 onions, chopped

3 celery stalks, chopped

6 garlic cloves, smashed

2 tbsps. freshly squeezed lemon juice

1 bay leaf

1 tsp. salt

1 tsp. black peppercorns

Directions
1. Roast the bones at 400ºF (205ºC) in a large roasting pan for about 20 to 25 minutes, or until browned.
2. Add the bones and the remaining ingredients in a 6-quart slow cooker.
3. Cover with the lid and cook on low for 8 to 10 hours, or until the broth is a deep brown.
4. Use tongs to remove the solids and discard. Strain

the broth through cheesecloth into a very large bowl.
5. Refrigerate the broth overnight. Remove the fat that rises to the surface with a ladle and discard.
6. Evenly divide the broth into 1-cup portions and freeze up to 3 months.

Nutritional Info per Serving (1 cup)
calories: 145, fat: 8g, protein: 13g, carbs: 3g, fiber: 1g, sugar: 1g, sodium: 325mg

Creamy Broccoli and Cauliflower Soup

Prep time: 9 minutes, Cook time: 1 hour, Serves 6

Ingredients
2 broccoli heads, coarsely chopped

1 cauliflower head, coarsely chopped

1 cup full-fat coconut milk

1 white onion, chopped

4 cups organic vegetable broth

Sea salt

Freshly ground black pepper

Directions
1. In a large pot, bring the broccoli, cauliflower, onion, vegetable broth, and coconut milk to a boil over high heat. Turn the heat to low, and simmer for about 30 minutes.
2. Sprinkle the soup with salt and pepper, and let the soup cool for 30 minutes.
3. Pout the soup into a blender to the marked maximum height, and blend on high until the consistency is smooth. Empty the puréed soup into a large bowl or a different pot. Repeat this until all the soup is blended. Alternatively, use an immersion blender to whisk the soup right in the pot while it is still warm.
4. Reheat the soup on the stove until warm, divide equally among 6 bowls, and serve immediately.

Nutritional Info per Serving
calories: 187, fat: 10g, protein: 8g, carbs: 22g, fiber: 7g, sugar: 8g, sodium: 342mg

Tex-Mex Black Bean, Corn and Tomato Soup

Prep time: 15 minutes, Cook time: 9 hours, Serves 9

Ingredients

4 large tomatoes, seeded and chopped
3 cups dried black beans
3 cups frozen corn
2 jalapeño peppers, minced
11 cups vegetable broth
2 onions, chopped
6 garlic cloves, minced
2 tbsps. chili powder
1 tsp. ground red chili
1 tsp. ground cumin

Directions

1. Mix all of the ingredients in a 6-quart slow cooker. Cover the slow cooker and cook on low for 8 to 9 hours, or until the beans are soft. Serve warm.

Nutritional Info per Serving

calories: 336, fat: 1g, protein: 18g, carbs: 63g, fiber: 20g, sugar: 13g, sodium: 229mg

Tomato-Fish Stock

Prep time: 11 minutes, Cook time: 6 hours, Makes 12 cups

Ingredients

2 pounds (907 g) shrimp shells, fish bones, and crab shells
1 (14-ounce / 397-g) BPA-free can diced tomatoes, undrained
11 cups water
½ cup chopped leek
1 onion, cut into 4
wedges
5 garlic cloves, peeled and smashed
1 tbsp. freshly squeezed lemon juice
½ tsp. dried thyme leaves
½ tsp. white peppercorns
½ tsp. salt

Directions

1. Mix all the ingredients in a 6-quart slow cooker. Cover the slow cooker and cook on low for 4 to 6 hours. Don't cook this stock longer, or it may become bitter.
2. Use tongs to remove the solids and discard. Strain the stock through cheesecloth into a large bowl.
3. Evenly divide the stock into 1-cup portions and freeze up to 3 months.

Nutritional Info per Serving (½ cup)

calories: 63, fat: 2g, protein: 8g, carbs: 2g, fiber: 0g, sugar: 1g, sodium: 234mg

Simple Roasted Vegetable Broth

Prep time: 9 minutes, Cook time: 8 hours, Makes 12 cups

Ingredients

1 tbsp. olive oil
10 cups water
3 carrots, cut into 2-inch pieces
2 onions, peeled and chopped
2 celery stalks, cut into
2-inch pieces
1 leek, chopped
4 garlic cloves, smashed
1 tbsp. freshly squeezed lemon juice
1 bay leaf
½ tsp. salt

Directions

1. Mix the onions, leek, carrots, celery, and garlic in a large roasting pan. Drizzle with the olive oil and toss to coat well. Roast at 375ºF (190ºC) for about 15 to 20 minutes, or until the vegetables are light brown.
2. Add the vegetables and remaining ingredients in a 6-quart slow cooker. Cover the slow cooker with lid and cook on low for 6 to 8 hours.
3. Use tongs to remove the solids and discard. Strain the broth through cheesecloth into a large bowl.
4. Evenly divide the broth into 1-cup portions and freeze up to 3 months.

Nutritional Info per Serving (1 cup)

calories: 30, fat: 1g, protein: 1g, carbs: 5g, fiber: 1g, sugar: 2g, sodium: 117mg

Chapter 10: Sides

Honey Beets and Onions

Prep time: 14 minutes, Cook time: 7 hours, Serves 10

Ingredients

2 tbsps. melted coconut oil

10 medium beets, peeled and sliced

3 red onions, chopped

⅓ cup honey

⅓ cup lemon juice

4 garlic cloves, minced

1 cup water

3 tbsps. cornstarch

½ tsp. salt

Directions

1. Mix the beets, onions, and garlic in a 6-quart slow cooker.
2. Mix the honey, lemon juice, water, coconut oil, cornstarch, and salt in a medium bowl, until well combined. Add this mixture over the beets.
3. Cover the slow cooker and cook on low for 5 to 7 hours, or until the beets are soft and the sauce has thickened. Serve warm.

Nutritional Info per Serving

calories: 140, fat: 4g, protein: 2g, carbs: 27g, fiber: 3g, sugar: 19g, sodium: 218mg

Crispy Air-Fryer Sweet Potato Tots

Prep time: 6 minutes, Cook time: 35 minutes, Serves 4

Ingredients

Cooking oil spray

1 (10- to 12-ounce / 283- to 340-g) sweet potato, peeled

1 tsp. cornstarch (plus more if needed)

½ tsp. cinnamon, plus 1 tsp. (optional)

A pinch of salt

1 to 2 tbsps. coconut sugar (optional)

Directions

1. Preheat the air fryer at 400ºF (205ºC), for 2 to 3 minutes. Spray the bottom of the air-fryer basket with oil spray.
2. Meanwhile, wrap the sweet potato in a damp paper towel. Microwave on high for 4 to 5 minutes until soft. Let cool.
3. Grate the sweet potato into a large bowl with a cheese grater.

4. Add the cornstarch and ½ tsp. of cinnamon to the grated sweet potato. Stir to combine.
5. Form the sweet potato mixture into tots that is as large as a thumb.
6. In a small dish, combine 1 tsp. of cinnamon and the sugar of your choice. Roll each tot in the cinnamon and sugar.
7. Place the tots in the bottom of the basket of the air fryer, working in batches. Cook for 15 minutes, shaking the insert halfway through.

Nutritional Info per Serving

calories: 65, fat: 0.2g, protein: 0.8g, carbs: 14g, fiber: 1.8g, sugar: 2.6g, sodium: 82mg

Mixed Potato Gratin with Thyme

Prep time: 18 minutes, Cook time: 9 hours, Serves 10

Ingredients

6 Yukon Gold potatoes, thinly sliced

3 sweet potatoes, peeled and thinly sliced

4 cups 2% milk, divided

1½ cups shredded Havarti cheese

1½ cups roasted

vegetable broth

2 onions, thinly sliced

4 garlic cloves, minced

3 tbsps. whole-wheat flour

3 tbsps. melted butter

1 tsp. dried thyme leaves

Directions

1. Grease a 6-quart slow cooker lightly with plain vegetable oil.
2. Layer the potatoes, onions, and garlic in the slow cooker.
3. Mix the flour with ½ cup of the milk until well combined in a large bowl. Gradually pour the remaining milk, stirring constantly with a wire whisk to avoid lumps. Stir in the melted butter, vegetable broth, and thyme leaves.
4. Add the milk mixture over the potatoes in the slow cooker and place the cheese on top.
5. Cover the slow cooker and cook on low for 7 to 9 hours, or until the potatoes are soft when pierced with a fork. Serve warm.

Nutritional Info per Serving

calories: 415, fat: 22g, protein: 17g, carbs: 42g, fiber: 3g, sugar: 10g, sodium: 431mg

Spicy Refried Pinto Beans

Prep time: 6 minutes, Cook time: 9 hours, Serves 8

Ingredients

⅓ cup olive oil

4 cups dried pinto beans, rinsed and drained

9 cups vegetable broth

1 jalapeño pepper, minced

2 onions, minced

4 garlic cloves, minced

1 tsp. dried oregano leaves

1 tsp. salt

Directions

1. Mix the beans, onions, garlic, jalapeño pepper, oregano, salt, and vegetable broth in a 6-quart slow cooker. Cover the slow cooker and cook on low for 8 hours, or until the beans have absorbed most of the liquid and are soft.

2. Remove the cover from the slow cooker and pour the olive oil. With a potato masher, mash the beans right in the slow cooker.

3. Cover the slow cooker and cook on low for 30 to 40 minutes more, then serve. If the beans aren't thick enough, remove the cover from the slow cooker and cook on high for 40 to 50 minutes longer, stirring occasionally. Serve warm.

Nutritional Info per Serving

calories: 444, fat: 10g, protein: 21g, carbs: 66g, fiber: 15g, sugar: 4g, sodium: 469mg

Chili Thai Noodle and Carrot Bowl

Prep time: 12 minutes, Cook time: 18 minutes, Serves 4

Ingredients

3 tbsps. extra-virgin olive oil

2 cups brown rice noodles

2 carrots, diced

¾ cup frozen shelled edamame, thawed

2 red bell peppers,

seeded and chopped

½ cup bean sprouts

⅓ cup red chili sauce

3 quarts water

2 garlic cloves, minced

Juice of 1½ limes

2 tbsps. chopped cashews

Directions

1. In a large pot over high heat, bring the water to a boil. Place the brown rice noodles and stir, leaving the heat on high and the pot uncovered, cooking them for about 10 minutes. Drain the water from the pot.

2. When the noodles are cooking, heat the olive oil over medium-high heat in a large skillet. Place the

garlic, bell peppers, carrots, and edamame, and cook for 5 to 7 minutes. Stir regularly to ensure all of the vegetables cook evenly. Add the bean sprouts and sauté the vegetable mixture for 1 minute more.

3. Place the vegetables into the pot with the drained noodles. Pour in the chili sauce and lime juice, and stir to combine well.

4. Divide the noodles equally among 4 bowls and top each with the cashews. Enjoy!

Nutritional Info per Serving

calories: 274, fat: 14g, protein: 7g, carbs: 33g, fiber: 4g, sugar: 4g, sodium: 49mg

Avocado Deviled Eggs

Prep time: 28 minutes, Cook time: 12 minutes, Serves 5

Ingredients

8 large eggs

1 large avocado, halved, pitted, and flesh scooped out

1½ tbsps. lemon juice, freshly squeezed

1½ tsps. white wine vinegar

½ tsp. salt

¼ tsp. garlic powder

⅛ tsp. onion, granulated

⅛ tsp. cayenne pepper

⅛ tsp. turmeric, ground

1 tbsp. hemp hearts (optional)

Directions

1. In a medium saucepan, combine the eggs with cold water to cover by 1 inch. Heat the saucepan over high heat and bring the water to a boil.

2. Turn off the heat and keep the pan on the hot burner. Cover the pan, and let sit for 10 to 12 minutes.

3. Drain the water and run cold water over the eggs. Once cool enough to handle, peel the eggs under cold running water.

4. Halve the eggs lengthwise. Scoop the egg yolks into a medium bowl.

5. Place 3 egg white halves, hollow-side up, in each of 5 small glass meal-prep containers with lids.

6. In the yolks bowl, add the avocado, lemon juice, vinegar, salt, garlic powder, granulated onion, cayenne, and turmeric. Mix thoroughly until no lumps remain. An electric handheld mixer works well here. Fill a piping bag with the egg yolk mixture. Alternatively, use a resealable zip-top bag with one bottom corner cut off. Evenly pipe the filling into the hollow of each egg white. Sprinkle with hemp hearts of your choice. Cover and refrigerate.

Nutritional Info per Serving (3 Halves)

calories: 201, fat: 13g, protein: 10g, carbs: 6g, fiber: 3.2g, sugar: 2g, sodium: 244mg

Herbed Leafy Greens

Prep time: 15 minutes, Cook time: 4 hours, Serves 10 to 12

Ingredients

2 bunches kale, washed and cut into large pieces
2 bunches Swiss chard, washed and cut into large pieces
2 bunches collard greens, washed and cut into large pieces

1½ cups vegetable broth
3 onions, chopped
¼ cup honey
2 tbsps. lemon juice
1 tsp. dried basil
1 tsp. dried marjoram
¼ tsp. salt

Directions

1. Mix the Swiss chard, collard greens, kale, and onions in a 6-quart slow cooker.
2. Mix the vegetable broth, honey, lemon juice, marjoram, basil, and salt in a medium bowl. Pour into the slow cooker.
3. Cover the slow cooker and cook on low for 3 to 4 hours, or until the greens are very soft. Serve warm.

Nutritional Info per Serving

calories: 80, fat: 0g, protein: 3g, carbs: 19g, fiber: 3g, sugar: 11g, sodium: 118mg

Sesame Noodle and Zucchini Bowl

Prep time: 4 minutes, Cook time: 15 minutes, Serves 2

Ingredients

3 tbsps. sesame oil, divided
1 quart water
1 zucchini, cut into small slices
1 cup brown rice noodles
2 Thai chiles
6 garlic cloves, minced

Juice of ½ lime
½ tsp. minced fresh ginger
¼ tsp. toasted sesame seeds
Sea salt
Freshly ground black pepper

Directions

1. In a large pot over high heat, bring the water to a boil. Place the brown rice noodles and stir, leaving the heat on high and the pot uncovered, cooking for about 10 minutes. Drain the water from the pot.
2. When the noodles are cooking, heat 2 tbsps. of sesame oil over medium heat in a large skillet. Put the zucchini, garlic, and Thai chiles, and cook for about 5 minutes, until the zucchini begins to soften.
3. Once the noodles have finished cooking, place them to the large skillet and mix to combine with the sesame oil mixture.
4. Stir in the lime juice, ginger, and remaining 1 tbsp. of sesame oil. Sprinkle with salt and pepper.
5. Divide the noodles equally between 2 bowls and garnish with the toasted sesame seeds. Enjoy!

Nutritional Info per Serving

calories: 296, fat: 20g, protein: 3g, carbs: 26g, fiber: 2g, sugar: 1g, sodium: 21mg

Shakshuka with Red Peppers

Prep time: 8 minutes, Cook time: 23 minutes, Serves 4

Ingredients

1 tbsp. extra-virgin olive oil
1 small yellow onion, diced
1 medium red bell pepper, cut into thin strips
2 garlic cloves, minced
2 cups kale, chopped
1 tbsp. red wine vinegar

1 tsp. Italian seasoning
½ tsp. black pepper, freshly ground
¼ tsp. red pepper flakes (optional)
¼ tsp. salt
1 (28-ounce / 794-g) can no-salt-added diced tomatoes with juice
8 large eggs

Directions

1. Heat the oil in a large cast-iron or nonstick skillet over medium heat. Add the onion and cook for 2 to 3 minutes, stirring frequently, until translucent.
2. Add the red bell pepper and cook for 5 minutes, stirring frequently, until the vegetables are soft.
3. Stir in the garlic.
4. Add the kale one handful a time. Cook, stirring continuously, adding more kale as it wilts.
5. Pour in the vinegar, stirring constantly for 1 minute to remove any stuck bits from the bottom.
6. Add the Italian seasoning, black pepper, red pepper flakes (if using), and salt. Stir.
7. Add the diced tomatoes and their juices and stir to fully combined. Cover the skillet and cook for 5 minutes.
8. Create 8 wells in the sauce with the back of a large spoon. Gently crack 1 egg into each well. Cover the skillet and cook for 6 minutes, or until the egg whites are set. You may want to slightly undercook the eggs, as they'll continue cooking when reheated.
9. With a serving spoon, portion 2 eggs and one-fourth of the sauce into each of 4 large single-compartment glass meal-prep containers. Cover and refrigerate.

Nutritional Info per Serving

calories: 243, fat: 14g, protein: 15g, carbs: 14g, fiber: 1.8g, sugar: 7g, sodium: 257mg

Zucchini, Red Cabbage and Carrot Ramen Bowl

Prep time: 11 minutes, Cook time: 58 minutes, Serves 2

Ingredients

4 cups water
2 zucchinis, cut into strips
2 carrots, cut into strips
1 cup chopped red cabbage
½ celery stalk, diced
½ red onion, cut into strips
½ white onion, diced
1 garlic clove, minced
1 tsp. miso paste
½ tsp. ground ginger

Directions

1. In a large pot, combine the water, white onion, celery, garlic, miso paste, and ground ginger over high heat. Bring to a boil, then turn the heat to low and simmer for about 55 minutes.
2. Increase the heat to high. Place the red cabbage and carrot noodles, zucchini noodles, and red onion noodles. Bring to a boil and cook for about 3 minutes.
3. Divide the noodles equally between 2 bowls. Spoon the hot broth over the noodles and serve immediately.

Nutritional Info per Serving

calories: 81, fat: 1g, protein: 4g, carbs: 17g, fiber: 4g, sugar: 9g, sodium: 152mg

Double Noodle Chicken Pho with Bean Sprouts

Prep time: 7 minutes, Cook time: 36 minutes, Serves 4

Ingredients

2 zucchinis, cut into strips
1½ cups cooked, shredded chicken breast
1 cup cellophane noodles
1 cup bean sprouts
4 cups chicken broth
3 cups boiling water
½ white onion, chopped
2 garlic cloves, minced
1 tbsp. tamari
1 tsp. ground ginger
½ tsp. ground cloves
½ tsp. Chinese five-spice powder
Lime wedges, for garnish

Directions

1. Add the garlic in a large pot over medium heat, and cook it for 30 seconds.
2. Place the onion, tamari, ginger, cloves, broth, and Chinese five-spice powder to the pot. Bring the mixture to a boil, cover, and turn the heat to low. Simmer the broth for about 30 minutes.
3. When the broth is cooking, put the cellophane noodles in a large bowl. Add the boiling water over the top so that the noodles are completely covered. Let the noodles soak for at least 15 minutes.
4. Toss the chicken and zucchini noodles into the broth. Cook for about 5 minutes, or until the zucchini noodles are soft.
5. Add the cellophane noodles to the pot with a pair of tongs. Take the pot from the heat.
6. Divide the pho equally among 4 bowls. Top with the bean sprouts and garnish with a lime wedge. Serve immediately.

Nutritional Info per Serving

calories: 264, fat: 3g, protein: 21g, carbs: 39g, fiber: 2g, sugar: 4g, sodium: 520mg

Garlicky Tofu and Brussels Sprouts

Prep time: 18 minutes, Cook time: 30 minutes, Serves 4

Ingredients

Nonstick cooking spray
1 (14-ounce / 397-g) package extra-firm organic tofu, drained and cut into 1-inch pieces
2 tbsps. balsamic vinegar
1 tbsp. extra-virgin olive oil plus 1 tsp.
1 tbsp. garlic, minced
¼ tsp. salt
¼ tsp. black pepper, freshly ground
1 pound (454 g) Brussels sprouts, quartered
½ cup dried cherries
¼ cup roasted salted pumpkin seeds
1 tbsp. balsamic glaze

Directions

1. Preheat the oven to 400ºF (205ºC). Line a large baking sheet with foil and coat it with cooking spray.
2. Place the tofu pieces between 2 clean towels. Rest for 15 minutes to wick away additional liquid.
3. In a large bowl, whisk the vinegar, 1 tbsp. of oil, the garlic, salt, and pepper. Add the tofu and Brussels sprouts and toss gently. Transfer the ingredients to the baking sheet and evenly spread into a layer. Roast for 20 minutes.
4. Remove from the oven and toss its contents. Sprinkle the cherries and pumpkin seeds on top of the Brussels sprouts and tofu. Return to the oven and roast for an additional 10 minutes. Remove from the oven and drizzle with balsamic glaze. Toss to coat.
5. Evenly portion into 4 large glass meal-prep containers with lids. Cover and refrigerate.

Nutritional Info per Serving

calories: 296, fat: 11g, protein: 16g, carbs: 34g, fiber: 8g, sugar: 18g, sodium: 197mg

Herbed Stewed Fruits

Prep time: 15 minutes, Cook time: 8 hours, Serves 12

Ingredients

2 cups dried apricots
2 cups dried apples
2 cups prunes
2 cups dried unsulfured pears
1 cup dried cranberries
6 cups water
¼ cup honey
1 tsp. dried basil leaves
1 tsp. dried thyme leaves

Directions

1. Mix all of the ingredients in a 6-quart slow cooker. Cover the slow cooker and cook on low for 6 to 8 hours, or until the fruits have entirely absorbed the liquid and are tender.
2. Store in the refrigerator up to 1 week. You can freeze the fruit in 1-cup portions for longer storage.

Nutritional Info per Serving

calories: 242, fat: 0g, protein: 2g, carbs: 61g, fiber: 9g, sugar: 43g, sodium: 11mg

Garlic Shrimp and Zucchini Noodle

Prep time: 5 minutes, Cook time: 23 minutes, Serves 4

Ingredients

20 jumbo shrimp, tails removed, peeled, and deveined
2 large zucchinis, cut into strips
1 medium white onion, cut into strips
1 yellow bell pepper, cut
into strips
5 garlic cloves, minced
5 tbsps. butter, divided
1 tsp. garlic powder
½ tsp. sea salt
½ tsp. freshly ground black pepper

Directions

1. Put the shrimp in a large bowl. Season the shrimp with the salt, pepper, and garlic powder, and toss to coat all the shrimp with the spices.
2. In a large skillet over medium heat, heat 4 tbsps. of butter and the garlic.
3. Place the bell pepper noodles and onion noodles to the butter and cook for 4 minutes, until the pepper noodles are tender.
4. Add the seasoned shrimp to the skillet. Sauté for about 10 to 15 minutes, until the shrimp are opaque.
5. In a medium skillet, heat the remaining 1 tbsp. of butter over medium heat. Place the zucchini noodles and cook for about 4 minutes.
6. Divide the zucchini noodles equally among 4 bowls and top with the shrimp and veggie noodle mixture.

Enjoy!

Nutritional Info per Serving

calories: 170, fat: 15g, protein: 5g, carbs: 5g, fiber: 1g, sugar: 1g, sodium: 465mg

Greens and Beans Stuffed Mushrooms

Prep time: 12 minutes, Cook time: 16 minutes, Serves 4

Ingredients

Nonstick cooking spray
4 tbsps. olive oil, divided
4 portabella mushroom caps
½ tsp. salt
½ tsp. black pepper, freshly ground
2 tbsps. garlic, minced
8 cups baby kale
1 cup vegetable broth
2 (15½-ounce / 439-g) cans white cannellini beans, drained and rinsed
¼ cup lemon juice, freshly squeezed
½ cup mozzarella, shredded

Directions

1. Preheat the oven to 375ºF (190ºC). Line a baking sheet with foil, coat it with cooking spray.
2. Drizzle 1 tbsp. of oil over the mushroom caps. Flip and drizzle 1 tbsp. of oil on the gill side. Season with salt and pepper. Place in the baking prepared sheet, gill-side up.
3. Roast for 10 minutes.
4. While the mushrooms cook, heat the remaining 2 tbsps. of oil in a cast-iron skillet over medium heat. Add the garlic and cook for 1 minute. Add 1 handful of kale. Once it begins to wilt, add a bit of the vegetable broth. Continue alternating handfuls of kale with a bit of vegetable broth. letting the kale cook down between additions until all of it is added.
5. Stir in the beans and lemon juice. Cook for 2 minutes, stirring frequently, until most of the liquid is evaporated.
6. Remove the roasted mushrooms from the oven. Portion the kale and beans evenly into the mushroom caps.
7. Sprinkle each mushroom cap with 2 tbsps. Of mozzarella. Return the mushrooms to the oven and bake for 3 minutes, or until the cheese has melted and is lightly golden brown.
8. Portion 1 stuffed mushroom into each of 4 glass meal-prep containers. Cover and refrigerate.

Nutritional Info per Serving

calories: 387, fat: 19g, protein: 16g, carbs: 41g, fiber: 11g, sugar: 4.7g, sodium: 357mg

Flavorful Garlic-Dijon Asparagus, page 121

Garlicky Parmesan Roasted Broccoli, page 123

Tasty Buffalo Cauliflower Bites, page 120

Honey Beets and Onions, page 114

Classic Tex-Mex Kale

Prep time: 11 minutes, Cook time: 5 hours, Serves 10

Ingredients

4 bunches kale, washed, stemmed, and cut into large pieces
4 large tomatoes, seeded and chopped
2 jalapeño peppers, minced
2 onions, chopped
8 garlic cloves, minced
1 tbsp. chili powder
½ tsp. salt
⅛ tsp. freshly ground black pepper

Directions

1. Mix the kale, onions, garlic, jalapeño peppers, and tomatoes in a 6-quart slow cooker.
2. Scatter with the chili powder, salt, and pepper, and stir to mix well.
3. Cover the slow cooker and cook on low for 4 to 5 hours, or until the kale is wilted and soft. Serve warm.

Nutritional Info per Serving

calories: 52, fat: 1g, protein: 3g, carbs: 11g, fiber: 3g, sugar: 5g, sodium: 223mg

Orange Balsamic Brussels Sprouts

Prep time: 7 minutes, Cook time: 30 minutes, Serves 4

Ingredients

1 pound (454 g) Brussels sprouts, trimmed and halved
2 tsps. olive oil
Salt
Pepper
Zest and juice of 1 small orange
3 tbsps. balsamic vinegar
1 tbsp. maple syrup

Directions

1. Preheat the oven to 400ºF (205ºC). Line a baking sheet with parchment paper.
2. Add the Brussels sprouts on the baking sheet and toss with the olive oil, salt, and pepper.
3. Roast for 20 to 30 minutes, or until crispy.
4. Meanwhile, combine the orange zest, orange juice, balsamic vinegar, and maple syrup and simmer in a small saucepan until thickened, about 5 minutes.
5. Once done, transfer them to a medium bowl and decorate them with orange balsamic glaze before serving.

Nutritional Info per Serving

calories: 103, fat: 3g, protein: 4g, carbs: 17g, fiber: 4.5g, sugar: 8g, sodium: 34mg

Simple Roasted Root Vegetables

Prep time: 17 minutes, Cook time: 8 hours, Serves 12

Ingredients

3 tbsps. olive oil
6 carrots, cut into 1-inch chunks
6 Yukon Gold potatoes, cut into chunks
2 sweet potatoes, peeled and cut into chunks
4 parsnips, peeled and cut into chunks
2 yellow onions, each cut into 8 wedges
8 whole garlic cloves, peeled
1 tsp. dried thyme leaves
½ tsp. salt
⅛ tsp. freshly ground black pepper

Directions

1. Mix all the ingredients in a 6-quart slow cooker. Cover the slow cooker and cook on low for 6 to 8 hours, or until the vegetables are soft. Serve warm.

Nutritional Info per Serving

calories: 214, fat: 5g, protein: 4g, carbs: 40g, fiber: 6g, sugar: 7g, sodium: 201mg

Tasty Buffalo Cauliflower Bites

Prep time: 4 minutes, Cook time: 30 minutes, Serves 4

Ingredients

½ cup water
½ cup flour
1 tsp. parsley, dried
2 tsps. garlic powder
1 head cauliflower,
chopped
⅔ cup hot sauce
¼ cup blue cheese crumbles (optional)
Pepper

Directions

1. Preheat the oven to 450ºF (235ºC). Line a baking sheet with parchment paper.
2. Mix together the water, flour, parsley, and garlic powder in large bowl.
3. Fold the cauliflower in the flour mixture.
4. Place the cauliflower in a single layer on a baking sheet. Bake for 10 minutes, then flip over. Bake for additional 5 to 10 minutes.
5. Remove the cauliflower from the oven. Glaze the hot sauce over the cauliflower. Return to the oven and bake for 8 to 10 minutes more.
6. Top the cauliflower with blue cheese of your choice. Broil for 1 to 2 minutes. Sprinkle with pepper.

Nutritional Info per Serving

calories: 132, fat: 0.2g, protein: 5g, carbs: 18g, fiber: 4g, sugar: 1.6g, sodium: 721mg

Quinoa with Brussels Sprouts and Avocado

Prep time: 14 minutes, Cook time: 6 hours, Serves 6 to 8

Ingredients
2 cups quinoa, rinsed
3 cups Brussels sprouts
2 avocados, peeled and sliced
1 cup broken walnuts
½ cup pomegranate seeds

4 cups vegetable broth
1 onion, finely chopped
3 garlic cloves, minced
2 tbsps. lemon juice
1 tsp. dried marjoram leaves

Directions
1. Mix the quinoa, onion, garlic, vegetable broth, Brussels sprouts, marjoram, and lemon juice in a 6-quart slow cooker. Cover the slow cooker and cook on low for 5 to 6 hours, or until the quinoa is tender.
2. Place the avocados, pomegranate seeds, and walnuts on top, and serve.

Nutritional Info per Serving
calories: 358, fat: 17g, protein: 10g, carbs: 42g, fiber: 8g, sugar: 6g, sodium: 83mg

Wheat Berry–Cranberry and Pecan Pilaf

Prep time: 13 minutes, Cook time: 10 hours, Serves 10 to 12

Ingredients
3 cups wheat berries, rinsed and drained
1½ cups dried cranberries
1½ cups shredded baby Swiss cheese
1 cup chopped pecans

2 leeks, peeled, rinsed, and chopped
7 cups vegetable broth
2 tbsps. lemon juice
1 tsp. dried thyme leaves
¼ tsp. salt

Directions
1. Mix the wheat berries, leeks, vegetable broth, lemon juice, cranberries, thyme, and salt in a 6-quart slow cooker. Cover the slow cooker and cook on low for 8 to 10 hours, or until the wheat berries are soft, but still slightly chewy.
2. Place the pecans and cheese. Cover and allow to stand for 10 minutes, then enjoy.

Nutritional Info per Serving
calories: 407, fat: 14g, protein: 13g, carbs: 59g, fiber: 10g, sugar: 14g, sodium: 129mg

Flavorful Garlic-Dijon Asparagus

Prep time: 7 minutes, Cook time: 30 minutes, Serves 4

Ingredients
Cooking oil spray
1 tbsp. olive oil
1 tbsp. Dijon mustard
Juice of ½ lemon
3 garlic cloves, minced

¼ tsp. salt
¼ tsp. black pepper
1 pound (454 g) asparagus, trimmed

Directions
1. Preheat the oven to 400ºF (205ºC). Line a baking sheet with aluminum foil. Spray the foil with cooking oil spray.
2. Whisk together the olive oil, mustard, lemon juice, garlic, salt, and pepper in a medium bowl.
3. Gently toss the asparagus to coat.
4. Lay the asparagus in a single layer on the baking sheet. Roast for 20 to 30 minutes, or until crispy.

Nutritional Info per Serving
calories: 67, fat: 3g, protein: 2.9g, carbs: 6g, fiber: 3g, sugar: 2.1g, sodium: 242mg

Thai Curry Roasted Veggies

Prep time: 10 minutes, Cook time: 8 hours, Serves 8 to 10

Ingredients
4 large carrots, peeled and cut into chunks
2 parsnips, peeled and sliced
2 jalapeño peppers, minced
½ cup vegetable broth
2 onions, peeled and sliced

6 garlic cloves, peeled and sliced
⅓ cup canned coconut milk
3 tbsps. lime juice
2 tbsps. grated fresh ginger root
2 tsps. curry powder

Directions
1. Mix the carrots, onions, garlic, parsnips, and jalapeño peppers in a 6-quart slow cooker.
2. Mix the vegetable broth, coconut milk, lime juice, ginger root, and curry powder in a small bowl, until well blended. Pour this mixture into the slow cooker.
3. Cover the slow cooker and cook on low for 6 to 8 hours, or until the vegetables are soft when pierced with a fork. Enjoy!

Nutritional Info per Serving
calories: 69, fat: 3g, protein: 1g, carbs: 13g, fiber: 3g, sugar: 6g, sodium: 95mg

Cheesy Mushroom Risotto

Prep time: 15 minutes, Cook time: 4 hours, Serves 8 to 10

Ingredients

8 ounces (227 g) shiitake mushrooms, stems removed and sliced
8 ounces (227 g) button mushrooms, sliced
8 ounces (227 g) cremini mushrooms, sliced
2 cups short-grain brown rice
6 cups vegetable broth
½ cup grated Parmesan cheese
2 onions, chopped
5 garlic cloves, minced
3 tbsps. unsalted butter
1 tsp. dried marjoram leaves

Directions

1. Mix the mushrooms, onions, garlic, rice, marjoram, and vegetable broth in a 6-quart slow cooker.
2. Cover the slow cooker and cook on low for 3 to 4 hours, or until the rice is tender.
3. Stir in the butter and cheese. Cover and allow to cook on low for 20 minutes, then serve warm.

Nutritional Info per Serving

calories: 331, fat: 10g, protein: 11g, carbs: 51g, fiber: 5g, sugar: 3g, sodium: 368mg

Root Vegetable Gratin with Barley

Prep time: 12 minutes, Cook time: 9 hours, Serves 10

Ingredients

2 cups hulled barley
4 Yukon Gold potatoes, cubed
3 large carrots, peeled and sliced
2 sweet potatoes, peeled and cubed
7 cups vegetable broth
½ cup grated Parmesan cheese
2 onions, chopped
5 garlic cloves, minced
1 tsp. dried tarragon leaves

Directions

1. Mix the barley, onions, garlic, carrots, sweet potatoes, and Yukon Gold potatoes in a 6-quart slow cooker. Pour the vegetable broth and tarragon leaves.
2. Cover the slow cooker and cook on low for 7 to 9 hours, or until the barley is tender and the vegetables are tender too.
3. Toss in the cheese and serve warm.

Nutritional Info per Serving

calories: 356, fat: 5g, protein: 13g, carbs: 64g, fiber: 12g, sugar: 6g, sodium: 424mg

Roasted Squashes Purée

Prep time: 16 minutes, Cook time: 7 hours, Serves 12

Ingredients

2 tbsps. olive oil
3 (1-pound / 454-g) acorn squash, peeled, seeded, and cut into 1-inch pieces
1 (3-pound / 1.4-kg) butternut squash, peeled, seeded, and cut into 1-inch pieces
2 onions, chopped
3 garlic cloves, minced
1 tsp. dried marjoram leaves
½ tsp. salt
⅛ tsp. freshly ground black pepper

Directions

1. Mix all the ingredients in a 6-quart slow cooker. Cover the slow cooker and cook on low for 6 to 7 hours, or until the squash is soft when pierced with a fork.
2. Mash the squash right in the slow cooker with a potato masher.

Nutritional Info per Serving

calories: 175, fat: 4g, protein: 3g, carbs: 38g, fiber: 3g, sugar: 1g, sodium: 149mg

Herbed Smashed Potatoes with Thyme

Prep time: 18 minutes, Cook time: 6 hours, Serves 12

Ingredients

3 tbsps. olive oil
3½ pounds (1.6 kg) red or creamer potatoes, rinsed
⅓ cup grated Parmesan cheese
2 onions, minced
12 garlic cloves, peeled and sliced
½ cup vegetable broth
1 tsp. dried thyme leaves
1 tsp. dried dill leaves
½ tsp. salt

Directions

1. Mix the potatoes, onions, garlic, vegetable broth, olive oil, thyme, dill, and salt in a 6-quart slow cooker. Cover the slow cooker and cook on low for 5 to 6 hours, or until the potatoes are soft.
2. Mash the potatoes with a potato masher in the slow cooker, leaving some chunky pieces. Toss in the Parmesan cheese and serve warm.

Nutritional Info per Serving

calories: 321, fat: 10g, protein: 10g, carbs: 48g, fiber: 7g, sugar: 8g, sodium: 439mg

Cilantro Lime Cauliflower Rice

Prep time: 3 minutes, Cook time: 5 minutes, Serves 4

Ingredients

1 head cauliflower, chopped
1 tbsp. olive oil
Juice of 1 lime
¼ cup cilantro, chopped
Salt

Directions

1. Place the cauliflower in a blender. Pulse until small, rice-like pieces form. Alternatively, you can mince the cauliflower.
2. Heat the oil over medium heat in a large skillet. Sauté the cauliflower for 3 to 5 minutes.
3. Remove from the heat. Add the lime, cilantro, and salt.

Nutritional Info per Serving

calories: 72, fat: 4g, protein: 2.8g, carbs: 7g, fiber: 3.8g, sugar: 0.9g, sodium: 44mg

Garlicky Parmesan Roasted Broccoli

Prep time: 6 minutes, Cook time: 30 minutes, Serves 4

Ingredients

3 heads broccoli, chopped
4 garlic cloves, minced
¼ cup Parmesan cheese, grated
2 tbsps. olive oil
Salt
Pepper
Red pepper flakes (optional)

Directions

1. Preheat the oven to 400ºF (205ºC). Line a baking sheet with parchment paper.
2. Mix all of the ingredients together on the lined baking sheet so the broccoli is evenly coated.
3. Evenly spread out the broccoli and bake for 30 minutes, or until crispy.

Nutritional Info per Serving

calories: 223, fat: 9g, protein: 15g, carbs: 24g, fiber: 13g, sugar: 3g, sodium: 238mg

Cranberry Green Beans with Walnut

Prep time: 15 minutes, Cook time: 7 hours, Serves 10

Ingredients

2 pounds (907 g) fresh green beans
1 cup dried cranberries
1 cup coarsely chopped toasted walnuts
1 onion, chopped
⅓ cup orange juice
½ tsp. salt
⅛ tsp. freshly ground black pepper

Directions

1. Mix the green beans, onion, cranberries, orange juice, salt, and pepper in a 6-quart slow cooker. Cover the slow cooker and cook on low for 5 to 7 hours, or until the green beans are soft.
2. Place the walnuts and serve warm.

Nutritional Info per Serving

calories: 100, fat: 3g, protein: 2g, carbs: 18g, fiber: 3g, sugar: 11g, sodium: 151mg

Herbed Cauliflower with Orange Juice

Prep time: 12 minutes, Cook time: 4 hours, Serves 10

Ingredients

2 heads cauliflower, rinsed and cut into florets
½ cup orange juice
2 onions, chopped
1 tsp. dried thyme leaves
1 tsp. grated orange zest
½ tsp. dried basil leaves
½ tsp. salt

Directions

1. Mix the cauliflower and onions in a 6-quart slow cooker. Top with the orange juice and orange zest, and sprinkle with the thyme, basil, and salt.
2. Cover the slow cooker and cook on low for 4 hours, or until the cauliflower is soft when pierced with a fork. Serve warm.

Nutritional Info per Serving

calories: 75, fat: 0g, protein: 5g, carbs: 16g, fiber: 5g, sugar: 8g, sodium: 212mg

Caramelized Onions and Garlic

Prep time: 8 minutes, Cook time: 10 hours, Serves 12

Ingredients

¼ cup olive oil

10 large yellow onions, peeled and sliced

20 garlic cloves, peeled

2 tbsps. balsamic vinegar

1 tsp. dried thyme leaves

¼ tsp. salt

Directions

1. Mix all the ingredients in a 6-quart slow cooker. Cover the slow cooker and cook on low for 8 to 10 hours, stirring once or twice if you have the time.
2. Refrigerate the onions up to 1 week, or evenly divide them into 1-cup portions and freeze up to 3 months.

Nutritional Info per Serving

calories: 109, fat: 4g, protein: 2g, carbs: 16g, fiber: 3g, sugar: 9g, sodium: 56mg

Chapter 11: Appetizers and Snacks

Classic Tex-Mex Nacho Dip

Prep time: 10 minutes, Cook time: 8 hours, Serves 12

Ingredients

1 (15-ounce / 425-g) BPA-free can no-salt-added black beans, drained and rinsed
4 (5-ounce / 142-g) boneless, skinless chicken breasts
2 avocados, peeled and chopped

1 cup plain Greek yogurt
1 cup shredded Monterey Jack cheese
3 onions, chopped
2 jalapeño peppers, minced
6 garlic cloves, minced
½ cup chicken stock
2 tbsps. chili powder

Directions

1. Mix the chicken, onions, garlic, and jalapeño peppers in a 6-quart slow cooker. Place the chicken stock and chili powder. Cover the slow cooker and cook on low for 5 to 7 hours, or until the chicken registers 165ºF (74ºC) on a food thermometer.
2. Remove the chicken from the slow cooker and use two forks to shred it. Take the chicken back to the slow cooker.
3. Place the black beans, yogurt, and cheese. Cover and cook on low 1 hour more, until hot.
4. Put the avocados on top and serve warm.

Nutritional Info per Serving

calories: 218, fat: 11g, protein: 18g, carbs: 13g, fiber: 4g, sugar: 4g, sodium: 286mg

Spinach and Goat Cheese Omelet

Prep time: 3 minutes, Cook time: 6 minutes, Serves 1

Ingredients

1 tbsp. extra-virgin olive oil
2 large eggs, beaten
1 cup baby spinach, roughly chopped
1 scallion (green and white parts), finely

chopped
1 tbsp. goat cheese
¼ tsp. Himalayan salt
Freshly ground black pepper (optional)
Spice it up:
¼ tsp. oregano

Directions

1. In a nonstick sauté pan or skillet, heat the olive oil over medium heat.
2. Add the scallions and cook for 1 minute, until wilted.
3. Place the spinach and cook for 1 minute more.
4. Put the beaten eggs, salt, pepper, and oregano (if using). Stir to combine well and cook on low heat until the bottom of the omelet seems firm.
5. Add the goat cheese and carefully fold the omelet in half with a wide spatula.
6. Cook for about 1 minute, then flip over and cook for an additional minute.
7. Serve hot.

Nutritional Info per Serving

calories: 294, fat: 25g, protein: 15g, carbs: 3g, fiber: 1g, sugar: 0g, sodium: 578mg

Spinach Stuffed Mushrooms

Prep time: 5 minutes, Cook time: 17 to 20 minutes, Serves 4

Ingredients

2 tbsps. extra-virgin olive oil, divided
1 (8-ounce / 227-g) package baby bella mushrooms

4 cups baby spinach
4 tbsps. goat cheese
1 large garlic clove, minced
¼ tsp. Himalayan salt

Directions

1. Preheat the oven to 400ºF (205ºC).
2. Peel the mushrooms, remove the stem and keep them aside. Place the mushroom caps in a bowl.
3. Pour 1 tbsp. of oil over the mushroom caps, then toss. Spread the mushrooms in a baking dish and keep aside.
4. Heat the remaining tbsp. of oil in a small, nonstick sauté pan or skillet.
5. Put the spinach and cook for 1 or 2 minutes. Place the garlic and salt, stir to combine well, and wilt the spinach, about 1 or 2 minutes.
6. Add some of the spinach mixture inside the cap of each mushroom. Scatter with goat cheese.
7. Bake for 15 to 20 minutes, until the mushrooms are tender and the cheese becomes soft.
8. Serve right away.

Nutritional Info per Serving

calories: 99, fat: 9g, protein: 3g, carbs: 4g, fiber: 1g, sugar: 2g, sodium: 139mg

Buffalo Cauliflower Wings with Ranch Dip

Prep time: 18 minutes, Cook time: 27 minutes, Serves 4

Ingredients

Cauliflower Wings:
1 large head cauliflower, broken into florets
2 cups almond flour
1 cup chickpea flour
1 cup unsweetened almond milk
1 tsp. paprika
1 tsp. garlic powder
½ tsp. sea salt, divided
½ tsp. ground black pepper

Buffalo Sauce:
2 tbsps. melted coconut oil
½ cup hot sauce
2 tbsps. pure maple syrup
1 tbsp. apple cider

vinegar
1 tsp. garlic powder
½ tsp. sea salt

Spicy Ranch Dip:
1 cup plain full-fat Greek yogurt
¼ cup unsweetened almond milk
1 tbsp. chopped fresh Italian parsley, plus more for garnish
1 tbsp. apple cider vinegar
½ tsp. coconut sugar
½ tsp. onion powder
¼ tsp. dried dill
¼ tsp. sea salt
¼ tsp. ground black pepper

Directions

Make the Cauliflower Wings:

1. Preheat the oven to 450ºF (235ºC), and carefully line a baking sheet with parchment paper.
2. In a mixing bowl, combine the almond milk, chickpea flour, paprika, garlic powder, ¼ tsp. salt, and pepper to make the batter.
3. Combine the almond flour and the remaining salt in a separate bowl.
4. Gently toss the cauliflower florets in the chickpea batter one at a time, shaking off any excess batter, then dip the floret in the almond flour mixture, and arrange it on the prepared baking sheet. Repeat this until all of the florets are coated.
5. Bake the florets for about 20 to 22 minutes.

Make the Sauce:

6. Make the sauce when the florets are baking. Combine the hot sauce, coconut oil, maple syrup, vinegar, garlic powder, and salt in a large bowl. Set the sauce aside.
7. Take the cauliflower from the oven, and toss it with the sauce. Take the cauliflower back to the baking sheet, and bake it for 5 minutes more to let the sauce soak in.

Make the Ranch Dip:

8. In a mixing bowl, combine the yogurt, milk, vinegar, parsley, onion powder, coconut sugar, dill, salt, and pepper, and whisk until smooth. Refrigerate the dip until it's needed.

9. Take the cauliflower from the oven, and serve right away with the ranch dip and extra parsley.

Nutritional Info per Serving
calories: 295, fat: 12g, protein: 13g, carbs: 36g, fiber: 5g, sugar: 20g, sodium: 598mg

Nutty Dark Chocolate Energy Bars

Prep time: 5 minutes, Cook time: 0 minutes, Makes 12 to 16 bars

Ingredients

24 pitted medjool dates
1 cup raw cashews
1 cup raw almonds
1¼ cups whey protein powder or egg white

¼ to ⅓ cup unsweetened almond milk
¼ cup unsweetened cocoa powder
½ tsp. coarse sea salt

Directions

1. Line an 8-inch square pan carefully with parchment paper, making sure that some of the parchment paper is overlapping on the sides, so you can use it to pull the mixture out of the pan.
2. Combine the almonds, cashews, and dates in a food processor, and process until the nuts are chopped. Place the protein powder and cocoa powder, and process again until the dates are broken down. Pour in ¼ cup of the almond milk, and process until the mixture starts to stick to itself and form a ball. Drizzle more of the remaining 1 tbsp. of almond milk, a little at a time, if needed for the ball to form.
3. Take the mixture to the prepared baking dish, and use your hands to press the mixture out as evenly as possible. Then, with an additional sheet of parchment paper on top, press the mixture out even more, until it's as smooth and even as possible. You can use the bottom of a glass as a small, makeshift rolling pin, which can help.
4. Scatter the salt evenly over the top of the mixture, and then carefully press to make the salt stick.
5. Refrigerate the bars for about 30 to 60 minutes, or until they are set and mostly solid. Then, take the bars by pulling the parchment paper up from the baking dish. Cut into 12 to 16 even bars with a fork.
6. Store the bars in an airtight container in the refrigerator, separated by parchment paper to keep the bars from sticking to each other.

Nutritional Info per Serving (1 bar)
calories: 290, fat: 12g, protein: 9g, carbs: 43g, fiber: 5g, sugar: 33g, sodium: 144mg

Crispy Chili-Lime Popcorn

Prep time: 4 minutes, Cook time: 5 minutes, Serves 4

Ingredients
3 tbsps. coconut oil
½ cup popcorn kernels
½ tsp. chili powder
Juice of ½ lime

A pinch of salt
Red pepper flakes
(optional)

Directions
1. Heat the oil over medium heat in a large pot until glistening.
2. Add 2 to 3 kernels to the pan until one pops to test the heat.
3. Add the rest of popcorn kernels, cover and cook until popping stops. Shake the pan frequently to prevent burning.
4. Remove from the heat. Transfer the popcorn to a large bowl. Sprinkle the popcorn with chili powder, lime juice, salt, and red pepper flakes of choice.

Nutritional Info per Serving
calories: 167, fat: 17g, protein: 2.3g, carbs: 16g, fiber: 4.7g, sugar: 0.8g, sodium: 43mg

Black Bean and Pork Carnitas Mini Tostadas

Prep time: 15 minutes, Cook time: 30 minutes, Serves 6

Ingredients
Carnitas:
1 tbsp. olive oil
½ pound (227 g) pork tenderloin, cut into 1-inch chunks
¼ cup low-sodium chicken broth
2 tbsps. freshly squeezed orange juice
1½ tsps. ground cumin
½ tsp. coconut sugar
½ tsp. chili powder
½ tsp. sea salt
¼ tsp. dried oregano
⅛ tsp. cayenne pepper
⅛ tsp. garlic powder
Spicy Black Beans:
1 tbsp. olive oil
1 (15-ounce / 425-g) can no-salt-added black beans, drained and rinsed

1 jalapeño pepper, seeded and minced
1 clove garlic, minced
¼ cup vegetable broth
1 tbsp. freshly squeezed lime juice
½ tsp. paprika
½ tsp. chili powder
½ tsp. ground cumin
½ tsp. sea salt
⅛ tsp. cayenne pepper
Yogurt-Lime Sauce:
3 tbsps. freshly squeezed lime juice
¼ cup plain full-fat Greek yogurt
2 to 3 tbsps. unsweetened almond milk, divided
Tostadas:
1 tbsp. olive oil, divided
6 small cassava flour tortillas
For Serving:
¼ cup chopped fresh

cilantro
2 tbsps. diced red onion
Lime wedges

Directions
Make the Carnitas:
1. Mix well the cumin, salt, chili powder, coconut sugar, oregano, garlic powder, and cayenne pepper in a medium bowl. Place the pork, and toss it with the seasoning mix to coat evenly.
2. In a large skillet over medium-high heat, heat the olive oil. Arrange the pork in a single layer in the skillet. Cook for about 6 to 8 minutes, or until the meat is cooked through, and golden brown on all sides. Pour in the chicken broth and orange juice, cover, and turn the heat to medium. Cook the pork for about 10 minutes, or until it's soft. Take the pork from the heat, and pull it apart with two forks to make shredded carnitas.

Make the Black Beans:
3. Meanwhile, make the black beans. In a skillet over medium-high heat, heat the olive oil, then add the jalapeño and garlic, and sauté until softened, 3 to 4 minutes, stirring frequently. Place the beans, broth, lime juice, chili powder, paprika, cumin, salt, and cayenne, and stir to combine well. Cook for 4 to 6 minutes, until the beans are heated through and the liquid cooks down. Then, use a potato masher to mash the beans until they are mostly smooth, but still a little chunky.

Make the Yogurt-Lime Sauce:
4. Combine the yogurt, lime juice, and 2 tbsps. of the almond milk in a small bowl, and whisk together. The texture should be thin enough to drizzle; if it's not, pour in more of the remaining milk until it is. Keep aside.

Make the Tostadas:
5. Heat a skillet or griddle over high heat. Place 1 tsp. of the olive oil to the pan, then spread 2 to 3 of the tortillas flat in the pan, taking care not to crowd them. Sauté on both sides, until they are golden brown and starting to become crisp and slightly burnt, about 1 to 2 minutes per side. Stack and wrap the tortillas in a clean dish towel or paper towels to keep them war. Repeat the cooking process with the remaining tortillas, drizzling more of the olive oil, 1 tsp. at a time, as needed.
6. To serve, evenly spread the beans onto the tortillas. Ladle the pork mixture over the beans. Garnish with the cilantro, lime, onion, and a drizzle of the yogurt-lime sauce. Enjoy!

Nutritional Info per Serving
calories: 290, fat: 12g, protein: 15g, carbs: 31g, fiber: 3g, sugar: 5g, sodium: 462mg

Spicy Mixed Nuts

Prep time: 8 minutes, Cook time: 3 hours, Makes 12 cups

Ingredients

3 cups pecans
3 cups raw cashews
3 cups walnuts
3 cups macadamia nuts
½ cup coconut sugar
¼ cup melted unsalted butter
2 tbsps. chili powder
2 tsps. paprika
¼ tsp. cayenne pepper

Directions

1. Mix the cashews, walnuts, pecans, and macadamia nuts in a 6-quart slow cooker. Drizzle with the melted butter and toss well.
2. In a small bowl, mix the chili powder, paprika, coconut sugar, and cayenne pepper until combined well. Sprinkle the mixture over the nuts and toss well.
3. Partially cover the slow cooker and cook on low for about 2 to 3 hours, stirring twice during the cooking time, until the nuts are golden and toasted. Enjoy!

Nutritional Info per Serving (½ cup)
calories: 393, fat: 38g, protein: 7g, carbs: 10g, fiber: 4g, sugar: 2g, sodium: 60mg

Caramelized Onion and Mushroom Dip

Prep time: 11 minutes, Cook time: 10½ hours, Serves 12

Ingredients

2 cups sliced cremini mushrooms
3 onions, sliced
2 white onions, chopped
2½ cups grated Gruyère cheese
6 garlic cloves, minced
1 bay leaf
2 tbsps. unsalted butter
2 tbsps. balsamic vinegar
2 tbsps. cornstarch
1 tsp. dried thyme leaves

Directions

1. Mix the onions, mushrooms, garlic, butter, bay leaf, thyme, and balsamic vinegar in a 6-quart slow cooker.
2. Cover the slow cooker and cook on low for 8 to 10 hours, or until the onions are deep golden brown and very tender. Remove the bay leaf and discard.
3. In a medium bowl, toss the cheese with the cornstarch and then add to the slow cooker.
4. Cover the slow cooker and cook on low for an additional 20 to 30 minutes, or until the cheese has melted.
5. Serve warm with crudités and tortilla chips.

Nutritional Info per Serving

calories: 263, fat: 17g, protein: 15g, carbs: 9g, fiber: 1g, sugar: 4g, sodium: 386mg

Shrimp Summer Rolls with Peanut Dipping Sauce

Prep time: 20 minutes, Cook time: 10 minutes, Serves 4

Ingredients

Spicy Peanut Dipping Sauce:
2 tsps. sesame oil
2 tbsps. natural peanut butter
1 to 2 tbsps. warm water, divided (optional)
1 tbsp. low-sodium soy sauce
1 tbsp. freshly squeezed lime juice, plus more for garnish
2 tsps. rice vinegar
¼ tsp. ground ginger
¼ tsp. crushed red pepper flakes

Summer Rolls:
1 pound (454 g) large, deveined cooked shrimp, sliced in half lengthwise
1 head butter or Bibb lettuce
2 carrots, cut into matchsticks
1 medium cucumber, cut into matchsticks
12 to 16 mint leaves
1 cup microgreens or bean sprouts
⅛ small red cabbage, thinly sliced

Directions

1. In a small saucepan over medium-high heat, heat the sesame oil, peanut butter, lime juice, soy sauce, ginger, rice vinegar, and crushed red pepper flakes. Stir the sauce gently until it's smooth. If you desire a thinner consistency for dipping, pour in the water, 1 tbsp. at a time, until you reach your preferred thickness. Take the sauce from the heat when you prepare the summer rolls.
2. Place the wrappers, lettuce, cucumber, cabbage, carrots, mint, microgreens, and shrimp in an assembly line.
3. One rice paper at a time, dip the wrapper in hot water for about 10 to 15 seconds. Put the wrapper flat on a cutting board. Beginning at the bottom third of wrapper, add the lettuce, cucumber, cabbage, carrots, mint, and microgreens, then top with the shrimp.
4. Gently fold the bottom of the wrapper up over the ingredients. Fold in the sides, then continue rolling up. Set seam side down on a plate. Repeat this with the remaining ingredients. Top the summer rolls with the dipping sauce and a lime wedge. Serve immediately.

Nutritional Info per Serving
calories: 386, fat: 21g, protein: 30g, carbs: 23g, fiber: 4g, sugar: 5g, sodium: 544mg

Homemade Guacamole

Prep time: 6 minutes, Cook time: 0 minutes, Serves 2 to 4

Ingredients
2 avocados, peeled, pitted, and mashed
¼ cup cherry tomatoes, diced small
½ shallot, minced
Juice of ½ lemon
1 tbsp. fresh cilantro, chopped
¼ tsp. Himalayan salt

Directions
1. Combine the avocado, salt, and lemon juice in a bowl. Mix well.
2. Place the tomatoes and shallots, and gently stir to combine well.
3. Put the cilantro on top.
4. Serve with some organic baked corn chips, celery, or romaine lettuce.

Nutritional Info per Serving
calories: 373, fat: 31g, protein: 7g, carbs: 26g, fiber: 17g, sugar: 2g, sodium: 163mg

Beet and White Bean Hummus

Prep time: 4 minutes, Cook time: 0 minutes, Makes about 2 cups

Ingredients
2 tbsps. extra-virgin olive oil
1 (13-ounce / 369-g) can cannellini beans, rinsed and drained
1 medium beet, peeled, cooked, and roughly chopped
2 tbsps. tahini
1 large garlic clove
¼ tsp. Himalayan salt

Directions
1. Combine the beans, beets, garlic, tahini, olive oil, and salt in a food processor or high-speed blender. Blend until smooth.
2. Serve on sourdough toast or your favorite crackers, or with some celery.

Nutritional Info per Serving (¼ cup)
calories: 107, fat: 6g, protein: 4g, carbs: 11g, fiber: 3g, sugar: 0g, sodium: 52mg

Baked Eggs with Zoodles

Prep time: 4 minutes, Cook time: 7 minutes, Serves 1

Ingredients
2 tbsps. extra-virgin olive oil
2 large eggs
1 zucchini, spiralized and patted dry
½ small red onion, finely sliced
1 tsp. chives, finely chopped
¼ tsp. Himalayan salt
Freshly ground black pepper (optional)
Spice it up:
¼ tsp. oregano

Directions
1. In a medium sauté pan or skillet, heat the olive oil over medium heat.
2. Add the onion and sauté until soft and translucent.
3. Place the zucchini, oregano (if using), and salt. Cook for about 2 minutes.
4. Using a slotted spoon, move the zucchini to make 2 circles where you can drop in the eggs. Put the eggs and cover. Cook for another 2 minutes for a runny yolk, or longer if you prefer them more well done.
5. Sprinkle with the fresh chives and black pepper, if desired.
6. Serve hot.

Nutritional Info per Serving
calories: 429, fat: 37g, protein: 15g, carbs: 10g, fiber: 3g, sugar: 2g, sodium: 549mg

Spinach, Artichoke and White Bean Dip

Prep time: 14 minutes, Cook time: 5 hours, Serves 10

Ingredients
2 tbsps. olive oil
2 (14-ounce / 397-g) BPA-free cans no-salt-added artichoke hearts, drained and quartered
1 (15-ounce / 425-g) BPA-free can no-salt-added cannellini beans, drained and rinsed
1 (10-ounce / 283-g) bag chopped frozen spinach, thawed and drained
1 cup shredded Swiss cheese
½ cup sour cream
1 red onion, chopped
3 garlic cloves, minced
2 tbsps. freshly squeezed lemon juice

Directions
1. In a 6-quart slow cooker, use a potato masher to mash the beans.
2. Stir in the garlic, onion, and artichoke hearts.
3. Stir in the olive oil, sour cream, spinach, lemon juice, and Swiss cheese.
4. Cover the slow cooker and cook on low for 4 to 5 hours, or until the dip is hot and bubbling. Serve warm.

Nutritional Info per Serving
calories: 145, fat: 9g, protein: 6g, carbs: 10g, fiber: 4g, sugar: 1g, sodium: 54mg

Raw Vegetables with Yogurt Tzatziki

Prep time: 9 minutes, Cook time: 0 minutes, Serves 4

Ingredients

1 tsp. extra-virgin olive oil
1 (6-ounce / 170-g) container Greek yogurt
1 garlic clove, crushed
1 tsp. lemon juice
1 tsp. fresh dill
⅛ tsp. Himalayan salt

Suggested Raw Vegetables:
Carrots, cut into thick sticks
Cucumbers, cut into thick sticks
Bell peppers, sliced

Directions

1. Combine the yogurt, garlic, lemon juice, olive oil, and salt in a bowl. Stir until well blended.
2. Place the dill, stir and spoon into a serving bowl. Spread the raw vegetables around the sides and serve right away.

Nutritional Info per Serving

calories: 39, fat: 3g, protein: 2g, carbs: 3g, fiber: 0g, sugar: 2g, sodium: 59mg

Protein Spinach Waffles

Prep time: 2 minutes, Cook time: 5 minutes, Makes 2 waffles

Ingredients

1½ tbsps. extra-virgin olive oil, divided
2 large eggs, beaten
1 cup baby spinach
½ cup almond flour
¼ cup tapioca flour

½ tsp. baking soda
¼ tsp. Himalayan salt
Spice it up:
¼ tsp. garlic powder
¼ tsp. oregano

Directions

1. In a nonstick sauté pan or skillet, heat ½ tbsp. of olive oil over medium heat.
2. Add the spinach and cook for about 3 minutes until spinach wilts. Keep aside.
3. In a bowl, combine the eggs, the remaining tbsp. of olive oil, tapioca flour, almond flour, baking soda, salt, oregano and garlic powder (if using). Mix to blend well.
4. Gently stir in the spinach.
5. Make the waffles according to your waffle maker instructions. Enjoy!

Nutritional Info per Serving (1 waffle)

calories: 361, fat: 27g, protein: 12g, carbs: 21g, fiber: 4g, sugar: 0g, sodium: 554mg

Onion and Carrot Hummus

Prep time: 4 minutes, Cook time: 15 minutes, Serves 10 to 12

Ingredients

¼ cup, plus 1 tsp. olive oil, divided
1 yellow onion, sliced
1 large carrot, chopped
1 (15-ounce / 425-g) can

chickpeas, drained and rinsed
Juice of 1 lemon
Salt
Pepper

Directions

1. Heat 1 tsp. of the olive oil over medium heat in a large skillet. Add the onion, stirring frequently until brown-colored, or 10 to 15 minutes.
2. Transfer the caramelized onion to blender. Add the carrot, chickpeas, lemon juice, the remaining ¼ cup olive oil, salt, and pepper. Pulse until smooth.
3. Serve with sliced vegetables.

Nutritional Info per Serving

calories: 108, fat: 6g, protein: 3g, carbs: 9g, fiber: 3.4g, sugar: 2.1g, sodium: 8mg

Easy Roasted Eggplant Dip

Prep time: 3 minutes, Cook time: 25 minutes, Makes 1 to 2 cups

Ingredients

1 large eggplant, cut lengthwise
2 small garlic cloves, crushed
2 tbsps. extra-virgin olive

oil, divided
1 tbsp. tahini
1 tsp. lemon juice
¼ tsp. Himalayan salt

Directions

1. Preheat the oven to 425ºF (220ºC). Line a baking sheet with parchment paper and keep aside.
2. Coat 1 tbsp. of olive oil on both insides of the eggplant.
3. Place the eggplant, cut-side down, on the prepared baking sheet and roast for about 25 minutes until soft.
4. While the eggplant is still hot, scrape out the meaty part into a glass bowl with a fork.
5. Put the tahini, crushed garlic, remaining tbsp. of olive oil, lemon, and salt. Mix well.
6. Serve right away.

Nutritional Info per Serving (¼ cup)

calories: 59, fat: 4g, protein: 1g, carbs: 5g, fiber: 2g, sugar: 2g, sodium: 42mg

Buffalo Cauliflower Wings with Ranch Dip, page 127

Shrimp Summer Rolls with Peanut Dipping Sauce, page 129

Crispy Chili-Lime Popcorn, page 128

Strawberry & Jalapeño Salsa, page 136

Garlic-Rosemary Potato Wedges

Prep time: 10 minutes, Cook time: 35 minutes, Serves 4

Ingredients

2 pounds (907 g) russet potatoes, washed and cut into wedges
2 tbsps. olive oil
3 garlic cloves, minced
½ tsp. salt
¼ tsp. pepper
2 tbsps. rosemary, fresh

Directions

1. Preheat the oven to 425ºF (220ºC). Line baking sheets with parchment paper.
2. In a large bowl, combine the potatoes with the olive oil, garlic, salt, pepper, and rosemary.
3. Evenly spread the potatoes on the baking sheets in a single layer. Bake for 35 minutes, turning halfway through.

Nutritional Info per Serving

calories: 234, fat: 7g, protein: 5g, carbs: 40g, fiber: 3.1g, sugar: 0.7g, sodium: 295mg

Spicy Broccoli Pizza Crust

Prep time: 6 minutes, Cook time: 45 minutes, Serves 3

Ingredients

Olive oil, for greasing the pan
3 cups broccoli, riced
1½ cups almond flour
1½ cups egg whites
1 tsp. baking powder
½ tsp. Himalayan salt
Spice it up:
½ tsp. oregano
¼ tsp. garlic powder

Directions

1. Preheat the oven to 400ºF (205ºC). Lightly grease a baking sheet with olive oil and keep aside.
2. Combine the broccoli, egg whites, almond flour, baking powder, salt, and garlic powder and oregano (if using) in a large bowl, and stir to combine well.
3. Distribute the mixture into thirds evenly and form pizzas on the prepared baking sheet. The mixture will be wet, but it will dry as it cooks.
4. Bake for about 30 minutes without opening the oven. After 30 minutes, take pizzas out, flip them over, and bake for 10 minutes more.
5. Place your favorite pizza toppings, such as tomato sauce, shredded mozzarella, and mushrooms, and return the pizzas in the oven until cheese is bubbly, about 5 minutes. Enjoy!

Nutritional Info per Serving

calories: 383, fat: 26g, protein: 26g, carbs: 18g, fiber: 8g, sugar: 1g, sodium: 547mg

Scrambled Tofu and Pepper

Prep time: 6 minutes, Cook time: 7 minutes, Serves 2

Ingredients

1 tbsp. extra-virgin olive oil
1 package extra-firm tofu, patted dry, crumbled
½ green bell pepper, thinly sliced
½ yellow onion, thinly sliced
Spice it up:
¼ tsp. garlic powder
¼ tsp. cumin
¼ tsp. Himalayan salt

Directions

1. In a small sauté pan or skillet over medium heat, heat the olive oil.
2. Add the onion and pepper, and sauté until the onion is translucent.
3. Add the crumbled tofu, and garlic, salt, and cumin (if using). Cook for 4 minutes, until all the flavors combine nicely.
4. Serve hot.

Nutritional Info per Serving

calories: 277, fat: 15g, protein: 20g, carbs: 8g, fiber: 2g, sugar: 3g, sodium: 234mg

Tuna and Carrot Lettuce Cups

Prep time: 7 minutes, Cook time: 0 minutes, Serves 2 to 4

Ingredients

2 tbsps. extra-virgin olive oil
2 (5-ounce / 142-g) cans skipjack tuna in water, drained
8 romaine or butter lettuce leaves, washed
and dried
¼ cup carrots, shredded
1 tbsp. chives, chopped
1 tbsp. whole-grain mustard
¼ tsp. Himalayan salt

Directions

1. Whisk together the olive oil, mustard, and salt in a bowl, and keep aside.
2. Combine the tuna, chives, and carrots and stir well in a separate bowl.
3. Add the dressing on the tuna mixture and gently toss to combine well.
4. Spread one leaf of lettuce and scoop some tuna on it. Repeat this until you've used all the tuna and lettuce leaves. Enjoy!

Nutritional Info per Serving

calories: 247, fat: 15g, protein: 24g, carbs: 6g, fiber: 3g, sugar: 1g, sodium: 342mg

Baked Seasoned Chickpeas

Prep time: 8 minutes, Cook time: 20 minutes, Serves 4

Ingredients
1 (15½-ounce / 439-g) can chickpeas, drained and rinsed

1 tsp. extra-virgin olive oil
½ tsp. sea salt
¼ tsp. cayenne pepper

Directions
1. Preheat the oven to 425ºF (220ºC). Line a baking sheet with foil.
2. Place the chickpeas between 2 kitchen paper towels and pat dry as thoroughly as possible. Transfer to a large bowl and coat with the oil. Stir in the salt and cayenne.
3. Place the chickpeas to the prepared baking sheet. Evenly spread into a single layer.
4. Bake for 10 minutes. Stir the chickpeas and bake for 10 minutes more, until crispy.
5. Evenly portion into 4 airtight silicone storage bags.

Nutritional Info per Serving
calories: 106, fat: 4g, protein: 6g, carbs: 14g, fiber: 5g, sugar: 2.5g, sodium: 434mg

Crunchy Homemade Chickpeas

Prep time: 6 minutes, Cook time: 45 minutes, Serves 6

Ingredients
1 (15½-ounce / 439-g) can chickpeas, drained, rinsed, and dried
1 tbsp. olive oil
½ tsp. salt

½ tsp. paprika
¼ tsp. onion powder
¼ tsp. garlic powder
Pinch black pepper

Directions
1. Preheat the oven to 350ºF (180ºC). Line a baking sheet with parchment paper.
2. Make sure the chickpeas are thoroughly dried. Discard any skins.
3. Toss the chickpeas with the oil and salt in a medium bowl.
4. Spread the chickpeas in a single layer on the baking sheet. Bake for 45 minutes or until crispy.
5. Remove from the oven and transfer to a medium bowl. add the paprika, onion powder, garlic powder, and pepper until well coated. Serve!

Nutritional Info per Serving
calories: 99, fat: 4.2g, protein: 4g, carbs: 12g, fiber: 3.6g, sugar: 0.7g, sodium: 203mg

Chia Seed Fresh Fruit Preserves

Prep time: 4 minutes, Cook time: 20 minutes, Makes 1 cup

Ingredients
1½ cups fresh blackberries
½ cup water
2 tbsps. honey

1 tbsp. lemon juice, freshly squeezed
⅛ tsp. pumpkin pie spice
2 tbsps. chia seeds

Directions
1. In a medium saucepan over medium heat, combine the berries, water, honey, lemon juice, and pumpkin pie spice. Bring them to a boil while stirring frequently.
2. Stir in the chia seeds, whisking constantly to prevent from clumping together. Lower the heat and simmer for 20 minutes, stirring occasionally. Let cool and then transfer to a 1-pint wide-mouth Mason jar with a lid.

Nutritional Info per Serving (¼ cup)
calories: 87, fat: 3g, protein: 3g, carbs: 16g, fiber: 4g, sugar: 10g, sodium: 12mg

Classic Mediterranean Snack Box

Prep time: 13 minutes, Cook time: 0 minutes, Serves 5

Ingredients
10 ounces (283 g) fresh mozzarella balls
10 ounces (283 g) green or Kalamata olives
1 tsp. extra-virgin olive oil

25 baby carrots
15 mini bell peppers
5 mini cucumbers, sliced
5 ounces (142 g) salted shelled pistachios

Directions
1. Gently stir together the mozzarella, olives, and oil in a medium bowl. Evenly portion the cheese and olive mixture into the medium compartments of 5 large three-compartment glass meal-prep containers with lids.
2. In the large compartment of the meal-prep containers, place 5 baby carrots, 3 mini bell peppers, and 1 sliced mini cucumber.
3. Place 1 ounce (28 g) of pistachios each in the smallest compartment. Cover and refrigerate.

Nutritional Info per Serving
calories: 443, fat: 32g, protein: 18g, carbs: 23g, fiber: 9g, sugar: 8g, sodium: 489mg

Cinnamon and Apple Chips

Prep time: 6 minutes, Cook time: 3 to 4 hours, Serves 4

Ingredients

3 apples, cored and sliced thinly   1 tsp. cinnamon

Directions

1. Preheat the oven to 200ºF (93ºC). Line a baking sheet with parchment paper.
2. Toss the apples and cinnamon in a bowl until evenly coated.
3. Place the apple slices in a single layer on the baking sheet. Bake for 1½ hours, then flip the apple slices and bake for an additional 1½ to 2 hours until the apples are crispy.

Nutritional Info per Serving

calories: 82, fat: 0g, protein: 0g, carbs: 18g, fiber: 4g, sugar: 12g, sodium: 3mg

Delicious Parmesan Crisps

Prep time: 2 minutes, Cook time: 5 minutes, Makes 8 crisps

Ingredients

½ cup Parmesan cheese, shredded   ½ tsp. black pepper

Directions

1. Preheat the oven to 400ºF (205ºC). Line a baking sheet with parchment paper.
2. Place 1 tbsp. of cheese at a time on the baking sheet to form 8 small mounds. Space each mound at least 1 inch apart. Sprinkle each with a pinch of pepper.
3. Gently press down on each mound with your hand.
4. Bake for 3 to 5 minutes or until crispy.

Nutritional Info per Serving (1 crisp)

calories: 29, fat: 3g, protein: 2g, carbs: 0g, fiber: 0g, sugar: 0.3g, sodium: 98mg

Flaxseed and Sesame Protein Crackers

Prep time: 2 minutes, Cook time: 20 minutes, Makes about 12 crackers

Ingredients

¼ cup extra-virgin olive oil   1 cup flax seeds
2 cups spelt flour   1 cup water
1 cup sesame seeds   1 tsp. Himalayan salt

Directions

1. Preheat the oven to 375ºF (190ºC). Line a baking sheet with parchment paper and keep aside.
2. Mix the flour with the seeds in a bowl, then pour in the water, oil, and salt. Gently stir until you get a thick dough-texture mixture.
3. On a clean, lightly floured surface, roll out the dough to about ¼-inch thickness with a rolling pin.
4. With a small coffee cup, cut out crackers and place them on the prepared baking sheet.
5. Bake for about 20 minutes, until crispy.
6. Allow the crackers to cool on a cooling rack before storing them in a glass container at room temperature. Enjoy!

Nutritional Info per Serving (1 cracker)

calories: 266, fat: 18g, protein: 8g, carbs: 21g, fiber: 7g, sugar: 0g, sodium: 107mg

Spicy Mole Chicken Bites

Prep time: 10 minutes, Cook time: 6 hours, Serves 4

Ingredients

6 (5-ounce / 142-g) boneless, skinless chicken breasts   6 garlic cloves, minced
4 large tomatoes, seeded and chopped   2 dried red chilies, crushed
1 jalapeño pepper, minced   ½ cup chicken stock
2 onions, chopped   3 tbsps. cocoa powder
    2 tbsps. chili powder
    2 tbsps. coconut sugar

Directions

1. Mix the onions, garlic, tomatoes, chili peppers, and jalapeño peppers in a 6-quart slow cooker.
2. In a medium bowl, mix the cocoa powder, chili powder, coconut sugar, and chicken stock.
3. Slice the chicken breasts into 1-inch strips crosswise and place to the slow cooker. Add the chicken stock mixture over all.
4. Cover the slow cooker and cook on low for 4 to 6 hours, or until the chicken registers 165ºF (74ºC) on a food thermometer. Serve warm with toothpicks or little plates and forks.

Nutritional Info per Serving

calories: 157, fat: 3g, protein: 23g, carbs: 12g, fiber: 2g, sugar: 8g, sodium: 249mg

Hard-Boiled Eggs with Everything Bagel-Seasoned

Prep time: 2 minutes, Cook time: 12 minutes, Serves 6

Ingredients

6 large eggs	1 tsp. garlic powder
1 tbsp. sesame seeds	1 tsp. onion powder
2 tsps. poppy seeds	1 tsp. sea salt

Directions

1. Cover the eggs with 1 inch of water in a large stockpot. Bring to a boil over high heat.
2. Cover the pot and remove from the heat. Let it sits, covered, for 12 minutes.
3. During the time, mix together the sesame seeds, poppy seeds, garlic powder, onion powder, and salt in a small bowl.
4. Remove the eggs from the water and cool in an ice water bowl for 10 minutes.
5. Peel the eggs and dip them in everything bagel seasoning.

Nutritional Info per Serving

calories: 89, fat: 5g, protein: 6g, carbs: 2.3g, fiber: 0.3g, sugar: 0.2g, sodium: 465mg

Spicy Shakshuka

Prep time: 8 minutes, Cook time: 10 minutes, Serves 2

Ingredients

3 tbsps. extra-virgin olive oil	Avocado (optional)
4 large eggs	Fresh parsley (optional)
3 bell peppers (green, yellow, red), cubed	¼ tsp. Himalayan salt
½ cup crushed tomatoes	**Spice it up:**
½ yellow onion, finely chopped	¼ tsp. basil
¼ cup crumbled feta	¼ tsp. oregano
	Freshly ground black pepper

Directions

1. In a large sauté pan or skillet, heat the olive oil over medium heat.
2. Add the onion and peppers, cover, and cook for 2 minutes.
3. Place the crushed tomatoes, salt, oregano, basil, and black pepper (if using). Cover and cook for about 5 minutes, until most of the liquid evaporates.
4. Use a slotted spoon to move the veggies around, making 4 circles in between the veggies where you can drop in the eggs. Gently crack an egg into each circle and cover the pan with a lid. Cook for 2

minutes for a runny yolk, or longer if you prefer them more well done.
5. Once the eggs are done, place some crumbled feta on top. Turn off the heat, cover, and allow the dish to rest for 1 or 2 minutes, until the feta melts.
6. Put some avocado and fresh parsley on top (if using), and serve warm.

Nutritional Info per Serving

calories: 467, fat: 34g, protein: 19g, carbs: 24g, fiber: 4g, sugar: 6g, sodium: 536mg

Energy Boosting Trail Mix

Prep time: 7 minutes, Cook time: 0 minutes, Serves 5

Ingredients

½ cup walnuts, chopped	½ cup hemp seeds
½ cup dark chocolate chips	½ cup unsweetened coconut flakes
½ cup cherries, dried	

Directions

1. In a large bowl, stir together the walnuts, chocolate chips, dried cherries, hemp seeds, and coconut flakes.
2. Portion the trail mix into 5 airtight silicone food bags.

Nutritional Info per Serving

calories: 378, fat: 27g, protein: 11g, carbs: 31g, fiber: 6g, sugar: 20g, sodium: 27mg

Strawberry & Jalapeño Salsa

Prep time: 6 minutes, Cook time: 0 minutes, Serves 8

Ingredients

1 pint strawberries, chopped and hulled	2 tbsps. cilantro, chopped
½ cup red onion, diced	1 lime, juiced and zested
1 jalapeño, seeded and diced	½ tsp. salt
	½ tsp. maple syrup (optional)

Directions

1. Combine all of the ingredients in a medium bowl. Refrigerate, covered, for 2 hours or until ready to serve.

Nutritional Info per Serving

calories: 23, fat: 0.1g, protein: 0.2g, carbs: 4g, fiber: 0.8g, sugar: 2.5g, sodium: 153mg

Simple Chocolate-Nut Clusters

Prep time: 18 minutes, Cook time: 2 hours, Makes 60 candies

Ingredients

¼ cup coconut oil

4 pounds (1.8 kg) dairy-free 70% to 80% cacao dark chocolate, chopped

4 cups roasted cashews

3 cups coarsely chopped pecans

2 tsps. vanilla extract

1 tsp. ground cinnamon

¼ tsp. ground cloves

Directions

1. Mix the chopped chocolate, coconut oil, vanilla, cinnamon, and cloves in a 6-quart slow cooker. Cover the slow cooker and cook on low for 2 hours, or until the chocolate melts.
2. Gently stir in the chocolate mixture until it is smooth.
3. Toss in the cashews and pecans.
4. Drop the mixture by tablespoons onto waxed paper or parchment paper. Allow to stand until set. Enjoy!

Nutritional Info per Serving

calories: 271, fat: 21g, protein: 4g, carbs: 17g, fiber: 4g, sugar: 8g, sodium: 6mg

Fluffy Chickpea Cookie Dough Bites

Prep time: 18 minutes, Cook time: 0 minutes, Serves 4

Ingredients

1 (15½-ounce / 439-g) can chickpeas, drained and rinsed

½ cup smooth or chunky all-natural peanut butter

¼ cup maple syrup

2 tbsps. powdered peanut butter

1 tsp. vanilla extract

¼ tsp. salt

¼ cup dark chocolate chips (optional)

Directions

1. Place the chickpeas in a food processor or blender. Process on high for 30 seconds.
2. Add the peanut butter, maple syrup, powdered peanut butter, vanilla, and salt. Purée until smooth, stopping to scrape down the sides as needed. Pour the mixture to a medium bowl. Gently fold in the chocolate chips (if using).
3. Chill the mixture for 5 minutes in fridge. Roll into 16 (1-inch) balls.
4. Portion 4 cookie dough bites into each of 4 silicone storage bags.

Nutritional Info per Serving (4 balls)

calories: 345, fat: 17g, protein: 13g, carbs: 34g, fiber: 8g, sugar: 16g, sodium: 475mg

Chapter 12: Desserts

Berries Oat Crisp

Prep time: 18 minutes, Cook time: 6 hours, Serves 12

Ingredients

⅓ cup coconut melted oil
3 cups frozen organic raspberries
3 cups frozen organic blueberries
3 cups frozen organic strawberries
2½ cups rolled oats
1 cup whole-wheat flour
⅓ cup maple sugar
2 tbsps. lemon juice
1 tsp. ground cinnamon

Directions

1. Do not thaw the berries. Mix the frozen berries in a 6-quart slow cooker. Pour in the lemon juice.
2. In a large bowl, mix the flour, maple sugar, oats, and cinnamon until well combined. Toss in the melted coconut oil until crumbly.
3. Place the oat mixture over the fruit in the slow cooker.
4. Cover the slow cooker and cook on low for 5 to 6 hours, or until the fruit is bubbling and the topping is browned.

Nutritional Info per Serving
calories: 219, fat: 8g, protein: 5g, carbs: 37g, fiber: 7g, sugar: 12g, sodium: 9mg

Dark Chocolate Avocado Strawberry Bowl

Prep time: 8 minutes, Cook time: 0 minutes, Serves 2

Ingredients

1 avocado, halved and pitted
8 fresh strawberries, chopped
⅓ cup cacao powder
¼ cup organic maple syrup
2 tbsps. pistachios, chopped
2 tbsps. unsweetened almond milk
1 tsp. pure vanilla extract
¼ tsp. sea salt

Directions

1. Combine the avocado, cacao powder, maple syrup, unsweetened almond milk, vanilla, and salt in a blender. Blend until thick and smooth, scraping down the sides of the blender if needed.
2. Divide the avocado pudding equally between 2 bowls. Refrigerate for about 30 minutes.
3. Top with the strawberries and pistachios. Serve right away.

Nutritional Info per Serving
calories: 341, fat: 20g, protein: 7g, carbs: 47g, fiber: 14g, sugar: 26g, sodium: 317mg

Raspberry Cherry Dessert Bowl

Prep time: 18 minutes, Cook time: 0 minutes, Serves 4

Ingredients

1 (13½-ounce / 383-g) can chilled full-fat coconut milk
1 cup fresh raspberries
1 cup cherries, pitted
2 tbsps. toasted almonds, chopped
2 tbsps. unsweetened coconut flakes
1 tbsp. organic maple syrup
1 tbsp. chia seeds
1½ tsps. pure vanilla extract, divided
1 tsp. freshly squeezed lemon juice
1 tsp. raw honey
Pinch sea salt

Directions

1. Add the raspberries, cherries, maple syrup, 1 tsp. vanilla, lemon juice, and salt in a food processor, and process until smooth. With the food processor running, gently add the chia seeds and continue processing until completely incorporated, about 5 to 10 seconds.
2. Scrape the jam into a glass jar, cover, and chill it in the refrigerator until gelled, about 15 to 20 minutes.
3. Remove the chilled can of coconut milk from the refrigerator; the solids will rise to the top. Gently turn the can upside down, open the bottom, and pour out the liquid.
4. Spoon the hardened coconut cream into a bowl, and whip it with an electric hand mixer until fluffy and smooth with soft peaks, for about 3 minutes. Place the remaining ½ tsp. vanilla and the honey to the coconut cream, and whip it again until creamy.
5. Alternate layers of the raspberry cherry jam and the coconut cream in 4 bowls. Top with the almonds and coconut flakes. Serve immediately.

Nutritional Info per Serving
calories: 306, fat: 25g, protein: 4g, carbs: 21g, fiber: 6g, sugar: 13g, sodium: 25mg

Classic Dark Chocolate-Sea Salt Popcorn

Prep time: 2 minutes, Cook time: 8 minutes, Serves 4

Ingredients
3 tbsps., plus 2 tsps. coconut oil
½ cup popcorn kernels
⅔ cup dark chocolate
Sea salt

Directions
1. Line a baking sheet with parchment paper.
2. Add 3 tbsps. of oil over high heat pot.
3. Testing out heat, add 2 to 3 kernels until one pops. Add the remaining popcorn kernels, cover, and cook, shaking the pot occasionally to prevent burning, until the popping stops.
4. Transfer the popcorn onto the baking sheet and cool for 5 minutes.
5. Meanwhile, melt the chocolate and the remaining 2 tsps. of coconut oil in the microwave in 30-second intervals. Stir between intervals and continue until the chocolate has melted.
6. Drizzle the chocolate over the popcorn, then sprinkle with salt before using.

Nutritional Info per Serving
calories: 320, fat: 21g, protein: 5g, carbs: 33g, fiber: 6g, sugar: 5g, sodium: 13mg

Grilled Peach, Plum and Coconut Cream Bowl

Prep time: 7 minutes, Cook time: 5 minutes, Serves 4

Ingredients
1 (13½-ounce / 383-g) can full-fat coconut milk, chilled
2 peaches, halved and pitted
2 plums, halved and pitted
2 tbsps. toasted walnuts, chopped
1 tsp. raw honey
½ tsp. pure vanilla extract
Dash ground cinnamon

Directions
1. Preheat the grill to high.
2. Remove the chilled can of coconut milk from the refrigerator; the solids will rise to the top. Gently turn the can upside down, open it from the bottom, and pour out the liquid.
3. Spoon the hardened coconut cream into a bowl, and whip it with an electric hand mixer until fluffy and smooth with soft peaks, for about 3 minutes. Place the vanilla and honey to the coconut cream, and whip it again until creamy. Keep aside.
4. Arrange a sheet of aluminum foil on the surface of the grill and put the peach and plum halves cut-side down on the foil. Grill them for about 4 to 5 minutes, until warmed through and evenly marked.
5. Divide the fruit equally among 4 bowls and top with a generous portion of coconut cream. Scatter with the walnuts and cinnamon. Enjoy!

Nutritional Info per Serving
calories: 296, fat: 25g, protein: 4g, carbs: 18g, fiber: 4g, sugar: 14g, sodium: 15mg

Chocolate Chip Zucchini Muffins

Prep time: 11 minutes, Cook time: 14 to 16 minutes, Makes 12 muffins

Ingredients
2 tbsps. melted coconut oil, plus more for greasing the pan
2 eggs
2 medium zucchinis, shredded
1½ cups spelt flour
1 cup unsweetened applesauce
½ cup dark chocolate chips, plus more for topping
½ cup chocolate protein powder
¼ cup coconut sugar
2 tbsps. rolled oats
2 tbsps. unsweetened cocoa powder
2 tsps. baking soda
1 tsp. ground cinnamon
¼ tsp. vanilla extract
¼ tsp. sea salt

Directions
1. Preheat the oven to 350ºF (180ºC), and lightly grease a 12-cup muffin pan with coconut oil.
2. Combine the coconut oil, coconut sugar, eggs, applesauce, and vanilla in a large mixing bowl. Whisk together until well blended.
3. Place the spelt flour, protein powder, baking soda, cocoa powder, cinnamon, and salt. Stir to combine well, taking care not to overmix.
4. Put the zucchinis and chocolate chips, and gently fold them into the mixture until well blended.
5. Ladle the batter into the muffin cups until each cup is filled almost full. Scatter a few dark chocolate chips and some rolled oats on top of each muffin.
6. Bake the muffins for about 14 to 16 minutes, or until they become golden brown on top and a toothpick inserted into the center comes out clean.
7. Take the muffins to a cooling rack to cool completely. Enjoy!

Nutritional Info per Serving (1 muffin)
calories: 169, fat: 7g, protein: 6g, carbs: 20g, fiber: 3g, sugar: 6g, sodium: 295mg

Homemade Granola with Walnut

Prep time: 2 minutes, Cook time: 15 minutes, Makes 15 ounces (425 g)

Ingredients

¼ cup coconut oil

1 cup walnuts

1 cup rolled oats

½ cup shredded coconut

¼ cup maple syrup

Directions

1. Preheat the oven to 400ºF (205ºC).
2. In a bowl, mix the walnuts, oats, and shredded coconut thoroughly, then keep aside.
3. Combine the maple syrup and coconut oil in a small saucepan, and bring just to a boil.
4. Add the warm maple and coconut oil mixture over the dry mixture. Mix to combine well.
5. Place the granola in a single layer on a baking sheet lined with parchment paper.
6. Bake for about 15 minutes.
7. Allow the granola to cool completely before storing it in a glass container with a lid.

Nutritional Info per Serving (3 ounces / 85 g)
calories: 389, fat: 30g, protein: 7g, carbs: 27g, fiber: 4g, sugar: 10g, sodium: 4mg

Fresh Raspberry Lemon Bars

Prep time: 8 minutes, Cook time: 40 minutes, Makes 12 bars

Ingredients

Almond Crust:

Cooking oil spray

1 cup almond flour

2 tbsps. ghee or butter, melted

2 tbsps. honey

1 large egg

½ tsp. pure vanilla extract

A pinch of salt

Lemon Filling:

4 large eggs

⅓ cup honey

Zest and juice of 4 lemons (½ cup lemon juice)

¼ cup tapioca flour

1 cup raspberries

Directions

Make the Almond Crust:

1. Preheat the oven to 350ºF (180ºC). Lightly coat the inside of an 8-by-8-inch baking dish with spray.
2. In a medium bowl, mix together all of the ingredients for the almond crust. Transfer the dough into the baking dish. Press the dough into the bottom of the baking dish with a spatula. The dough should cover the bottom of the dish in an even layer. Bake for 15 to 20 minutes.

Make the Lemon Filling:

3. Mix together the eggs, honey, lemon zest, lemon juice, and tapioca flour.
4. When the almond crust has set, remove it from the oven and sprinkle the raspberries on top in an even layer. Pour the lemon filling over the raspberries.
5. Bake for 20 minutes more, or until cooked through.

Nutritional Info per Serving (1 bar)
calories: 164, fat: 10g, protein: 6g, carbs: 16g, fiber: 2.4g, sugar: 9g, sodium: 48mg

Sweet Potato Chocolate Chip Pancakes

Prep time: 7 minutes, Cook time: 15 minutes, Makes 8 (4-inch) pancakes

Ingredients

Pancakes:

1 egg

1 cup cooked and mashed sweet potato

¾ cup unsweetened almond milk

⅔ cup rolled oats

2 tbsps. dark chocolate chips, plus more for topping

1 tbsp. melted coconut oil and divided

2 tsps. baking powder

½ tsp. ground cinnamon

½ tsp. vanilla extract

⅛ tsp. ground nutmeg

⅛ tsp. sea salt

For Serving:

1 ripe banana, sliced

Pure maple syrup

Directions

1. To make the pancakes, in a blender or food processor, place the sweet potato, milk, oats, egg, cinnamon, vanilla, baking powder, nutmeg, and salt. Blend until entirely smooth. Gently fold in the chocolate chips.
2. In a griddle or skillet over medium-high heat, heat about 1 tsp. of the coconut oil. Once the pan is hot, add about ¼ cup of the batter onto the surface.
3. Cook the pancake for about 3 to 4 minutes, until the edges start to turn from shiny to dull and bubbles appear in the center of the pancake. The entire top of the pancake should look dull. The pancake will be tender, so flip gently.
4. Flip and cook for 2 to 3 minutes more, or until golden brown. Repeat this with the remaining batter, drizzling more of the remaining coconut oil, a tsp. at a time, to grease the griddle, as needed.
5. For serving, place the chocolate chips, maple syrup, and banana slices on the pancakes. Enjoy!

Nutritional Info per Serving (1 pancake)
calories: 111, fat: 4g, protein: 3g, carbs: 18g, fiber: 3g, sugar: 6g, sodium: 70mg

Salted Chocolate Coconut Macaroons

Prep time: 8 minutes, Cook time: 20 minutes, Makes 24 macaroons

Ingredients
½ cup maple syrup
1 tsp. pure vanilla extract
2 large eggs
2 cups unsweetened

coconut flakes
½ cup dark chocolate
1 tsp. coconut oil
A pinch of salt

Directions
1. Preheat the oven to 350ºF (180ºC). Line a large baking sheet with parchment paper.
2. In a large bowl, whisk together the maple syrup, vanilla, and eggs. Add the coconut and mix well.
3. Form the coconut mixture into 24 even-size balls. Space out the macaroons evenly on the baking sheet. Bake for 20 minutes.
4. Remove from the oven and cool for about 5 minutes.
5. Meanwhile, melt the chocolate and the coconut oil in the microwave in 30-second intervals. Stir between intervals and continue until melted.
6. Drizzle the chocolate over macaroons and sprinkle with salt before serving.

Nutritional Info per Serving
calories: 98, fat: 6.2g, protein: 1.5g, carbs: 7g, fiber: 1.3g, sugar: 4g, sodium: 18mg

Chocolate Peanut Butter Truffles with Date

Prep time: 35 minutes, Cook time: 0 minutes, Makes 12 truffles

Ingredients
1 cup walnuts
1 cup tahini
12 fresh dates, pitted
3½ ounces (99 g) dark

chocolate (at least 85% dark)
½ cup chocolate peanut butter powder

Directions
1. Soak the walnuts and dates under cold water for at least 30 minutes.
2. In a blender or food processor, combine the walnuts and dates and blend until the mixture is thick and sticky. Transfer the mixture to a bowl.
3. Place the tahini and chocolate peanut butter powder and mix until incorporated well.
4. Shape the batter into 12 bite-size balls, arrange them on a plate, and freeze for 15 minutes.
5. Melt most of the chocolate and ladle some over the semi-frozen truffles. Use a fork to shred the rest of the chocolate for topping.
6. Top with some shredded chocolate. Place the truffles back in the freezer overnight.
7. The next day, take the truffles to a covered glass container and refrigerate for up to a few days.

Nutritional Info per Serving (1 truffle)
calories: 180, fat: 14g, protein: 5g, carbs: 10g, fiber: 3g, sugar: 6g, sodium: 42mg

Clean Eating Chocolate Brownies

Prep time: 7 minutes, Cook time: 5 hours, Serves 12

Ingredients
5 tbsps. melted coconut oil
4 eggs
1½ cups whole-wheat pastry flour
1 cup mashed ripe bananas (about 2 medium)

1 cup mashed peeled ripe pears
¾ cup unsweetened cocoa powder
½ cup coconut sugar
½ cup honey
1 tsp. baking powder
2 tsps. vanilla extract

Directions
1. Tear off two long strips of heavy-duty foil and gently fold to make long thin strips. Put in a 6-quart slow cooker to make an X. Then line the slow cooker with parchment paper on top of the foil.
2. In a medium bowl, combine the whole-wheat pastry flour, baking powder and cocoa powder, and stir to mix well.
3. In another medium bowl, combine the melted coconut oil, mashed bananas, mashed pears, honey, eggs, coconut sugar, and vanilla and mix well.
4. Pour the banana mixture into the flour mixture just until combined.
5. Ladle the batter into the slow cooker onto the parchment paper.
6. Cover the slow cooker and cook on low for 4 to 5 hours or until a toothpick inserted near the center comes out with just a few moist crumbs attached to it.
7. Gently remove the brownie with the foil sling. Let cool, then transfer the brownie from the parchment paper and cut into squares to serve.

Nutritional Info per Serving
calories: 260, fat: 8g, protein: 2g, carbs: 43g, fiber: 5g, sugar: 25g, sodium: 47mg

Baked Apples and Walnuts Oatmeal

Prep time: 4 minutes, Cook time: 35 minutes, Serves 4

Ingredients

Coconut oil spray (optional)
2 apples, peeled, cored, and halved
1 cup steel-cut oats
2 cups water
4 tbsps. chopped walnuts
1 tsp. cinnamon

Directions

1. Preheat the oven to 375ºF (190ºC).
2. Place the apples cut-side up on a small baking sheet, then lightly spray with coconut oil (if using), and scatter with cinnamon.
3. Bake for about 15 minutes, or until tender.
4. Meanwhile, bring the water to a boil in a small saucepan.
5. Place the oats, reduce the heat to low, cover, and cook for 20 minutes.
6. Remove from the heat and keep aside.
7. In each of 4 serving bowls, add a quarter of the oatmeal, ½ apple, and a tbsp. of walnuts on top.

Nutritional Info per Serving

calories: 248, fat: 7g, protein: 6g, carbs: 43g, fiber: 6g, sugar: 10g, sodium: 0mg

Chocolate Peanut Butter Freezer Fudge

Prep time: 10 minutes, Cook time: 0 minutes, Serves 10

Ingredients

Chocolate:
2 ounces (57 g) 70 percent dark chocolate
¼ cup creamy unsweetened peanut butter
Peanut Butter Layer:
1 cup creamy unsweetened peanut butter
3 tbsps. coconut oil
3 tbsps. maple syrup
½ tsp. pure vanilla extract

Directions

Make the Chocolate:
1. Melt the chocolate and the peanut butter in the microwave in 30-second intervals. Stir between intervals and continue until the chocolate has melted.

Make the Peanut Butter Layer:
2. Combine the peanut butter, coconut oil, maple syrup, and vanilla. Microwave on high in 30-second intervals. Stir between intervals and continue until the coconut oil has melted. Mix well.

Make the Fudge:
3. Line an 8-by-8-inch baking dish with parchment paper.
4. Pour in the peanut butter layer.
5. Scoop dollops of chocolate on the top of the peanut butter layer. Swirl the chocolate dollops with a knife.
6. Place the fudge in the freezer for 45 to 60 minutes.
7. Lift up on the parchment paper. Cut into squares with a serrated knife.
8. Serve immediately or seal in a freezer-safe bag and store in the freezer for up to 1 month.

Nutritional Info per Serving

calories: 287, fat: 22g, protein: 8g, carbs: 12g, fiber: 2.2g, sugar: 7g, sodium: 148mg

Mocha Cheesecake Brownies

Prep time: 9 minutes, Cook time: 30 minutes, Makes 12 brownies

Ingredients

Brownies:
½ cup butter, softened, plus more for greasing
1 cup coconut sugar
⅔ cup unsweetened cocoa powder
2 large eggs
1 tsp. pure vanilla extract
2 tbsps. brewed coffee
(at room temperature) or cold brew
½ cup chocolate chips
Cheesecake:
8 ounces (227 g) cream cheese
1 large egg
2 tbsps. maple syrup

Directions

Make the Brownies:
1. Preheat the oven 350ºF (180ºC). Grease the inside of an 8-by-8-inch baking dish with butter.
2. In a large bowl, mix together the butter, sugar, cocoa, eggs, vanilla, and coffee, then fold in the chocolate chips.
3. Pour the brownie batter into the baking dish.

Make the Cheesecake:
4. In a separate large bowl, use a whisk or an electric mixer to mix the cream cheese, egg, and maple syrup.
5. Scoop dollops of cheesecake on the top of the brownie batter. Swirl the cheesecake dollops with a knife.
6. Bake the brownies for 30 minutes or until the center is no longer tacky. Test with a toothpick which should be inserted in the center but comes out clean.

Nutritional Info per Serving

calories: 284, fat: 18g, protein: 6g, carbs: 27g, fiber: 2.3g, sugar: 12g, sodium: 142mg

Strawberry Shortcake Cake

Prep time: 9 minutes, Cook time: 5 minutes, Serves 1

Ingredients
1 tbsp. butter or ghee
2 tbsps. milk of choice
½ tsp. pure vanilla extract
¼ cup oat flour (or flour of choice)
½ tsp. baking powder
1 tbsp. maple syrup
1 large egg
A pinch of salt
2 chopped strawberries, plus 1 strawberry, sliced, for topping

Directions
1. Put the butter in a mug and microwave it for 30 seconds to 1 minute, checking every 20 seconds.
2. Whisk in the milk and the vanilla. Add the flour, baking powder, syrup, egg, salt, and chopped strawberries. Combine.
3. Microwave until firm, for 90 seconds to 2 minutes.
4. Adorn with the remaining strawberry and serve immediately!

Nutritional Info per Serving
calories: 374, fat: 17g, protein: 11g, carbs: 42g, fiber: 6g, sugar: 29g, sodium: 247mg

Apple-Cranberries Oatmeal Bread Pudding

Prep time: 11 minutes, Cook time: 8 hours, Serves 8

Ingredients
3 tbsps. melted coconut oil
8 slices oatmeal bread, cubed
3 apples, peeled and chopped
3 eggs, beaten
2 cups quick-cooking oatmeal
2 cups canned coconut milk
1 cup dried cranberries
⅓ cup coconut sugar
2 tsps. vanilla extract
1 tsp. ground cinnamon

Directions
1. Mix the bread cubes, oatmeal, apples, and cranberries in a 6-quart slow cooker.
2. In a large bowl, mix the eggs, coconut milk, coconut sugar, cinnamon, vanilla, and melted coconut oil, and mix until well combined. Pour the mixture into the slow cooker.
3. Cover the slow cooker and cook on low for 6 to 8 hours, or until a food thermometer registers 165ºF (74ºC). Serve warm.

Nutritional Info per Serving
calories: 491, fat: 21g, protein: 10g, carbs: 69g, fiber: 9g, sugar: 32g, sodium: 147mg

Lemon Poppy Seed Pancakes with Yogurt Topping

Prep time: 5 minutes, Cook time: 20 minutes, Makes 8 (4-inch) pancakes

Ingredients
Lemon Yogurt Topping:
1 tbsp. pure maple syrup
¼ cup plain full-fat Greek yogurt
1 tsp. freshly squeezed lemon juice
¼ tsp. lemon zest, plus more for topping
Lemon Poppy Seed Pancakes:
Coconut oil, for greasing the pan
2 eggs
1⅓ cups rolled oats
¾ cup full-fat cottage cheese
¼ cup freshly squeezed lemon juice
2 tbsps. pure maple syrup
1 to 2 tbsps. water, divided (optional)
1 tbsp. baking powder
1 tbsp. lemon zest
2 tsps. poppy seeds
⅛ tsp. sea salt
For Serving:
½ cup fresh blueberries

Directions
1. To make the lemon yogurt topping, in a small mixing bowl, combine the yogurt, maple syrup, lemon juice, and lemon zest. Keep it aside.
2. For the pancakes, in a blender, combine the cottage cheese, eggs, maple syrup, oats, lemon zest, lemon juice, baking powder, salt, and poppy seeds. Blend until mixed well. If the batter is too thick, pour in 1 tbsp. of the water at a time, until the batter is a pourable, but not watery, consistency.
3. Heat a griddle or large skillet over medium heat, and lightly grease it with the coconut oil. When the pan is hot, ladle about ¼ cup of the batter into a 4-inch circle, and let the pancake cook for about 2 to 3 minutes until the edges look dull, a few small bubbles appear on the top in the center, and the bottom is golden brown. Flip gently, and continue to cook for about 2 to 3 minutes until the second side is golden brown.
4. Take the pancake from the heat, and repeat with the remaining batter, drizzling more coconut oil for greasing the griddle, as needed.
5. To serve, pour the yogurt sauce over the pancakes, and garnish with the blueberries and lemon zest. Enjoy!

Nutritional Info per Serving (1 pancake)
calories: 110, fat: 3g, protein: 6g, carbs: 19g, fiber: 2g, sugar: 6g, sodium: 133mg

Homemade Chocolate-Covered Orange Slices

Prep time: 22 minutes, Cook time: 0 minutes, Serves 8

Ingredients
3 to 4 Mandarin oranges, peeled and separated into sections

¾ cup dark chocolate

Flaked salt (optional)

Directions
1. Place the oranges on a paper towel-lined dish to absorb excess liquid.
2. Line a baking sheet with parchment.
3. Melt the chocolate in the microwave in 30-second intervals. Stir between intervals and continue until melted.
4. Dip half of each orange section in the chocolate before placing on the baking sheet. Repeat until all of the orange slices are dipped halfway in chocolate.
5. Sprinkle with salt if desired and refrigerate for 15 minutes to make sure the chocolate has set.

Nutritional Info per Serving
calories: 103, fat: 5g, protein: 0.2g, carbs: 12g, fiber: 2.4g, sugar: 6g, sodium: 18mg

Cinnamon Nutty Baked Apples

Prep time: 15 minutes, Cook time: 6 hours, Serves 8

Ingredients
8 large apples

1½ cups buckwheat flakes

1 cup chopped walnuts

½ cup apple juice

⅓ cup coconut sugar

6 tbsps. unsalted butter, cut into pieces

2 tbsps. freshly squeezed lemon juice

1 tsp. ground cinnamon

¼ tsp. salt

Directions
1. Peel a strip of skin around the top of each apple to prevent splitting. Gently remove the apple core, making sure not to cut all the way through to the bottom. Coat the apples with lemon juice and keep aside.
2. Mix the buckwheat flakes, walnuts, coconut sugar, cinnamon, and salt in a medium bowl.
3. Pour the melted butter over the buckwheat mixture and mix until crumbly. Stuff the apples with this mixture, rounding the stuffing on top of each apple.
4. In a 6-quart slow cooker, arrange the stuffed apples. Add the apple juice around the apples.
5. Cover the slow cooker and cook on low for 4 to 6 hours, or until the apples are very soft. Enjoy!

Nutritional Info per Serving
calories: 369, fat: 17g, protein: 4g, carbs: 53g, fiber: 6g, sugar: 36g, sodium: 112mg

Sweet Potato and Pecan Casserole Muffins

Prep time: 6 minutes, Cook time: 20 to 22 minutes, Makes 12 muffins

Ingredients
Muffins:
¼ cup coconut oil, softened, plus more for greasing the pan

2 eggs

2 cups cooked and mashed sweet potato

1½ cups spelt flour

½ cup coconut sugar

⅓ cup unsweetened almond milk

1 tsp. vanilla extract

1 tsp. ground cinnamon

1 tsp. baking powder

½ tsp. baking soda

½ tsp. ground nutmeg

¼ tsp. ground ginger

¼ tsp. sea salt

Topping:
¼ cup melted coconut oil

⅓ cup chopped pecans

⅓ cup almond flour

¼ cup coconut sugar

1 tsp. ground cinnamon

Directions
1. For the muffins, preheat the oven to 350ºF (180ºC), and lightly grease a 12-cup muffin pan with coconut oil.
2. Whisk together the spelt flour, coconut sugar, baking powder, baking soda, cinnamon, nutmeg, ginger, and salt in a large mixing bowl.
3. In a separate bowl, whisk together the eggs, coconut oil, milk, vanilla, and sweet potato.
4. Place the egg mixture to the flour mixture, and stir until just mixed. Evenly divide the batter among the muffin cups, filling each about three-quarters full.
5. For the topping, combine the pecans, almond flour, coconut sugar, coconut oil, and ground cinnamon in a small bowl. Mix well to fully incorporate the flour.
6. Scatter the topping generously and equally over all the muffins.
7. Bake the muffins for about 20 to 22 minutes, or until a toothpick inserted into the center comes out clean. Allow the muffins to cool in the pan for about 5 minutes, then serve, or take them to a wire rack to cool completely.
8. The muffins can be stored in an airtight container for up to 5 days.

Nutritional Info per Serving (1 muffin)
calories: 252, fat: 13g, protein: 4g, carbs: 31g, fiber: 3g, sugar: 11g, sodium: 137mg

Dark Chocolate Avocado Strawberry Bowl, page 139

Chocolate Chip Zucchini Muffins, page 140

Chunky Monkey Chocolate Waffles, page 147

Clean Eating Chocolate Brownies, page 142

Mocha Ricotta Mousse

Prep time: 4 minutes, Cook time: 0 minutes, Serves 8

Ingredients

¼ cup chocolate chips, melted, plus 2 tbsps. for topping
2 tbsps. strongly brewed coffee or cold brew
1 (16-ounce / 454-g) container ricotta
Berries, melon, pineapple, or other fruit, for dipping or for topping

Directions

1. Combine the melted chocolate and coffee into the ricotta well in a medium bowl.
2. Garnish with chocolate chips. Serve with fruit for dipping.

Nutritional Info per Serving

calories: 172, fat: 10g, protein: 9g, carbs: 8g, fiber: 0.2g, sugar: 0.4g, sodium: 62mg

Jalapeño Pepper and Cheddar Cornmeal Muffins

Prep time: 5 minutes, Cook time: 15 to 20 minutes, Makes 12 muffins

Ingredients

¼ cup melted coconut oil, plus more for greasing the pan
2 eggs
1 cup unsweetened almond milk
1 cup almond flour
1 cup coarse yellow cornmeal
½ cup shredded sharp
Cheddar cheese
1 jalapeño pepper, seeded and minced, plus more for slicing and topping
1 tbsp. coconut sugar
2 tsps. baking powder
Raw honey, for serving
½ tsp. sea salt

Directions

1. Preheat the oven to 400ºF (205ºC), and grease a 12-cup muffin pan lightly with coconut oil.
2. In a large bowl, place the almond flour, cornmeal, coconut sugar, baking powder, and salt, and whisk to combine well.
3. Combine the milk, eggs, and coconut oil in a separate mixing bowl.
4. Place the milk mixture to the cornmeal mixture, and stir to combine well. Gently fold in the cheese and the jalapeño.
5. Divide the batter evenly among the muffin cups, and top it with a slice of jalapeño.
6. Bake the muffins for about 15 to 20 minutes, until they are golden brown and a toothpick inserted into the center comes out clean.
7. Allow the muffins to cool briefly in the pan before removing them. Drizzle the muffins with the honey. Serve immediately.

Nutritional Info per Serving (1 muffin)

calories: 172, fat: 7g, protein: 5g, carbs: 21g, fiber: 2g, sugar: 2g, sodium: 149mg

Chunky Monkey Chocolate Waffles

Prep time: 12 minutes, Cook time: 12 to 16 minutes, Makes 2 waffles

Ingredients

Chocolate Sauce:
2 tbsps. plain full-fat Greek yogurt
1 tbsp. pure maple syrup
1 tbsp. unsweetened cocoa powder
1 tbsp. unsweetened almond milk
Waffles:
Coconut oil, for greasing the waffle iron
2 egg whites
1 ripe banana, mashed
⅓ cup rolled oats
¼ cup chocolate protein powder
2 tbsps. natural peanut butter
1 tbsp. unsweetened almond milk
½ tsp. baking powder
½ tsp. vanilla extract
¼ tsp. cinnamon
For Serving:
1 ripe banana, sliced
Chopped peanuts
Dark chocolate chips

Directions

Make the Chocolate Sauce:
1. Whisk together the yogurt, maple syrup, cocoa powder, and almond milk until smooth in a small bowl. Keep aside.
Make the Waffles:
2. Combine the oats, protein powder, peanut butter, banana, egg whites, baking powder, cinnamon, vanilla, and almond milk in a food processor or blender. Blend until smooth.
3. Heat a waffle iron, and lightly grease it with coconut oil. Ladle about ¼ cup of the batter onto the hot iron, and cook the waffle for about 3 to 4 minutes, or until golden brown. Repeat this with the remaining batter. With a clean kitchen towel, cover the cooked waffles to keep them warm.
4. For serving, top the waffles with the chocolate sauce, banana, peanuts, and chocolate chips. Enjoy!

Nutritional Info per Serving (½ waffle)

calories: 190, fat: 7g, protein: 11g, carbs: 25g, fiber: 4g, sugar: 11g, sodium: 89mg

Tropical Pineapple Fruit Leather

Prep time: 6 minutes, Cook time: 4 to 5 hours, Serves 6

Ingredients
1 pineapple, cored and chopped
1 mango, peeled and chopped
1 tbsp. honey
Juice and zest of 1 lemon

Directions
1. Preheat the oven to 200ºF (93ºC). Line a baking sheet with a silicone baking mat or parchment paper.
2. Blend all of the ingredients into on high until smooth.
3. Transfer the mixture onto the baking sheet. Evenly spread it out in a layer. Bake for 4 to 5 hours or until a inserted toothpick comes out clean.
4. Cool completely, cut into strips and roll up in parchment paper.
5. Store in an airtight container for up to a week.

Nutritional Info per Serving
calories: 78, fat: 0.3g, protein: 0.2g, carbs: 18g, fiber: 2.5g, sugar: 15g, sodium: 6mg

Apple-Peach Oatmeal Crumble

Prep time: 14 minutes, Cook time: 5 hours, Serves 8 to 10

Ingredients
6 large Granny Smith apples, peeled and cut into chunks
4 large peaches, peeled and sliced
3 cups quick-cooking oatmeal
1 cup almond flour
½ cup slivered almonds
½ cup melted coconut oil
⅓ cup coconut sugar
3 tbsps. honey
2 tbsps. lemon juice
1 tsp. ground cinnamon

Directions
1. Mix the apples, peaches, honey, and lemon juice in a 6-quart slow cooker.
2. In a large bowl, mix the almond flour, oatmeal, coconut sugar, cinnamon, and almonds until well combined.
3. Place the coconut oil and mix until crumbly.
4. Scatter the almond mixture over the fruit in the slow cooker.
5. Cover the slow cooker and cook on low for 4 to 5 hours, or until the fruit is soft and the crumble is bubbling around the edges. Enjoy!

Nutritional Info per Serving
calories: 547, fat: 26g, protein: 10g, carbs: 75g, fiber: 11g, sugar: 42g, sodium: 0mg

Peaches and Cream Pancakes

Prep time: 9 minutes, Cook time: 25 minutes, Makes 8 (4-inch) pancakes

Ingredients
Cream:
½ cup plain full-fat Greek yogurt
1 tbsp. pure maple syrup, plus more for topping
½ tsp. vanilla extract
Peaches:
2 large peaches, peeled and sliced
2 tbsps. water
1½ tbsps. coconut sugar
¼ tsp. ground cinnamon
Pancakes:
Coconut oil, for greasing the pan
2 egg whites
1½ cups whole wheat pastry flour
1 to 1¼ cups unsweetened almond milk, divided
2 tbsps. ground flaxseed
2 tbsps. coconut sugar
1 tsp. vanilla extract
1 tsp. baking soda
1 tsp. baking powder
⅛ tsp. sea salt

Directions
1. For the cream, in a small bowl, combine the yogurt, maple syrup, and vanilla. Refrigerate the cream until you are ready to use it.
2. For the peaches, combine the peaches, coconut sugar, cinnamon, and water in a small saucepan. Simmer slowly over medium heat, stirring occasionally, until the peaches are tender, about 6 to 8 minutes. Keep the pan aside.
3. For the pancakes, in a large mixing bowl, combine the flour, flaxseed, coconut sugar, baking soda, baking powder, and salt. Whisk together well.
4. Combine 1 cup of the almond milk, the egg whites, and vanilla in a separate mixing bowl, and mix well.
5. Add the milk mixture into the flour mixture, and whisk them together. Pour in more of the remaining ¼ cup of milk, a little at a time, if it's needed to reach a thick, but pourable consistency. Allow the batter to stand for 5 minutes. It will thicken as it sets.
6. Heat a griddle or skillet over medium-high heat until hot. Grease it lightly with the coconut oil. Place ¼ cup of the batter onto the griddle in a circle. Cook the pancake for about 2 to 4 minutes, until bubbles form on the surface and the bottom is golden. Gently flip the pancake, and cook for about 1 more minute until done. Repeat with all the remaining batter.
7. For serving, place the yogurt topping, and the warm peaches on the pancakes.

Nutritional Info per Serving (1 pancake)
calories: 158, fat: 2g, protein: 6g, carbs: 29g, fiber: 3g, sugar: 11g, sodium: 76mg

Peach Brown Betty with Cranberries

Prep time: 20 minutes, Cook time: 6 hours, Serves 10

Ingredients

⅓ cup melted coconut oil
8 ripe peaches, peeled and cut into chunks
3 cups cubed whole-wheat bread
1½ cups whole-wheat bread crumbs

1 cup dried cranberries
⅓ cup coconut sugar
3 tbsps. honey
2 tbsps. freshly squeezed lemon juice
¼ tsp. ground cardamom

Directions

1. Mix the peaches, dried cranberries, lemon juice, and honey in a 6-quart slow cooker.
2. In a large bowl, mix the bread crumbs, bread cubes, coconut sugar, and cardamom. Pour the melted coconut oil over all and toss to coat well.
3. Place the bread mixture on the fruit in the slow cooker.
4. Cover the slow cooker and cook on low for 5 to 6 hours, or until the fruit is bubbling and the topping is browned. Serve warm.

Nutritional Info per Serving
calories: 322, fat: 9g, protein: 6g, carbs: 57g, fiber: 6g, sugar: 31g, sodium: 69mg

Chocolate Peanut Butter Cup Pudding Bowl

Prep time: 9 minutes, Cook time: 0 minutes, Serves 2

Ingredients

1 banana, sliced
1 cup unsweetened almond milk, divided
4 tbsps. chia seeds, divided
2 tbsps. cacao powder
2 tbsps. organic maple syrup, divided
1 tbsp. natural peanut

butter
1 tbsp. dark chocolate chips
1 tbsp. unsweetened shredded coconut
1 tsp. pure vanilla extract, divided
Dash ground cinnamon
¼ tsp. salt

Directions

1. Combine 2 tbsps. chia seeds, ½ cup unsweetened almond milk, the cacao powder, 1 tbsp. maple syrup, ½ tsp. vanilla, and the salt in a medium bowl. Mix well until combined.
2. Add the remaining 2 tbsps. chia seeds, the remaining ½ cup unsweetened almond milk, peanut butter, the

remaining 1 tbsp. maple syrup, and the remaining ½ tsp. vanilla in a small bowl. Mix well until combined.
3. Put both bowls in the refrigerator and chill for at least 3 hours.
4. Divide the peanut butter pudding mixture (from the small bowl) equally between 2 bowls. Distribute the chocolate pudding mixture (from the medium bowl) on top of the peanut butter pudding. Top with the dark chocolate chips, banana slices, shredded coconut, and a dash cinnamon. Enjoy!

Nutritional Info per Serving
calories: 200, fat: 15g, protein: 8g, carbs: 38g, fiber: 11g, sugar: 14g, sodium: 412mg

Berries-Chocolate Waffles

Prep time: 5 minutes, Cook time: 12 to 18 minutes, Makes 4 waffles

Ingredients

Waffles:
2 tbsps. melted coconut oil, plus more for greasing
1 egg
1 cup whole wheat pastry flour
1 cup unsweetened almond milk
¼ cup unsweetened cocoa powder

2 tbsps. coconut sugar
2 tsps. baking powder
1 tsp. vanilla extract
1 tsp. chili powder, plus more for garnish
1 tsp. ground cinnamon
¼ tsp. sea salt
For Serving:
Pure maple syrup
Fresh berries
Plain full-fat Greek yogurt

Directions

1. In a large bowl, add the flour, cocoa powder, coconut sugar, baking powder, chili powder, cinnamon, and salt. Whisk together to combine well.
2. Whisk together the milk, egg, coconut oil, and vanilla in a separate bowl. Place the milk mixture into the flour mixture, and then whisk together until a smooth batter is formed. Do not overmix.
3. Preheat the waffle iron, and lightly grease it with the coconut oil. Place ⅓ cup of the batter onto the hot waffle iron and close it.
4. Cook for about 4 to 6 minutes until the waffles are crisp and cooked through, depending on the size and shape of your waffle iron.
5. For serving, garnish with a light sprinkle of chili powder and the maple syrup, berries, and yogurt. Enjoy!

Nutritional Info per Serving (1 waffle)
calories: 239, fat: 10g, protein: 8g, carbs: 34g, fiber: 5g, sugar: 7g, sodium: 212mg

Strawberry Lemonade Slushie

Prep time: 4 minutes, Cook time: 0 minutes, Serves 4

Ingredients
1 pound (454 g) frozen strawberries
1 cup water
2 cups ice
Juice of 3 lemons
1 tbsp. honey

Directions
1. Put all of the ingredients in a blender. Pulse on high until smooth.
2. Pour into four glasses. Decorate with fresh strawberry and lemon slices.

Nutritional Info per Serving
calories: 65, fat: 0.2g, protein: 0.6g, carbs: 17g, fiber: 1.7g, sugar: 9g, sodium: 3mg

Homemade Strawberry Ice Pops

Prep time: 5 minutes, Cook time: 0 minutes, Makes 4 to 6 pops

Ingredients
2 cups fresh strawberries
2 tbsps. raw honey
½ cup orange juice

Directions
1. Combine the strawberries, honey, and orange juice in a high-speed blender.
2. Blend to your desired consistency.
3. Fill up the ice pop molds and freeze overnight. Enjoy!

Nutritional Info per Serving
calories: 70, fat: 0g, protein: 1g, carbs: 18g, fiber: 2g, sugar: 14g, sodium: 2mg

Chili-Spiced Fruit Cups

Prep time: 7 minutes, Cook time: 0 minutes, Serves 8

Ingredients
1 pineapple
2 mangos
1 small seedless watermelon
1 cucumber
Juice of 1 lime
1 tsp. chili powder
½ tsp. salt

Directions
1. Chop the fruits listed above to equal-size cubes.
2. Place the fruit and cucumber cubes into a large bowl. Toss with the lime juice, chili powder, and season with salt.

Nutritional Info per Serving
calories: 118, fat: 0.3g, protein: 3g, carbs: 28g, fiber: 4g, sugar: 24g, sodium: 154mg

Nutty Carrot Pudding

Prep time: 10 minutes, Cook time: 7 hours, Serves 12

Ingredients
3 cups finely grated carrots
2 eggs, beaten
2 cups canned coconut milk
1½ cups chopped pecans
1 cup golden raisins
1 cup almond flour
1 cup coconut flour
½ cup coconut sugar
1½ tsps. ground cinnamon
1 tsp. baking powder

Directions
1. Mix all of the ingredients in a 6-quart slow cooker. Cover the slow cooker and cook on low for 5 to 7 hours, or until the pudding is set.
2. Serve hot, either plain or with softly whipped heavy cream.

Nutritional Info per Serving
calories: 359, fat: 24g, protein: 7g, carbs: 31g, fiber: 7g, sugar: 22g, sodium: 70mg

Chocolate Banana Cream Bowl

Prep time: 6 minutes, Cook time: 0 minutes, Serves 2

Ingredients
3 frozen bananas, peeled and sliced
4 fresh strawberries, sliced
½ cup dehydrated banana chips
2 tbsps. dark chocolate chips
2 tbsps. cacao powder
2 tbsps. unsweetened shredded coconut
1 tbsp. organic maple syrup

Directions
1. Combine the frozen bananas, cacao powder, and maple syrup in a blender. Blend until thick and smooth, scraping down the sides of the blender if needed.
2. Divide the ice cream equally between 2 bowls. Top with the coconut, banana chips, chocolate chips, and strawberries. Serve right away.

Nutritional Info per Serving
calories: 326, fat: 7g, protein: 1g, carbs: 73g, fiber: 10g, sugar: 39g, sodium: 21mg

Raisin Rice Pudding

Prep time: 5 minutes, Cook time: 6 hours, Serves 16

Ingredients

2 tbsps. coconut oil
6 cups canned coconut milk
1⅔ cups brown Arborio rice
1 cup raisins

1 cup dark chocolate chips (optional)
3 cups water
½ cup coconut sugar
1 tbsp. vanilla extract

Directions

1. Mix the coconut milk and water in a 6-quart slow cooker. Place the rice and coconut sugar and mix well. Pour in the coconut oil and the raisins.
2. Cover the mixture and cook on low for 5 to 6 hours, or until the rice is very soft.
3. Gently stir in the vanilla. Sprinkle the pudding with chocolate chips, if using. Serve warm.

Nutritional Info per Serving

calories: 383, fat: 24g, protein: 5g, carbs: 41g, fiber: 2g, sugar: 22g, sodium: 27mg

Chocolate & Banana Chia Seed Pudding

Prep time: 12 minutes, Cook time: 0 minutes, Serves 4

Ingredients

3 cups milk
½ cup chia seeds
1 tbsp. unsweetened cocoa powder

2 tsps. maple syrup
½ tsp. pure vanilla extract
2 bananas, sliced

Directions

1. In a quart-size glass container with lid, combine the milk, chia seeds, cocoa powder, maple syrup, and vanilla. Seal the lid and shake the mixture vigorously for at least 1 minute until no clumps remain.
2. Evenly portion the pudding into 4 pint-size Mason jars with lids. Top each with banana slices and seal the lids.
3. Refrigerate the jars for at least 1 hour or overnight, to allow them to set.

Nutritional Info per Serving

calories: 271, fat: 8g, protein: 10g, carbs: 35g, fiber: 11g, sugar: 18g, sodium: 87mg

Vanilla Strawberry Chia Jam

Prep time: 5 minutes, Cook time: 23 minutes, Makes about ¾ cup

Ingredients

2 cups frozen strawberries
1 cup water

3 tbsps. coconut sugar
2 tbsps. chia seeds
2 tbsps. vanilla extract

Directions

1. Combine the strawberries, coconut sugar, water, and vanilla in a medium stockpot, and bring to boil.
2. Cover and cook for about 15 to 20 minutes, until the strawberries have cooked down and the mixture has thickened.
3. Place the chia seeds and cook for another 3 minutes.
4. Allow the jam to cool before transferring it to a glass jar for storage.

Nutritional Info per Serving (1 tablespoon)

calories: 37, fat: 0g, protein: 0g, carbs: 7g, fiber: 1g, sugar: 4g, sodium: 1mg

Fruit & Nut Chocolate Bark

Prep time: 30 minutes, Cook time: 0 minutes, Serves 12

Ingredients

16 ounces (454 g) dark chocolate
1 tsp. coconut oil

1 cup walnuts, chopped
½ cup dried cranberries
¼ tsp. flaked salt

Directions

1. Line a baking sheet with parchment.
2. Melt the chocolate and the coconut oil in the microwave in 30-second intervals. Stir between intervals and continue until melted.
3. Pour the melted chocolate onto baking sheet in an even layer.
4. Evenly sprinkle the walnuts, cranberries, and salt over the chocolate.
5. Freeze for 20 minutes or until it can be broken into pieces.
6. Break into bars. Keep in the refrigerator for up to 1 week or in the freezer for up to 1 month.

Nutritional Info per Serving

calories: 264, fat: 17g, protein: 4g, carbs: 28g, fiber: 5g, sugar: 11g, sodium: 68mg

Creamy Lime Protein Pancakes

Prep time: 5 minutes, Cook time: 15 minutes, Makes 8 pancakes

Ingredients
Creamy Lime Topping:
1 tbsp. pure maple syrup
½ cup plain full-fat Greek yogurt
⅛ tsp. vanilla extract
¼ tsp. lime zest
Pancakes:
Coconut oil, for greasing the pan
2 egg whites
¾ cup rolled oats
½ cup almond flour
½ cup vanilla protein powder
¼ cup unsweetened almond milk
¼ cup freshly squeezed lime juice
2 tbsps. pure maple syrup, plus more for topping
2 tsps. baking powder
1 tsp. lime zest, plus more for topping
1 tsp. baking soda
¼ tsp. sea salt

Directions
Make the Creamy Lime Topping:
1. In a small bowl, combine the yogurt, maple syrup, vanilla, and lime zest, and stir until well mixed. Keep aside.
Make the Pancakes:
2. In a mixing bowl, place the oats, almond flour, protein powder, baking powder, baking soda, and salt. Whisk to combine well.
3. Whisk together the lime juice, milk, egg whites, maple syrup, and lime zest in a separate bowl.
4. Place the milk mixture to the oat mixture, and stir until just combined. Do not overmix.
5. Preheat a griddle or a skillet over medium-high heat and lightly grease with coconut oil.
6. Add ¼ cup of the batter onto the griddle, and slowly spread it into a circle shape, with the measuring cup or by tilting the griddle.
7. Cook for about 2 to 3 minutes, until the edges start to become crisp and look dull. Flip the pancake gently and cook for 1 to 2 minutes more. Repeat with the remaining batter.
8. To serve, place the creamy lime topping, a drizzle of maple syrup, and lime zest on the pancakes. Enjoy!

Nutritional Info per Serving (1 pancake)
calories: 133, fat: 3g, protein: 9g, carbs: 21g, fiber: 3g, sugar: 6g, sodium: 136mg

Maple-Yogurt Chia Pudding

Prep time: 6 minutes, Cook time: 0 minutes, Serves 1

Ingredients
1 (6-ounce / 170-g) container plain Greek yogurt
1 tbsp. maple syrup
3 tbsps. chia seeds
½ tsp. vanilla extract

Directions
1. In a glass bowl or jar with a lid, combine the yogurt, chia seeds, maple syrup, and vanilla.
2. Stir until combined well.
3. Cover and allow to rest for 20 minutes on the kitchen counter or in the refrigerator.
4. Mix and place your favorite fruit toppings, if desired.

Nutritional Info per Serving
calories: 368, fat: 19g, protein: 13g, carbs: 40g, fiber: 15g, sugar: 17g, sodium: 88mg

Overnight Chia and Quinoa Pudding with Date

Prep time: 5 minutes, Cook time: 0 minutes, Serves 2

Ingredients
1⅛ cups vanilla almond milk
¼ cup chia seeds
2 dates, pitted and finely chopped
6 tbsps. crunchy quinoa
3 tbsps. unsweetened shredded coconut

Directions
1. In a glass bowl, mix together the vanilla almond milk and chia seeds, stirring well.
2. Add the chopped dates, quinoa, and shredded coconut. Stir to combine well.
3. Cover and refrigerate overnight. Enjoy!

Nutritional Info per Serving
calories: 355, fat: 15g, protein: 10g, carbs: 48g, fiber: 14g, sugar: 12g, sodium: 93mg

Chapter 13: Drink and Smoothie

Citrus & Coconut Rehydration Drink

Prep time: 5 minutes, Cook time: 0 minutes, Serves 2

Ingredients
1 small cucumber
1 orange
1 lemon
½ cup packed fresh spinach
1 (½-inch) piece fresh

ginger, peeled
¼ tsp. salt
¼ tsp. honey
⅛ tsp. cayenne pepper, ground
2 cups coconut water

Directions
1. To a juicer, slowly add the cucumber, orange, lemon, spinach, ginger, salt, honey, and cayenne.
2. Evenly divide the juice mixture into 2 pint-size Mason jars with tight-fitting lids. Pour 1 cup of coconut water into each jar. Seal the lids and store.

Nutritional Info per Serving
calories: 114, fat: 2g, protein: 4g, carbs: 25g, fiber: 7g, sugar: 14g, sodium: 562mg

Strawberry-Banana Sunrise Smoothie

Prep time: 4 minutes, Cook time: 0 minutes, Serves 2

Ingredients
1 cup hulled strawberries, plus extra for topping
1 frozen ripe banana
½ orange, peeled and seeded, plus orange

slices for topping
½ cup plain full-fat Greek yogurt
Raw honey (optional)
Ice (optional)

Directions
1. Use a high-speed blender to blend the strawberries, banana, orange, and yogurt until the mixture is smooth enough to pour. Taste for sweetness, and pour in some honey, if needed. Add the ice if the smoothie is too thin.
2. Top with a strawberry and an orange slice. Enjoy!

Nutritional Info per Serving
calories: 130, fat: 2g, protein: 4g, carbs: 26g, fiber: 4g, sugar: 16g, sodium: 30mg

Berries and Banana Smoothie Bowl

Prep time: 8 minutes, Cook time: 0 minutes, Serves 1

Ingredients
Smoothie Bowl:
1 cup frozen mixed berries
½ frozen banana
½ cup baby spinach
½ cup unsweetened almond milk

1 tbsp. chia seeds
Topping:
½ banana, sliced
8 fresh raspberries
6 fresh blackberries
2 tbsps. pomegranate seeds

Directions
1. In a blender, add all the smoothie bowl ingredients in the order listed and blend until smooth, scraping down the sides of the blender if needed.
2. Place the smoothie into a bowl and garnish with the topping. Serve right away.

Nutritional Info per Serving
calories: 318, fat: 6g, protein: 6g, carbs: 67g, fiber: 17g, sugar: 29g, sodium: 102mg

Blueberry, Pineapple and Banana Smoothie Bowl

Prep time: 10 minutes, Cook time: 0 minutes, Serves 1

Ingredients
Smoothie Bowl:
½ frozen banana
½ cup frozen blueberries
½ cup frozen pineapple
½ cup unsweetened almond milk
¼ cup mint leaves

Topping:
¼ cup diced pineapple
¼ cup fresh blueberries
2 tbsps. pumpkin seeds
1 tbsp. flaxseed
Mint leaves

Directions
1. In a blender, add all the smoothie bowl ingredients in the order listed. Blend until smooth, scraping down the sides of the blender if needed.
2. Place the smoothie into a bowl and garnish with the topping. Serve right away.

Nutritional Info per Serving
calories: 317, fat: 13g, protein: 8g, carbs: 50g, fiber: 10g, sugar: 30g, sodium: 93mg

Cheese Raspberry Smoothie

Prep time: 5 minutes, Cook time: 0 minutes, Serves 2

Ingredients

1 cup unsweetened coconut milk or milk of choice, plus more if needed
2 cups frozen or fresh raspberries, plus more
frozen for topping
½ cup whole-milk cottage cheese
1 tbsp. raw honey
1½ tsps. vanilla extract
Ice (optional)

Directions

1. Blend the coconut milk, cottage cheese, raspberries, honey, and vanilla until smooth in a high-speed blender.
2. If the smoothie is too thin, which is likely if you use fresh raspberries, add the ice. If it's too thick, you can thin it with additional coconut milk or water.
3. Top with the frozen raspberries. Enjoy!

Nutritional Info per Serving

calories: 256, fat: 9g, protein: 13g, carbs: 32g, fiber: 8g, sugar: 21g, sodium: 118mg

Chocolate Avocado and Banana Smoothie

Prep time: 4 minutes, Cook time: 0 minutes, Serves 2

Ingredients

1¼ cups unsweetened almond milk, plus more if needed
1 frozen ripe banana
½ avocado, plus more for topping
2 pitted dried dates
Shaved dark chocolate, for topping
2 tbsps. unsweetened cocoa powder
½ tsp. vanilla extract

Directions

1. In a blender, combine the almond milk, banana, dates, avocado, cocoa powder, and vanilla. Blend until smooth. Pour in more almond milk, as needed, to achieve your desired consistency.
2. Top with the dark chocolate and extra diced avocado. Enjoy!

Nutritional Info per Serving

calories: 273, fat: 12g, protein: 4g, carbs: 43g, fiber: 8g, sugar: 26g, sodium: 113mg

Lemon Kale and Mango Smoothie

Prep time: 7 minutes, Cook time: 0 minutes, Serves 4

Ingredients

2 cups frozen mango chunks
2 cups roughly chopped fresh kale, stems removed
½ cup diced cucumber, plus cucumber slices for topping
¼ cup freshly squeezed
lemon juice
¼ cup fresh cilantro, plus more for topping
2 cups water, plus more if needed
1 tsp. chopped ginger
¼ tsp. lemon zest
Ice (optional)

Directions

1. Blend the kale and the water together until smooth in a high-speed blender.
2. Place the mango, lemon zest, lemon juice, cucumber, ginger, and cilantro. Blend again until the mixture is smooth. Pour in the ice to thicken, if desired, and additional water to thin the smoothie, if needed.
3. Top with the cucumber slices and extra cilantro. Enjoy!

Nutritional Info per Serving

calories: 119, fat: 1g, protein: 2g, carbs: 29g, fiber: 4g, sugar: 24g, sodium: 14mg

Green Smoothie Bowl

Prep time: 6 minutes, Cook time: 0 minutes, Serves 1

Ingredients

3 cups spinach
½ cup milk of choice
½ cup pineapple, chopped
½ cup pumpkin, puréed
1 kiwi, peeled and chopped
¼ avocado, peeled and sliced
2 tbsps. pumpkin seed butter (or nut or seed
butter of choice)
1 scoop vanilla or unflavored protein powder (optional)
Ice (optional)
Chia seeds, granola, hemp seeds, kiwi slices, sliced banana, unsweetened shredded coconut, walnuts, for topping (optional)

Directions

1. In a blender, place the spinach, milk, pineapple, pumpkin, kiwi, avocado, and pumpkin seed butter. Run on high until smooth.
2. Add the protein powder and ice, if preferred, and blend until smooth.
3. Pour the smoothie into a medium bowl. Top with the fruits, nuts, or seeds, if desired.

Nutritional Info per Serving

calories: 457, fat: 27g, protein: 18g, carbs: 47g, fiber: 12g, sugar: 21g, sodium: 179mg

Coconut Banana Smoothie Bowl

Prep time: 6 minutes, Cook time: 0 minutes, Serves 1

Ingredients
Smoothie Bowl:
1 frozen banana
½ cup coconut milk
½ cup Greek yogurt
½ cup ice
Topping:

3 fresh strawberries, sliced
2 tbsps. toasted coconut flakes
2 tbsps. dark chocolate chips

Directions
1. In a blender, add all the smoothie bowl ingredients in the order listed. Blend until smooth, scraping down the sides of the blender if needed.
2. Place the smoothie into a bowl and garnish with the topping. Serve right away.

Nutritional Info per Serving
calories: 576, fat: 36g, protein: 13g, carbs: 57g, fiber: 7g, sugar: 34g, sodium: 145mg

Vanilla Almond Milk

Prep time: 12 minutes, Cook time: 0 minutes, Makes 3 cups

Ingredients
2 cups raw almonds, soaked for 12 hours
4 Medjool dates, pitted
2½ cups water
1 whole vanilla bean,

chopped, or 1 tsp. pure vanilla extract
¼ tsp. ground cinnamon
Pinch sea salt

Directions
1. Rinse and drain the soaked almonds well.
2. In a blender, add the almonds, water, dates, and vanilla. Blend on the highest speed for about 60 seconds.
3. Add the almond mixture into a cheesecloth or nut milk bag over a large bowl. Slowly squeeze the bottom to release the milk.
4. Rinse out the blender and then take the milk back in. Place the cinnamon and a pinch salt. Blend on low to combine well and strain the milk through the cheesecloth again.
5. Store the milk in a tightly sealed glass jar in the refrigerator for up to 5 days. Just be sure to give it a good shake before serve.

Nutritional Info per Serving (½ cup)
calories: 224, fat: 15g, protein: 7g, carbs: 19g, fiber: 5g, sugar: 12g, sodium: 28mg

Spicy Green Mango and Pineapple Smoothie

Prep time: 6 minutes, Cook time: 0 minutes, Serves 2

Ingredients
1 cup unsweetened coconut milk, plus more if needed
1 cup fresh spinach
½ cup frozen mango
½ medium frozen ripe banana
¼ cup frozen pineapple

chunks, plus more for topping
½ jalapeño pepper, seeded and chopped, plus jalapeño slices for topping
1 tsp. chopped ginger
¼ tsp. ground cinnamon

Directions
1. Blend the coconut milk, banana, mango, pineapple, spinach, jalapeño, ginger, and cinnamon until smooth in a high-speed blender. If needed, add additional coconut milk to reach your desired consistency.
2. Top with the cilantro and jalapeño. Enjoy!

Nutritional Info per Serving
calories: 148, fat: 6g, protein: 5g, carbs: 21g, fiber: 2g, sugar: 17g, sodium: 65mg

Vanilla Latte

Prep time: 5 minutes, Cook time: 0 minutes, Serves 1

Ingredients
4 ounces (113 g) strong coffee (or 2 to 3 shots espresso)
¾ cup milk

¼ tsp. pure vanilla extract
1 scoop unflavored collagen peptides (optional)

Directions
1. Brew the coffee. Set aside, but keep warm.
2. Pour the milk and vanilla into a 2-cup glass jar that has a lid.
3. Place the milk uncovered in the microwave and turn on high for 2 minutes, checking every 30 seconds to see if hot enough and to make sure that a film does not form the on top.
4. Remove the milk from the microwave. Let the glass cool enough to handle safely, put the lid on the glass and shake vigorously for 30 seconds.
5. Carefully remove lid, add the coffee and collagen, if using. Replace the lid and shake for an additional 10 to 15 seconds.

Nutritional Info per Serving
calories: 134, fat: 5g, protein: 7g, carbs: 9g, fiber: 0.3g, sugar: 8g, sodium: 81mg

Healthy Green Smoothie

Prep time: 5 minutes, Cook time: 0 minutes, Serves 1

Ingredients

2 cups baby spinach
½ cucumber
½ apple
¼ avocado
½ lemon, squeezed
1 cup water

Directions

1. Combine the spinach, avocado, cucumber, lemon, apple, and water in a high-speed blender. Blend until smooth.
2. Enjoy immediately or refrigerate for up to several hours.

Nutritional Info per Serving

calories: 180, fat: 8g, protein: 5g, carbs: 28g, fiber: 9g, sugar: 12g, sodium: 53mg

Protein PB&J Smoothie

Prep time: 2 minutes, Cook time: 0 minutes, Serves 1

Ingredients

1 cup milk
1 cup berries, frozen
1 tbsp. peanut butter, smooth and unsweetened
1 tbsp. raspberry jelly
1 scoop vanilla or unflavored protein powder (optional)

Directions

1. Place all of the ingredients in a blender. Blend on high for 30 seconds or until smooth.
2. Serve immediately.

Nutritional Info per Serving

calories: 387, fat: 16g, protein: 12g, carbs: 46g, fiber: 7g, sugar: 22g, sodium: 167mg

Cinnamon Latte

Prep time: 7 minutes, Cook time: 0 minutes, Serves 2

Ingredients

12 ounces (340 g) unsweetened vanilla almond milk
1 tsp. raw honey
1 tsp. turmeric
¼ tsp. cinnamon
½ tsp. ground ginger

Directions

1. Bring the vanilla almond milk to a boil in a small saucepan.

2. Turn off the heat and add the turmeric, ginger, cinnamon, and honey. Whisk until well combined.
3. Serve warm.

Nutritional Info per Serving

calories: 75, fat: 2g, protein: 1g, carbs: 13g, fiber: 2g, sugar: 11g, sodium: 108mg

Strawberry and Peach Smoothie

Prep time: 6 minutes, Cook time: 0 minutes, Serves 1

Ingredients

10 large strawberries, hulled
1 cup unsweetened almond milk
½ peach, frozen
2 tbsps. oat bran
1 tbsp. raw honey

Directions

1. Combine the strawberries, peach, almond milk, oat bran, and honey in a high-speed blender.
2. Blend until smooth.
3. Enjoy right away or refrigerate for up to several hours.

Nutritional Info per Serving

calories: 271, fat: 4g, protein: 5g, carbs: 62g, fiber: 8g, sugar: 38g, sodium: 154mg

Kale and Avocado Smoothie Bowl

Prep time: 9 minutes, Cook time: 0 minutes, Serves 1

Ingredients

Smoothie Bowl:
1 cup kale, chopped
1 cup unsweetened almond milk
½ frozen banana
½ avocado
½ cup ice
1 tbsp. agave
Topping:
1 kiwi, peeled and sliced
½ banana
½ cup fresh raspberries
1 tsp. chia seeds

Directions

1. In a blender, add all the smoothie bowl ingredients in the order listed. Blend until smooth, scraping down the sides of the blender if needed.
2. Place the smoothie into a bowl and garnish with the topping. Serve right away.

Nutritional Info per Serving

calories: 399, fat: 20g, protein: 7g, carbs: 58g, fiber: 18g, sugar: 25g, sodium: 188mg

Cheese Raspberry Smoothie, page 155

Healthy Green Smoothie, page 157

Cinnamon Latte, page 157

Vanilla Almond Milk, page 156

Spinach and Banana Smoothie

Prep time: 4 minutes, Cook time: 0 minutes, Serves 2

Ingredients
12 ounces (340 g) vanilla almond milk
1 cup baby spinach
1 banana, frozen
1 measure plant-based, vanilla protein powder
1 tbsp. peanut butter

Directions
1. Combine the milk, banana, protein powder, peanut butter, and spinach in a high-speed blender.
2. Blend until creamy. Enjoy.

Nutritional Info per Serving
calories: 256, fat: 8g, protein: 16g, carbs: 34g, fiber: 5g, sugar: 16g, sodium: 123mg

Green Detox Juice

Prep time: 4 minutes, Cook time: 0 minutes, Serves 2

Ingredients
1 cup packed fresh spinach
1 cup packed baby kale
2 cored green apples
2 celery stalks
½ lemon, peeled and seeded
½ tsp. lemon zest, grated
1 (½-inch) piece fresh ginger, peeled

Directions
1. To a juicer, slowly add the spinach, kale, apples, celery, lemon, lemon zest, and ginger.
2. Evenly portion into 2 pint-size Mason jars with lids.

Nutritional Info per Serving
calories: 123, fat: 2g, protein: 3g, carbs: 25g, fiber: 7g, sugar: 17g, sodium: 35mg

Strawberry & Watermelon Lemonade

Prep time: 6 minutes, Cook time: 0 minutes, Serves 2

Ingredients
1 cup fresh strawberries, stemmed
1½ cups diced seedless watermelon
¼ cup lemon juice, freshly squeezed
1 tbsp. honey

Directions
1. In a blender, add the strawberries, watermelon, lemon juice, and honey. Blend on high speed until completely puréed, for 2 minutes.
2. Evenly portion into 2 pint-size Mason jars with tight-fitting lids.

Nutritional Info per Serving
calories: 87, fat: 0.2g, protein: 2g, carbs: 21g, fiber: 3g, sugar: 19g, sodium: 5mg

Carrot and Banana Smoothie

Prep time: 5 minutes, Cook time: 0 minutes, Serves 2

Ingredients
1 frozen ripe banana
2 medium carrots, chopped
¾ cup coconut milk, plus more if needed
1 (½ inch) piece ginger
1 tbsp. pure maple syrup
¼ tsp. ground turmeric
Ice (optional)

Directions
1. Combine the banana, carrots, ginger, turmeric, coconut milk, and maple syrup in a high-speed blender. Blend until smooth. If you'd like a thicker consistency, place some ice cubes and blend again. For a thinner consistency, pour in additional coconut milk. Enjoy!

Nutritional Info per Serving
calories: 297, fat: 20g, protein: 3g, carbs: 31g, fiber: 5g, sugar: 19g, sodium: 58mg

Strawberry and Banana Bowl

Prep time: 10 minutes, Cook time: 0 minutes, Serves 1

Ingredients
Smoothie Bowl:
1 cup frozen strawberries
½ frozen banana
½ beet, peeled and chopped
½ cup unsweetened almond milk

Topping:
3 fresh strawberries, sliced
¼ cup fresh blueberries
1 tbsp. goji berries
1 tbsp. unsweetened coconut flakes

Directions
1. In a blender, add all the smoothie bowl ingredients in the order listed. Blend until smooth, scraping down the sides of the blender if needed.
2. Place the smoothie into a bowl and garnish with the topping. Serve right away.

Nutritional Info per Serving
calories: 216, fat: 4g, protein: 4g, carbs: 45g, fiber: 10g, sugar: 24g, sodium: 138mg

Banana and Kale Smoothie Bowl

Prep time: 9 minutes, Cook time: 0 minutes, Serves 1

Ingredients
Smoothie Bowl:
1 frozen banana
½ cup frozen mango
½ cup kale, chopped
½ cup coconut water
Juice of ½ lemon
1 (½-inch) piece fresh ginger

2 tbsps. hemp seeds
1 tbsp. flaxseed
¼ tsp. ground turmeric
Topping:
½ kiwi, peeled and sliced
¼ cup fresh blueberries
2 tbsps. unsweetened coconut flakes

Directions
1. In a blender, add all the smoothie bowl ingredients in the order listed. Blend until smooth, scraping down the sides of the blender if needed.
2. Place the smoothie into a bowl and garnish with the topping. Serve right away.

Nutritional Info per Serving
calories: 249, fat: 11g, protein: 6g, carbs: 36g, fiber: 9g, sugar: 22g, sodium: 165mg

Berry Smoothie Bowl

Prep time: 3 minutes, Cook time: 0 minutes, Serves 1

Ingredients
1½ cups berries, fresh or frozen
½ cup plain unsweetened Greek yogurt
½ cup milk
2 tbsps. peanut butter (or nut or seed butter)
1 scoop vanilla or

unflavored protein powder (optional)
Ice (optional)
Berries, chia seeds, flax seeds, granola, sliced almonds, unsweetened shredded coconut, for topping (optional)

Directions
1. Place the berries, yogurt, milk, and peanut butter in a blender. Process on high for 30 seconds or until smooth.
2. Add the protein powder and ice, if desired, and blend until smooth.
3. Pour the smoothie into a medium bowl and sprinkle the toppings you like.

Nutritional Info per Serving
calories: 496, fat: 27g, protein: 16g, carbs: 47g, fiber: 10g, sugar: 22g, sodium: 284mg

Carrot and Banana Smoothie Bowl

Prep time: 7 minutes, Cook time: 0 minutes, Serves 1

Ingredients
Smoothie Bowl:
1 frozen banana
½ cup carrot juice
½ cup ice
2 Medjool dates, pitted
¼ tsp. pure vanilla extract
¼ tsp. ground cinnamon

Topping:
2 Medjool dates, pitted and torn
¼ cup walnuts
2 tbsps. unsweetened shredded coconut
Ground cinnamon

Directions
1. In a blender, add all the smoothie bowl ingredients in the order listed. Blend until smooth, scraping down the sides of the blender if needed.
2. Place the smoothie into a bowl and garnish with the topping. Serve right away.

Nutritional Info per Serving
calories: 484, fat: 17g, protein: 7g, carbs: 64g, fiber: 9g, sugar: 37g, sodium: 111mg

Healthy Rainbow Smoothie Bowl

Prep time: 7 minutes, Cook time: 0 minutes, Serves 1

Ingredients
Smoothie Bowl:
1 packet frozen dragon fruit (pitaya) purée, thawed
½ cup unsweetened almond milk
½ cup frozen mango
½ cup frozen pineapple
½ kiwi, peeled

¼ cup baby spinach
Topping:
½ kiwi, peeled and sliced
½ banana, sliced
3 fresh strawberries, sliced
¼ cup fresh blueberries
¼ cup diced mango

Directions
1. In a blender, add all the smoothie bowl ingredients in the order listed. Blend until smooth, scraping down the sides of the blender if needed.
2. Place the smoothie into a bowl and garnish with the topping. Serve right away.

Nutritional Info per Serving
calories: 260, fat: 3g, protein: 4g, carbs: 61g, fiber: 10g, sugar: 42g, sodium: 97mg

Raspberry & Peach Smoothie

Prep time: 6 minutes, Cook time: 0 minutes, Serves 2

Ingredients

1 peach, pitted and cut into slices	yogurt
1 cup raspberries, fresh	1 tbsp. honey
1 cup ice	1 tbsp. flaxseed, ground
¾ cup milk	½ tsp. turmeric, ground
¼ cup full-fat plain Greek	¼ tsp. cinnamon, ground
	¼ tsp. vanilla extract

Directions

1. In a blender, combine the peach slices, raspberries, ice, milk, yogurt, honey, flaxseed, turmeric, cinnamon, and vanilla. Pulse on high speed for 2 minutes, or until completely smooth. Scrape down the sides if necessary.
2. Portion evenly into 2 pint-size Mason jars with lids.

Nutritional Info per Serving

calories: 178, fat: 5g, protein: 9g, carbs: 32g, fiber: 7g, sugar: 23g, sodium: 49mg

Cocoa-Mint Smoothie

Prep time: 4 minutes, Cook time: 0 minutes, Serves 2

Ingredients

2 bananas	yogurt
1 cup lightly packed fresh spinach	1 tbsp. cocoa powder
1 cup ice	1 tsp. fresh mint, chopped
¾ cup milk	¼ tsp. vanilla extract
¼ cup full-fat plain Greek	

Directions

1. In a blender, add the bananas, spinach, ice, milk, yogurt, cocoa powder, mint, and vanilla.
2. Blend on high speed for 2 minutes, or until completely smooth, scraping down the sides as needed.
3. Portion evenly into 2 pint-size Mason jars with tight-fitting lids.

Nutritional Info per Serving

calories: 187, fat: 4g, protein: 9g, carbs: 33g, fiber: 5g, sugar: 18g, sodium: 73mg

Hemp Seed Milk

Prep time: 5 minutes, Cook time: 0 minutes, Serves 4

Ingredients

1 cup hemp seeds, hulled	½ tsp. vanilla extract
4 cups water	¼ tsp. salt
1 tsp. maple syrup	

Directions

1. In a blender, place the hemp seeds and water. Soak for 20 minutes.
2. Blend on high for 1 minute.
3. Add the maple syrup, vanilla, and salt. Process on high speed for 30 seconds more.
4. If you prefer creamier texture, pour the mixture through a fine-mesh strainer, nut milk bag, or cheesecloth over a bowl.
5. Evenly portion into 4 half-pint Mason jars with lids.

Nutritional Info per Serving

calories: 231, fat: 19g, protein: 12g, carbs: 6g, fiber: 3g, sugar: 3g, sodium: 154mg

Tropical Fruits Smoothie Bowl

Prep time: 11 minutes, Cook time: 0 minutes, Serves 1

Ingredients

Smoothie Bowl:	1 kiwi, peeled and sliced
½ frozen banana	½ banana, sliced
½ cup frozen mango	2 tbsps. unsweetened
½ cup frozen pineapple	shredded coconut
½ cup fresh baby spinach	1 tsp. chia seeds
½ cup coconut milk	Drizzle raw honey
Topping:	

Directions

1. In a blender, add all the smoothie bowl ingredients in the order listed and blend until smooth, scraping down the sides of the blender if needed.
2. Place the smoothie into a bowl and garnish with the topping. Serve right away.

Nutritional Info per Serving

calories: 556, fat: 30g, protein: 7g, carbs: 70g, fiber: 11g, sugar: 39g, sodium: 62mg

Classic Lemon Meringue Smoothie

Prep time: 2 minutes, Cook time: 0 minutes, Serves 1

Ingredients

1½ cups ice
1 cup milk or water
¾ cup plain unsweetened Greek yogurt
1 tbsp. maple syrup

Juice and zest of 1 lemon
1 scoop vanilla or unflavored protein powder
(optional)

Directions

1. Place all of the ingredients in a blender. Run on high until smooth, for 30 seconds.

Nutritional Info per Serving

calories: 384, fat: 17g, protein: 14g, carbs: 40g, fiber: 0.3g, sugar: 31g, sodium: 223mg

Pineapple and Coconut Smoothie

Prep time: 4 minutes, Cook time: 0 minutes, Serves 1

Ingredients

1 cup fresh pineapple
1 cup iceberg lettuce

¼ cup shredded, unsweetened coconut
1 cup water

Directions

1. Combine the pineapple, coconut, lettuce, and water in a high-speed blender.
2. Blend to your desired consistency.
3. Serve immediately or refrigerate for up to several hours.

Nutritional Info per Serving

calories: 163, fat: 7g, protein: 2g, carbs: 27g, fiber: 5g, sugar: 18g, sodium: 13mg

Chapter 14: Sauces and Dressing

Basic Almond Butter

Prep time: 2 minutes, Cook time: 0 minutes, Makes 2 cups

Ingredients
16 ounces (454 g) raw almonds

Directions
1. Place the almonds in a blender until creamy. Pulse a few times and scrape down the sides every few minutes if necessary.
2. Store in an airtight container in the fridge for up to 1 week.

Nutritional Info per Serving (2 tablespoons)
calories: 165, fat: 13g, protein: 6.2g, carbs: 5g, fiber: 4g, sugar: 1.1g, sodium: 0mg

Mayo

Prep time: 7 minutes, Cook time: 0 minutes, Makes 1½ cups

Ingredients
1 large egg
1 tbsp. Dijon mustard
1 tbsp. apple cider vinegar
¼ tsp. salt, plus more as desired
¾ cup avocado oil
Pinch garlic powder
1 tsp. lemon juice

Directions
1. Put the egg in a 2-cup liquid measuring cup or bowl. Blend on high for 20 seconds or until frothy.
2. Add the mustard, vinegar, and salt, and blend for another 20 seconds.
3. Do not stop blending and add the oil drop by drop until creamy and emulsified.
4. Drizzle the rest of the oil while still blending until all of the oil is used up.
5. Add an extra ¼ cup of oil in a slow and steady stream to reach a creamier or thicker consistency.
6. Season with more salt as needed and the garlic powder and lemon juice. Refrigerate in an airtight container for up to 2 weeks.

Nutritional Info per Serving (2 tablespoons)
calories: 142, fat: 13g, protein: 0.3g, carbs: 0.2g, fiber: 0.4g, sugar: 0.2g, sodium: 85mg

Easy Taco Seasoning

Prep time: 1 minute, Cook time: 0 minutes, Makes ⅔ cup

Ingredients
¼ cup chili powder
1 tbsp. paprika
1 tbsp. cumin
1 tbsp. salt
1 tsp. garlic powder
1 tsp. onion powder
1 tsp. oregano
½ tsp. ground black pepper

Directions
1. Combine all of the ingredients in a glass container, cover and shake to combine. Store in your pantry until ready to use.

Nutritional Info per Serving (1 tablespoon)
calories: 9, fat: 0g, protein: 0.2g, carbs: 0.6g, fiber: 0.2g, sugar: 0g, sodium: 652mg

Quick Almond Butter

Prep time: 3 minutes, Cook time: 5 minutes, Makes 1 cup

Ingredients
2 tbsps. coconut oil
2 cups raw almonds
2 tbsps. raw honey
Dash sea salt

Directions
1. In a medium container, cover the almonds with water. Sprinkle with a dash salt, and allow them to soak overnight. Drain the almonds well, and put them on a paper towel to dry.
2. Preheat the oven to 350ºF (180ºC).
3. Cover a baking sheet with parchment paper, and arrange the almonds on the sheet in a single layer. Roast them for about 5 minutes.
4. Grind the almonds in a food processor, until they become a fine powder. Pour the coconut oil to the food processor, and continue to grind the nuts for about 10 to 15 minutes, stopping to scrape down the sides as needed.
5. Put the honey, and grind for an additional 10 minutes, stopping to scrape down the sides as needed, until the butter is smooth and creamy.

Nutritional Info per Serving (1 tablespoon)
calories: 101, fat: 8g, protein: 3g, carbs: 5g, fiber: 2g, sugar: 3g, sodium: 10mg

Fresh Salsa

Prep time: 12 minutes, Cook time: 0 minutes, Makes 2 cups

Ingredients

1 tbsp. extra-virgin olive oil
3 tomatoes, diced
1 jalapeño, chopped
½ onion, chopped
Juice of 1 lime
Fresh cilantro, chopped
Sea salt

Directions

1. Stir together the tomatoes, onion, and jalapeño in a large bowl.
2. Place the lime juice and olive oil, and stir until the mixture has an even consistency.
3. Sprinkle with the cilantro, season with salt, and enjoy!

Nutritional Info per Serving (1 tablespoon)

calories: 5, fat: 0g, protein: 0g, carbs: 1g, fiber: 0g, sugar: 0g, sodium: 77mg

Fresh Maple Vinaigrette

Prep time: 5 minutes, Cook time: 0 minutes, Makes ½ cup

Ingredients

¼ cup extra-virgin olive oil
¼ cup maple syrup
1 tbsp. Dijon mustard
½ tbsp. apple cider
vinegar
Juice of 1 lemon
A pinch of salt
Pinch pepper

Directions

1. Stir all of the ingredients and refrigerate until ready to use.
2. Warm the dressing in the microwave for short and shake well before serving, since the maple syrup and the oil will congeal in the refrigerator.
3. Store in an airtight container for up to 1 week.

Nutritional Info per Serving (2 tablespoons)

calories: 178, fat: 12g, protein: 0.3g, carbs: 13g, fiber: 0.2g, sugar: 5g, sodium: 128mg

BBQ Sauce

Prep time: 3 minutes, Cook time: 25 minutes, Makes 4 cups

Ingredients

1 tbsp. avocado oil
4 garlic cloves, minced
1 (14½-ounce / 411-g) can diced tomatoes
1 (6-ounce / 170-g) can tomato paste
2 tbsps. soy sauce
2 tbsps. Dijon mustard
2 tbsps. maple syrup
1 tbsp. apple cider vinegar
1 tsp. garlic powder
1 tsp. onion powder
1 tsp. chili powder
½ tsp. salt
½ tsp. pepper

Directions

1. In a large saucepan, heat the oil over medium heat.
2. Add the garlic cloves and sauté until slightly golden, for 3 to 4 minutes.
3. Add all of the remaining ingredients and mix well. Simmer the barbecue sauce.
4. Blend the ingredients until smooth. Add water to reach a thin consistency, as needed.
5. Reduce the heat to low and simmer for 20 minutes, stirring occasionally.
6. Store in a sealed airtight container in the refrigerator for up to 2 weeks.

Nutritional Info per Serving (½ cup)

calories: 69, fat: 2.3g, protein: 3g, carbs: 10g, fiber: 1.8g, sugar: 7g, sodium: 685mg

Tomato Sauce

Prep time: 15 minutes, Cook time: 11 hours, Makes 13 cups

Ingredients

3 tbsps. extra-virgin olive oil
4 pounds (1.8 kg) Roma tomatoes, seeded and chopped
2 cups bottled tomato juice
2 onions, chopped
5 garlic cloves, minced
3 tbsps. tomato paste
2 tsps. dried basil leaves
½ tsp. salt
⅛ tsp. white pepper

Directions

1. Place all the tomatoes in a 6-quart slow cooker. Partially cover the slow cooker and cook the tomatoes on high for 3 hours, stirring tomatoes twice during the cooking time.
2. Put the remaining ingredients. Cover and cook on low for 6 to 8 hours longer, until the sauce is bubbling and the consistency you want.
3. You can make the sauce smoother if you want by working the sauce with a potato masher, or leave it as is.
4. Evenly divide the sauce into 2-cup portions and freeze up to 3 months.

Nutritional Info per Serving (1 cup)

calories: 76, fat: 3g, protein: 2g, carbs: 11g, fiber: 2g, sugar: 6g, sodium: 210mg

Greek Avocado-Cilantro Cream

Prep time: 6 minutes, Cook time: 0 minutes, Makes 1 cup

Ingredients
1 ripe avocado, pitted and skinned
½ cup Greek yogurt
¼ cup chopped fresh cilantro
1 jalapeño, chopped and seeded
Juice of 1 lime
Sea salt

Directions
1. Combine the yogurt, avocado, cilantro, lime juice, and jalapeño in a blender. Sprinkle with salt. Blend until smooth.
2. The cream can be stored in an airtight container in the refrigerator for 4 to 5 days.

Nutritional Info per Serving (1 tablespoon)
calories: 25, fat: 2g, protein: 1g, carbs: 2g, fiber: 1g, sugar: 1g, sodium: 17mg

Quick Guacamole

Prep time: 6 minutes, Cook time: 0 minutes, Serves 4

Ingredients
¼ cup red onion, diced
1 jalapeño, seeded and diced
Juice of 2 limes
½ tsp. salt
¼ tsp. black pepper
3 avocados, pitted and peeled

Directions
1. Mix together the onion, jalapeño, lime juice, salt, and pepper In a large bowl.
2. Add the avocados and press the avocados with the back of fork. Combine with the onion-and-jalapeño mixture until relatively smooth and well combined.
3. Season with additional salt or pepper to taste.

Nutritional Info per Serving
calories: 152, fat: 12g, protein: 2g, carbs: 7g, fiber: 5g, sugar: 0.7g, sodium: 203mg

Homemade Pesto

Prep time: 9 minutes, Cook time: 8 minutes, Makes 2 cups

Ingredients
3 cups packed fresh basil
½ cup pine nuts
½ cup extra-virgin olive oil
⅓ cup finely grated Parmesan cheese
3 garlic cloves, roughly chopped
1 tsp. sea salt, plus additional for seasoning
Freshly ground black pepper

Directions
1. Preheat the oven to 375ºF (190ºC).
2. Cover a baking sheet with parchment paper. Arrange the pine nuts on the baking sheet in a single layer and roast them for about 8 minutes. Take the sheet from the oven and keep the nuts aside to cool.
3. Combine the pine nuts, basil, garlic, and salt in a food processor. With the food processor running, gently add the olive oil until the ingredients are completely combined.
4. Place the Parmesan cheese to the processor and pulse to combine. Sprinkle the pesto with more salt and the pepper.
5. The pesto can be stored in an airtight container in the refrigerator for 4 to 5 days.

Nutritional Info per Serving (1 tablespoon)
calories: 49, fat: 5g, protein: 1g, carbs: 1g, fiber: 0g, sugar: 0g, sodium: 92mg

Spicy Bolognese Sauce

Prep time: 14 minutes, Cook time: 9 hours, Makes 12 cups

Ingredients
3 pounds (1.4 kg) Roma tomatoes, seeded and chopped
2 pounds (907 g) lean grass-fed ground beef
2 cups bottled tomato juice
2 onions, chopped
1 large carrot, grated
7 garlic cloves, minced
¼ cup tomato paste
1 bay leaf
1 tsp. dried oregano leaves
½ tsp. salt

Directions
1. Mix the ground beef, onions, and garlic in a large skillet. Cook over medium heat, stirring constantly to break up the meat, until the beef is browned. Drain.
2. Mix the beef mixture with the remaining ingredients in a 6-quart slow cooker. Cover the slow cooker and cook on low for 7 to 9 hours, or until the sauce is thickened.
3. Remove and discard the bay leaf.
4. Evenly divide the sauce into 3-cup portions and freeze up to 3 months. To use, allow the sauce to thaw in the refrigerator overnight, then slowly heat in a saucepan until the sauce is bubbling.

Nutritional Info per Serving (1 cup)
calories: 167, fat: 6g, protein: 18g, carbs: 12g, fiber: 2g, sugar: 6g, sodium: 265mg

Homemade Ghee

Prep time: 2 minutes, Cook time: 35 minutes, Makes 3 cups

Ingredients
2 pounds (907 g)   unsalted butter, chunked

Directions
1. In a large saucepan, melt the butter over medium heat and bring to a slow boil. Reduce the heat and simmer for 15 minutes.
2. Remove the white solids with a spoon. Continue to simmer for another 15 minutes. Brown solids will form on the bottom of the pan. Continue to skim white solids off the top. Cool for 5 minutes.
3. Line a fine mesh strainer with cheesecloth. Pour the ghee into a medium bowl through the strainer to seperate the remaining milk solids.
4. Store in an airtight container in a dark cool place in your pantry for up to 1 month or longer in the refrigerator, for up to 3 months.

Nutritional Info per Serving (1 tablespoon)
calories: 137, fat: 14g, protein: 0.3g, carbs: 0.2g, fiber: 0g, sugar: 0.2g, sodium: 3mg

Classic Marinara Sauce

Prep time: 12 minutes, Cook time: 8 hours, Makes 12 cups

Ingredients
4 pounds (1.8 kg) Roma tomatoes, chopped
4 beefsteak tomatoes, seeded and chopped
1 (6-ounce / 170-g) can BPA-free tomato paste
½ cup shredded carrot
2 onions, peeled and chopped
4 garlic cloves, peeled and minced
1 bay leaf
2 tsps. dried basil leaves
1 tsp. dried oregano leaves

Directions
1. Mix all the ingredients in a 6-quart slow cooker. Cover the slow cooker and cook on low for 6 to 8 hours.
2. Remove the bay leaf and discard.
3. You can freeze this sauce as is, or you can puree it with a potato masher to crush some of the tomatoes.
4. Evenly divide the sauce into 2-cup portions and freeze up to 4 months.

Nutritional Info per Serving (1 cup)
calories: 77, fat: 1g, protein: 3g, carbs: 16g, fiber: 4g, sugar: 8g, sodium: 19mg

Homemade Ketchup

Prep time: 6 minutes, Cook time: 0 minutes, Makes 2½ cups

Ingredients
12 ounces (340 g) tomato paste
¼ cup coconut sugar
¾ cup water
½ cup apple cider vinegar
1 tsp. onion powder
1 tsp. garlic powder
Pinch red pepper flakes
½ tsp. salt
Pinch pepper

Directions
1. In a large bowl, combine all of the ingredients together until smooth.
2. Refrigerate overnight. Add water to reach desired consistency, if necessary. Store in an airtight jar in the refrigerator for up to 2 weeks.

Nutritional Info per Serving (¼ cup)
calories: 82, fat: 0.4g, protein: 4g, carbs: 18g, fiber: 4g, sugar: 8g, sodium: 637mg

Creamy Chipotle Taco Hummus

Prep time: 13 minutes, Cook time: 0 minutes, Serves 8

Ingredients
1 (15½-ounce / 439-g) can chickpeas, drained, and liquid reserved
2 tbsps. tahini
1 tbsp. lemon juice, freshly squeezed
2 tsps. chopped chipotle peppers in adobo sauce
2 scallions, sliced, white and green parts
1 tsp. garlic, minced
½ tsp. salt
½ tsp. black pepper, freshly ground
Cut veggies of choice, for serving

Directions
1. In a food processor or blender, combine the chickpeas, tahini, lemon juice, chipotle peppers in adobo, scallions, garlic, salt, and pepper. Process on high speed for 1 to 1½ minutes, or until completely smooth, scraping down the sides halfway, as needed. If you prefer thinner hummus, add the reserved chickpea liquid, 1 tbsp. at a time, blending until the hummus reaches your desired consistency.
2. Place ¼-cup portions into each of 5 half-pint Mason jars with tight-fitting lids, and refrigerate. Top with veggies of your choice for a quick grab-and-go snack.

Nutritional Info per Serving
calories: 74, fat: 4g, protein: 4g, carbs: 11g, fiber: 2g, sugar: 3g, sodium: 218mg

Mayo, page 164

BBQ Sauce, page 165

Famous Tzatziki, page 172

Garlic-Tahini Dressing, page 169

Homemade Kefir Marinade

Prep time: 5 minutes, Cook time: 0 minutes, Makes about 1 cup

Ingredients
1 cup kefir
3 garlic cloves, minced
Juice of ½ lemon
1 tsp. oregano
½ to 1 tsp. Himalayan salt

Directions
1. Combine the kefir, lemon juice, garlic, oregano, and salt in a large bowl. Combine together well.
2. Remove and discard any marinade after using.

Nutritional Info per Serving (2 tablespoons)
calories: 17, fat: 0g, protein: 1g, carbs: 3g, fiber: 0g, sugar: 1g, sodium: 85mg

Lemony Tahini Dressing

Prep time: 4 minutes, Cook time: 0 minutes, Makes about ½ cup

Ingredients
2 tbsps. extra-virgin olive oil
2 tbsps. tahini
Juice of ½ lemon
1 clove garlic, crushed
1 tsp. honey
¼ tsp. Himalayan salt

Directions
1. Whisk together the tahini, olive oil, lemon juice, garlic, honey, and salt in a small bowl. Give it a stir right before serving.

Nutritional Info per Serving (2 tablespoons)
calories: 112, fat: 11g, protein: 1g, carbs: 4g, fiber: 1g, sugar: 1g, sodium: 87mg

Easy Greek Yogurt Marinade

Prep time: 5 minutes, Cook time: 0 minutes, Makes about ¾ cup

Ingredients
1 (6-ounce / 170-g) container plain Greek yogurt
Juice from ½ lemon
½ tsp. cumin
½ tsp. turmeric
½ tsp. garlic powder
½ tsp. Himalayan salt

Directions
1. Combine the yogurt with the cumin, turmeric, garlic powder, salt, and lemon juice in a large bowl. Stir to combine well.
2. Remove and discard any marinade after using.

Nutritional Info per Serving (2 tablespoons)
calories: 22, fat: 1g, protein: 1g, carbs: 2g, fiber: 0g, sugar: 1g, sodium: 111mg

Lime-Jalapeño Vinaigrette

Prep time: 5 minutes, Cook time: 0 minutes, Makes 2 cups

Ingredients
1 cup freshly squeezed lime juice
1 jalapeño, seeded and minced
½ cup extra-virgin olive oil
1½ tsps. sea salt
¾ tsp. freshly ground black pepper

Directions
1. Whisk together the lime juice, olive oil, jalapeño, salt, and pepper in a medium bowl.
2. The vinaigrette can be stored in an airtight container in the refrigerator for 4 to 5 days.

Nutritional Info per Serving (1 tablespoon)
calories: 33, fat: 3g, protein: 0g, carbs: 1g, fiber: 0g, sugar: 0g, sodium: 109mg

Garlic-Tahini Dressing

Prep time: 6 minutes, Cook time: 0 minutes, Makes 1 cup

Ingredients
¼ cup extra-virgin olive oil
¼ cup tahini
¼ cup water
3 garlic cloves, minced
2 tbsps. tamari
1½ tbsps. freshly squeezed lemon juice
2 tsps. minced fresh ginger
1½ tsps. red wine vinegar
1½ tsps. white wine vinegar
Freshly ground black pepper

Directions
1. Combine the tahini, olive oil, water, tamari, lemon juice, red wine vinegar, white wine vinegar, ginger, and garlic in a blender. Sprinkle with pepper and blend until smooth.
2. The dressing can be stored in an airtight container in the refrigerator for 4 to 5 days.

Nutritional Info per Serving (1 tablespoon)
calories: 55, fat: 5g, protein: 1g, carbs: 1g, fiber: 0g, sugar: 0g, sodium: 130mg

Easy Guacamole

Prep time: 14 minutes, Cook time: 0 minutes, Makes 2 cups

Ingredients

4 avocados, halved and pitted
½ tomato, chopped
1 jalapeño, diced
¼ red onion, finely chopped
Juice of 1 lime
¼ tsp. garlic salt
Fresh cilantro, chopped, for garnish
½ tsp. sea salt
Freshly ground black pepper

Directions

1. Combine the onion and salt. Add the lime juice in a large bowl, and allow to sit for 10 minutes.
2. Use a knife to score the avocados and scoop the flesh into the bowl. Stir in the jalapeño and tomato. Sprinkle with the garlic salt, pepper, and cilantro. Stir until the desired consistency is reached.

Nutritional Info per Serving (1 tablespoon)
calories: 41, fat: 4g, protein: 1g, carbs: 2g, fiber: 2g, sugar: 0g, sodium: 38mg

Marinara Sauce

Prep time: 10 minutes, Cook time: 40 minutes, Makes 8 cups

Ingredients

1 tbsp. olive oil
1 yellow onion, chopped
5 garlic cloves, minced
1 green bell pepper, chopped
2 (28-ounce / 794-g) cans crushed tomatoes
1 (6-ounce / 170-g) can tomato paste
2 tsps. oregano
¼ cup fresh parsley, chopped
¼ cup fresh basil, chopped
½ cup water, as needed for thinning
Salt
Pepper
Red pepper flakes (optional)

Directions

1. In a large pot, heat the oil over medium heat. Add the onion and cook for 2 to 3 minutes. Add the garlic and cook for 1 to 2 minutes.
2. Add the bell pepper and cook for 2 minutes.
3. Stir in the tomatoes, tomato paste, oregano, parsley, and basil.
4. Add about ¼ cup water to each can of tomatoes, churn and pour into the pot.
5. Bring the sauce to a boil, lower the heat and simmer for 30 minutes uncovered, stirring frequently.

6. Season with salt, pepper, and red pepper flakes, if using.
7. Make it thin by adding additional water, if needed.
8. Leave the sauce chunky if you use an immersion blender.
9. Store in an airtight container in the refrigerator for up to 1 week or freeze for up to 3 months.

Nutritional Info per Serving (½ cup)
calories: 42, fat: 2g, protein: 3g, carbs: 8g, fiber: 1.7g, sugar: 3g, sodium: 156mg

Lemony Mustard Dressing

Prep time: 3 minutes, Cook time: 0 minutes, Makes about ½ cup

Ingredients

¼ cup extra-virgin olive oil
Juice of 1 large lemon
1 tsp. Dijon mustard
½ tsp. Himalayan salt

Directions

1. Whisk together the Dijon, olive oil, lemon, and salt in a bowl. Give a stir again before serving.

Nutritional Info per Serving (2 tablespoons)
calories: 123, fat: 14g, protein: 0g, carbs: 1g, fiber: 0g, sugar: 0g, sodium: 160mg

Quick Lemon Dressing

Prep time: 9 minutes, Cook time: 0 minutes, Makes 1 cup

Ingredients

½ cup extra-virgin olive oil
2 garlic cloves, minced
4 tbsps. freshly squeezed lemon juice
2 tbsps. Dijon mustard
2 tsps. minced shallot
Sea salt
Freshly ground black pepper

Directions

1. Whisk the lemon juice, mustard, shallot, and garlic until well combined in a medium bowl.
2. Gently add the olive oil, while continuing to whisk, until the dressing has thickened.
3. Sprinkle with salt and pepper. Store the dressing in an airtight container in the refrigerator for 4 to 5 days.

Nutritional Info per Serving (1 tablespoon)
calories: 62, fat: 7g, protein: 0g, carbs: 1g, fiber: 0g, sugar: 0g, sodium: 41mg

Spinach Walnut Pesto

Prep time: 3 minutes, Cook time: 0 minutes, Makes 1 cup

Ingredients

2 cups spinach, lightly packed
⅓ cup walnuts
⅓ cup shredded Parmesan
½ cup extra-virgin olive oil
3 garlic cloves
½ tsp. salt
¼ tsp. pepper

Directions

1. Place all of the ingredients in a food processor or blender. Pulse until well blended and smooth.
2. Store in an airtight container in the refrigerator for up to 1 week.

Nutritional Info per Serving (¼ cup)
calories: 327, fat: 33g, protein: 3.2g, carbs: 4g, fiber: 0.9g, sugar: 0.3g, sodium: 411mg

Lemon Vinaigrette

Prep time: 9 minutes, Cook time: 0 minutes, Makes 2 cups

Ingredients

¼ cup lemon juice, freshly squeezed
¼ cup white balsamic vinegar
2 tbsps. white wine vinegar
1½ tsps. sliced scallion, white parts only
1½ tsps. fresh Parmesan, grated
1⅛ tsps. garlic, granulated
1⅛ tsps. onion, granulated
¾ tsp. honey
¾ tsp. salt
½ tsp. black pepper, freshly ground
½ tsp. Dijon mustard
½ tsp. garlic, minced
⅛ tsp. red pepper flakes
1½ cups avocado oil

Directions

1. In blender, add the lemon juice, balsamic vinegar, white wine vinegar, scallions, Parmesan, granulated garlic, granulated onion, honey, salt, black pepper, Dijon, minced garlic, and red pepper flakes. Process on high until smooth.
2. With the blender still running, slowly drizzle in the oil until emulsified.
3. Portion 2 tbsps. of dressing per serving into individual 1½-ounce (43-g) stainless-steel salad dressing containers for storage and refrigerate.

Nutritional Info per Serving (2 tablespoons)
calories: 191, fat: 19g, protein: 0.2g, carbs: 2g, fiber: 0.4g, sugar: 0.8g, sodium: 127mg

Taco Seasoning

Prep time: 6 minutes, Cook time: 0 minutes, Makes 1 cup

Ingredients

6 tbsps. cumin, ground
3 tbsps. chili powder, ground
3 tbsps. corn flour
1 tbsp. garlic, granulated
1 tbsp. onion, granulated
1 tbsp. coriander, ground
2 tsps. paprika
2 tsps. turmeric, ground
2 tsps. kosher salt
2 tsps. black pepper, freshly ground
1 tsp. chipotle pepper, ground
1 tsp. oregano, ground
½ tsp. red pepper flakes

Directions

1. In a large bowl, well incorporate the cumin, chili powder, corn flour, granulated garlic, granulated onion, coriander, paprika, turmeric, salt, black pepper, chipotle pepper, oregano, and red pepper flakes.
2. Pour to a quart-size wide-mouth Mason jar with a lid for storage.

Nutritional Info per Serving (1 tablespoon)
calories: 29, fat: 2g, protein: 0.9g, carbs: 5g, fiber: 0.7g, sugar: 0.3g, sodium: 386mg

Ranch Dressing

Prep time: 7 minutes, Cook time: 0 minutes, Makes 1 cup

Ingredients

1 cup full-fat plain Greek yogurt
1 tbsp. milk
1 tsp. white vinegar
1 tsp. lemon juice, freshly squeezed
1 tsp. garlic powder
1 tsp. onion powder
1 tsp. chives, dried
1 tsp. parsley, dried
½ tsp. dill, dried
½ tsp. salt
¼ tsp. black pepper, freshly ground

Directions

1. In a large bowl, combine the yogurt, milk, vinegar, lemon juice, garlic powder, onion powder, chives, parsley, dill, salt, and pepper. Whisk until incorporated, smooth and creamy.
2. Portion 2 tbsps. of dressing per serving into individual 1½-ounce (43-g) stainless-steel salad dressing containers. Store in the fridge.

Nutritional Info per Serving (2 tablespoons)
calories: 34, fat: 2g, protein: 4g, carbs: 3g, fiber: 0.2g, sugar: 0.8g, sodium: 227mg

Famous Tzatziki

Prep time: 9 minutes, Cook time: 0 minutes, Serves 4

Ingredients
1 cucumber, finely grated
A pinch of salt, plus more for seasoning
7 ounces (198 g) full-fat plain unsweetened Greek yogurt

¼ cup feta cheese, crumbled
Juice of ½ lemon
Pinch pepper

Directions
1. Mix the cucumber with a pinch of salt in a medium bowl. Spread the cucumber on the cheesecloth. Wait 2 minutes, then squeeze the cheesecloth to remove the excess water from the cucumbers.
2. Mix the cucumber with the rest of the ingredients until well combined. Season with salt and pepper to taste.
3. Store in an airtight jar in the fridge for 4 to 5 days.

Nutritional Info per Serving
calories: 101, fat: 4g, protein: 5g, carbs: 5g, fiber: 0.7g, sugar: 2.6g, sodium: 188mg

Simple EVOO and Lemon Dressing

Prep time: 2 minutes, Cook time: 0 minutes, Makes about ¼ cup

Ingredients
Juice of ½ lemon
⅛ cup extra-virgin olive oil

½ tsp. Himalayan salt

Directions
1. In a small bowl, whisk together the olive oil, lemon, and salt. Give a fresh stir right before serving.

Nutritional Info per Serving (2 tablespoons)
calories: 127, fat: 14g, protein: 0g, carbs: 1g, fiber: 0g, sugar: 0g, sodium: 291mg

Gochugaru EVOO with Sesame Seed Dressing

Prep time: 5 minutes, Cook time: 0 minutes, Makes about ½ cup

Ingredients
¼ cup extra-virgin olive oil
¼ cup rice vinegar
¼ tsp. gochugaru (Korean chili flakes)

1 tbsp. sesame seeds
¼ tsp. Himalayan salt

Directions
1. Whisk together the olive oil, rice vinegar, gochugaru, sesame seeds, and salt in a medium bowl. Give a fresh stir right before serving.

Nutritional Info per Serving (2 tablespoons)
calories: 136, fat: 15g, protein: 0g, carbs: 0g, fiber: 0g, sugar: 0g, sodium: 84mg

Appendix 1: Measurement Conversion Chart

Volume Equivalents (Dry)

US STANDARD	METRIC (APPROXIMATE)
1/8 teaspoon	0.5 mL
1/4 teaspoon	1 mL
1/2 teaspoon	2 mL
3/4 teaspoon	4 mL
1 teaspoon	5 mL
1 tablespoon	15 mL
1/4 cup	59 mL
1/2 cup	118 mL
3/4 cup	177 mL
1 cup	235 mL
2 cups	475 mL
3 cups	700 mL
4 cups	1 L

Temperatures Equivalents

FAHRENHEIT (F)	CELSIUS(C) (APPROXIMATE)
225 °F	107 °C
250 °F	120 °C
275 °F	135 °C
300 °F	150 °C
325 °F	160 °C
350 °F	180 °C
375 °F	190 °C
400 °F	205 °C
425 °F	220 °C
450 °F	235 °C
475 °F	245 °C
500 °F	260 °C

Volume Equivalents (Liquid)

US STANDARD	US STANDARD (OUNCES)	METRIC (APPROXIMATE)
2 tablespoons	1 fl.oz.	30 mL
1/4 cup	2 fl.oz.	60 mL
1/2 cup	4 fl.oz.	120 mL
1 cup	8 fl.oz.	240 mL
1 1/2 cup	12 fl.oz.	355 mL
2 cups or 1 pint	16 fl.oz.	475 mL
4 cups or 1 quart	32 fl.oz.	1 L
1 gallon	128 fl.oz.	4 L

Weight Equivalents

US STANDARD	METRIC (APPROXIMATE)
1 ounce	28 g
2 ounces	57 g
5 ounces	142 g
10 ounces	284 g
15 ounces	425 g
16 ounces (1 pound)	455 g
1.5 pounds	680 g
2 pounds	907 g

Appendix 2: Dirty Dozen and Clean Fifteen

The Environmental Working Group (EWG) is a widely known organization that has an eminent guide to pesticides and produce. More specifically, the group takes in data from tests conducted by the US Department of Agriculture (USDA) and then categorizes produce into a list titled "Dirty Dozen," which ranks the twelve top produce items that contain the most pesticide residues, or alternatively the "Clean Fifteen," which ranks fifteen produce items that are contaminated with the least amount of pesticide residues.

The EWG has recently released their 2021 Dirty Dozen list, and this year strawberries, spinach and kale – with a few other produces which will be revealed shortly – are listed at the top of the list. This year's ranking is similar to the 2020 Dirty Dozen list, with the few differences being that collards and mustard greens have joined kale at number three on the list. Other changes include peaches and cherries, which having been listed subsequently as seventh and eighth on the 2020 list, have now been flipped; the introduction – which the EWG has said is the first time ever – of bell and hot peppers into the 2021 list; and the departure of potatoes from the twelfth spot.

DIRTY DOZEN LIST

Strawberries	Apples	Pears
Spinach	Grapes	Bell and hot peppers
Kale, collards and mustard greens	Cherries	Celery
Nectarines	Peaches	Tomatoes

CLEAN FIFTEEN LIST

Avocados	Sweet peas (frozen)	Kiwi
Sweet corn	Eggplant	Cauliflower
Pineapple	Asparagus	Mushrooms
Onions	Broccoli	Honeydew melon
Papaya	Cabbage	Cantaloupe

These lists are created to help keep the public informed on their potential exposures to pesticides, which then allows for better and healthier food choices to be made.

This is the advice that ASEQ-EHAQ also recommends. Stay clear of the dirty dozen by opting for their organic versions, and always be mindful of what you are eating and how it was grown. Try to eat organic as much as possible – whether it is on the list, or not.

Appendix 3: Recipes Index

Don't forget to get a free PDF with color pictures!

Getting it is easy, just take out your phone, scan the QR code below! Your PDF is available and will be displayed in color.

To bring you a better shopping experience, we are always working hard. This is the only way we can send you recipes with color pictures and make the book as affordable as possible.

Once you've downloaded the PDF file with your phone, you can take it with you, which means you can cook these recipes anywhere!

Made in the USA
Las Vegas, NV
03 December 2024

13315232R00105